The Apocalypse and
the End of History

The Apocalypse and the End of History

Modern Jihad and the Crisis of Liberalism

Suzanne Schneider

VERSO
London • New York

First published by Verso 2021
© Suzanne Schneider 2021

1 3 5 7 9 10 8 6 4 2

Verso
UK: 6 Meard Street, London W1F 0EG
US: 20 Jay Street, Suite 1010, Brooklyn, NY 11201
versobooks.com

Verso is the imprint of New Left Books

ISBN-13: 978-1-83976-241-3
ISBN-13: 978-1-83976-244-4 (US EBK)
ISBN-13: 978-1-83976-243-7 (UK EBK)

British Library Cataloguing in Publication Data
A catalogue record for this book is available from the British Library

Library of Congress Cataloging-in-Publication Data

Names: Schneider, Suzanne, 1983– author.
Title: The apocalypse and the end of history : modern jihad and the crisis
of liberalism / Suzanne Schneider.
Description: First edition hardback. | London ; New York : Verso, 2021. |
Includes bibliographical references and index. | Summary: "Historian
Suzanne Schneider examines the politics and ideology of the Islamic
State (better known as ISIS). Schneider argues that today's jihad is not
the residue from a less enlightened time, nor does it have much in
common with its classical or medieval form, but it does bear a striking
resemblance to the reactionary political formations and acts of
spectacular violence that are upending life in Western democracies"–
Provided by publisher.
Identifiers: LCCN 2021020086 (print) | LCCN 2021020087 (ebook) | ISBN
9781839762413 (hardback) | ISBN 9781839762444 (ebk)
Subjects: LCSH: Liberalism. | Jihad. | IS (Organization) | Islamic
fundamentalism.
Classification: LCC JC574 .S356 2021 (print) | LCC JC574 (ebook) | DDC
320.55/7–dc23
LC record available at https://lccn.loc.gov/2021020086
LC ebook record available at https://lccn.loc.gov/2021020087

Typeset in Fournier by MJ & N Gavan, Truro, Cornwall
Printed and bound by CPI Group (UK) Ltd, Croydon, CR0 4YY

For David, ז״ל

Could there be, Echo wondered, laughing silently, unheeded tears still falling, each with a little sun or moon or planet at its epicenter, could there be echoes that rang out before their noises, echoes more vibrant than their originals, echoes of the future here on earth?

—Rebecca Ariel Porte, "On Earthly Delights"

Contents

Acknowledgments

Though writing is a solitary project, it cannot be completed without the aid, support, and suggestions of others. It is my great pleasure to recognize their contributions, in varied forms, to the book before you.

This work was long in process—in articles, partial drafts, seminar classrooms, and conversations with friends—prior to rapidly meeting the page during the wee morning hours of the Covid-19 lockdown. I first began researching the Islamic State in 2014 while a Visiting Scholar at the Center for Religion and Media at New York University, and I was able to develop my early ideas through a number of articles published by the center's magazine, *The Revealer*. I am thankful to Kali Handelman and Angela Zito for affording me this opportunity. Students in my Brooklyn Institute for Social Research seminar, On Religious Violence, helped hone many of the theoretical and methodological standpoints I have adopted, and I thank them for their insights. I was also fortunate to receive feedback at the early stages of this project from Robin Varghese and the late David Landes, a dear friend and mentor, to whom this book is dedicated. Conrad Fischer has been a champion of this project from the beginning, and I can't thank him enough for his support.

Many of my colleagues at the Brooklyn Institute have provided critical feedback as the work progressed, particularly Mark DeLucas, Rebecca Ariel Porte, Abby Kluchin, Patrick Blanchfield, and last but certainly not least, Ajay Singh Chaudhary, from whom I continue to learn so much. I further benefited from discussions along the way with Wael Hallaq, Suleiman Mourad, Ahmed Dailami, and Martyn Frampton. Particular thanks is due to Tareq Mahmud, Richard Bulliet, and Faisal Devji, who generously read and offered valuable feedback on the manuscript. I was lucky to work with three great research assistants over the years, Sam Osterfeld, Huzaifa Taquee, and Arooj Alam, and wish to recognize their contributions. Finally, it has been an absolute pleasure to work with Jessie Kindig from Verso Books, who has deftly shepherded the project from proposal to final form. Each of these individuals has given greatly to the book; what it lacks is due to my limitations alone.

A whole cadre of friends has patiently listened to my ramblings and offered insights and encouragement in equal parts. To Elizabeth Marcus, Daniel Lee, Samantha Hill, Emily Wenner, Tamar Huberman, Tanya Everett, Eliana Meirowitz-Nelson, and the esteemed members of the Park Slope Crew and 79.6 millimeters (especially Abby Deift, Rebecca Miller, and Joanna Kabat), all my love. Thank you for sustaining me. Nicola Robinson, my right-hand woman in all things, has allowed me to do this work by loving our children dearly in my absence. I cannot thank her enough for her help and companionship over the years. Yaron and Lisa Reich have supported me in ways too numerous to list, and I owe them a great deal of thanks for their years of kindness. My parents, Joel and Mary Sue Schneider, whose love is truly unconditional, were particularly vital to helping me complete this manuscript with twins in Zoom school and a toddler running amok. And finally, Yono Reich deserves all the love and gratitude I can express and then some. He believed in this project even when I did not and facilitated it at every point. He is my anchor in a world that sometimes spins too fast. To Sophia and Charlotte, thank you for your patience with me, your help with your baby sister, and your loving if misguided belief that I can do all things. Madeline, please don't rip the pages out of this book. Mommy worked hard on it.

Introduction: Two Presents

On November 14, 1914, the chief jurist of the Ottoman Empire issued a fatwa declaring jihad on the empire's enemies. The empire had recently, if reluctantly, been pulled into the Great War on the side of the Central Powers and suddenly found itself at war with Britain and France in addition to its historic rival, Russia. On the one hand this jihad was a largely traditional affair: declared during wartime by a recognized religious authority within the state administration, and in consultation with the Sultan-Caliph. The declaration was also right at home among propaganda efforts by other combatants, many of whom cast the struggle as a battle for God and country. On the other, the circumstances surrounding the Ottoman declaration were quite unusual. This was a "holy war" fought in alliance with major Christian powers. It was, moreover, a "jihad made in Germany," in the words of one contemporary observer.[1] Eyeing the millions of Muslims living under British and French colonial rule, German Orientalists and administrators hoped that a declaration of jihad from the Sultan-Caliph would stir the masses to revolt. In this regard the scheme was an utter failure, having no measurable impact beyond the empire's boundaries. But it remains illustrative of the exotic quality Western observers have tended to ascribe to jihad— envisioning "holy war" as something apart from the quotidian mass slaughter taking place all around them.

During the closing years of the twentieth century, a wealthy Saudi man named Osama bin Laden declared a different type of jihad in his 1996 fatwa, "Declaration of Jihad Against the Americans Occupying the land of the Two Holiest Sites [Mecca and Medina]."[2] In contrast to the Ottoman Empire, al-Qaeda was not a state, had no organized army or administration to speak of, and no citizens to draft. The organization's structure more closely resembled an NGO or corporate entity, and it spoke in distinctly moralizing terms rather than those of realpolitik. Bin Laden's jihad was not declared in the midst of a major war, but during what was supposed to be peacetime. Whereas the Ottoman jihad remained steeped in traditional forms of religious and political authority—of the Sultan-Caliph and the empire's chief jurist—bin Laden, who studied civil engineering and business administration, was neither a ruler nor a religious scholar. Still, his networked organization managed to inflict serious harm to US targets overseas, like the 1998 embassy bombings in Nairobi and Dar es Salaam, before bringing the war home in the attacks of September 11, 2001.

Fifteen years later, on June 12, 2016, Omar Mateen opened fire in the Pulse nightclub in Orlando, Florida, killing forty-nine people and injuring fifty-three more. Twenty-nine years old with a penchant for violence and (in all likelihood) an undiagnosed mental illness—not to mention turmoil stemming from his own conflicted sexuality—Mateen fit well into the pantheon of American mass shooters. He used a semi-automatic rifle and 9 mm Glock, both purchased legally in the weeks leading up to the attack. With the benefit of hindsight, law enforcement officials, gun vendors, and his former employers all pointed to numerous red flags whose warnings went unheeded. Though this was the 133rd American mass shooting of 2016 alone, the mystical conception of jihad proved irresistible for commentators eager to differentiate homegrown, white assailants from Muslim terrorists. Thus, Mateen was not a "troubled" young man like Adam Lanza or Devin Patrick Kelley—the perpetrators behind mass shootings at the Sandy Hook Elementary School and Sutherland Springs First Baptist Church, respectively—but rather a religious fanatic who had sworn allegiance to the Islamic State and its leader, Abu Bakr al-Baghdadi. Joining the jihad no longer required migrating to a safe harbor for training or coordinating with operatives online, as it might have a generation earlier, but was rather a wholly self-directed affair. All that was necessary was a target and a gun, which—this being America—were easily available.

Between these three declarations of jihad there lies a world of difference so substantive that one hesitates to place them into a single category. We could do it, of course, but we would miss most of what's important in the pursuit of commonality. Indeed, it would be akin to thinking that some great unifying thread links World War I with the war on terror, rather than acknowledging that war itself has changed. Taking these moments of rupture as a starting point, this book argues that contemporary jihad is neither the natural heir to its earlier forms nor a phenomenon that can be accounted for within the bounds of Islam alone. Yet, and despite the clear points of overlap that link jihad to the broader transformation of violence, the idea of "holy war" maintains its mystifying hold on much of public discourse. Jihad is most often regarded as a culturally specific phenomenon best accounted for by looking backward into Islamic history rather than sideways at the contemporary world. Such frameworks do the important job of Othering, of creating a sense of distance between "our" violence (which is supposed to be rational, proportionate, and just) and "theirs." Useful as such paradigms are for nurturing a sense of Western exceptionalism, they are not much help in understanding the emergence of a particular type of jihad over the last four decades or what its continued salience might teach us about the world as a whole.

In turning to these questions, I advance a number of overlapping arguments. The most elemental is that jihad became unmoored from its traditional keeper, the state, during the course of the twentieth century in a fashion that mirrors the broader shift toward factional and private violence. From a communal obligation that resembled traditional warfare (as in the Ottoman example above), jihad has morphed into an individual, globalized, and ethical struggle against the forces of "evil" everywhere. No longer a weapon of states, jihad has become a revolutionary force turned *against* them—a dialectical move that culminated in the Islamic State's attempt to revive the Caliphate as a political alternative to the nation-state. Each of these pivots generated new ideas about authority, subjectivity, community, governance, and conflict that are firmly rooted in modernity and its crises. Indeed, we find that across the globe a series of changes are occurring that make violence less democratic, states more fragmented, knowledge less esteemed, identity more exclusive, and politics more fraught. Today's jihad is not the leftover residue from a less enlightened time, but rather a political and social form that belongs firmly to the current era. Further, examining modern jihad's intricacies offers insight into the political and social conditions that are reshaping life far outside the obvious boundaries of Islam—indeed, in the very heart of the West.

Understanding the hypermodernity of jihad requires first tackling the narratives that, despite their widespread acceptance, drive us to regard it as either an undifferentiated phenomenon or a medieval one. Such arguments are not only historically indefensible, but they serve to obscure the much more fascinating question at hand: not how people and traditions remain essentially the same, but how, and why, they change.

An Unbroken Chain?

Among his many contributions, the late historian Salo Baron is famous for criticizing what he called the "lachrymose conception of Jewish history," that which narrated the past as a string of perpetual persecutions and expulsions, with little room for anything that did not fit the privileged narrative.[3] Though he was working with a different pool of historical sources, we might nonetheless borrow from Baron's observation as we consider how the Islamic past is narrated and mobilized for particular contemporary ends.

Within the West there are two primary views about Islam that circulate today. The first is a dystopian narrative that trades in camp images of bloodthirsty horsemen riding out of the desert "with a sword in one hand and the Qur'an in the other."[4] Forged against the background of long-standing political conflicts between European powers and their Muslim rivals to the south and east, this Orientalist vision depends on an ontological divide between "the West" and Islam, in which the latter is associated with all those undesirable traits supposedly vanquished by European rationalism and modernity. Of course the opposing narrative, which conjures up idyllic images of Islamic "Golden Ages" characterized by effortless interreligious harmony, does not hold up to much scrutiny either—though it is worth noting that most historians agree that Islamic governments and societies prior to the twentieth century were more hospitable to minority populations than their contemporary European peers.[5] All of this is to say that Muslims, like other people who have inhabited planet Earth, have acted in varied ways toward both those within and outside their communities over a long and geographically distributed history. Let us therefore cast aside the utopian and the dystopian as we try to make sense of contemporary jihad.

In the years since 9/11, an entire industry has grown up around the question of Islam and violence: from threat assessment experts to the ever-expanding counterterrorism sector and talking heads of quite varied quality. Figures like

Sam Harris, Bill Maher, Frank Gafney, and Laura Ingraham unfortunately command more airtime than scholars such as Suleiman Mourad, Roxanne Euben, or Khaled Abou El Fadl, and they use it to perpetuate the view that there is a fundamental link between Islam and violence. According to this view, the seventh century Islamic conquest of much of the Middle East and North Africa inaugurated a continuous history of jihad that culminated in the attacks of September 11, 2001, and those that have occurred since. For partisans of this view, violence within Islam is both essential—you can't escape it without abandoning Islam—and eternal—it is a consistent, rather than exceptional, state of affairs. Casting aside "apologists" who contest this narrative, these pundits assert their own prerogative to adjudicate what Islam is really about: namely, jihad, the purpose of which is supposedly to spread the faith by force. The problem is not that this argument lacks nuance or misses out on finer points evident only to academic specialists. It is that it is historically, verifiably false.

Luckily, empirical data point toward an alternative framework, one that clarifies that the history of jihad is not an unbroken chain. We are in fact living through a unique period in Islamic history, one characterized by the proliferation of militant and separatist groups. Over the last four decades, we have seen the emergence of Islamic Jihad (established 1979), al-Qaeda (1988), al-Shabaab (whose parent organization, the Islamic Courts Union, dates to the late 1990s), Boko Haram (2002), and the Islamic State, in addition to many lesser known groups.

One of the best ways to understand the scale of this phenomenon is to visualize it using data from the Mapping

Militant Organizations (MMO) project at Stanford University. Its research indicates a compelling trend that is stable across many conflict zones, wherein the relative quiet of the 1960s and 1970s gave way in the 1980s to a new wave of militancy by Islamist actors, who both supplanted earlier organizations and drastically outnumbered them. The pattern in Pakistan is rather typical: the Balochistan Liberation Front—described as an "ethno-nationalist separatist military organization … fighting against the Pakistani government for an independent Balochi state"[6]—was superseded in the 1980s by a dizzying assortment of Islamist groups, splinters and rivals. These include Harakat ul-Jihadi al-Islami, Harakat ul-Mujahedeen (formed to fight against the Soviet occupation of Afghanistan on one hand and Indian control of Kashmir on the other), Lashkar-e-Jhangvi (which perpetrates violent attacks on Shi'ites), and the Taliban (established 1994 and straddling the border with neighboring Afghanistan). Approximately a dozen new groups have emerged since 2000 alone.

The story in Iraq is strikingly similar, but this time the role of aspiring nationalist movement is played by the Kurds. Secular organizations were eventually eclipsed by the creation of the Islamic Movement of Kurdistan in 1987, which went on to spawn a number of affiliates and rivals. The next wave of organizations emerged as a direct response to the US-led invasion in 2003, from Ansar al-Sunna to the Mahdi Army (created by that perpetual thorn in the occupation's side, Muqtada al-Sadr) and the Islamic State of Iraq (known also as al-Qaeda Iraq), which was born during these same years at the hands of Abu Mus'ab al-Zarqawi.

Surveying this data raises an important question, one that must be addressed in historical rather than theological terms: Why now? That is to say, why have we witnessed the rise and proliferation of so many Islamic militant groups in so many regions over the course of the last forty years, and not prior? That is to say, why not in 1850 or 1930? While Islamic history is replete with instances of rebellion, the simultaneous existence of so many militants justifying their struggles as jihad is without precedent. Why have the last several decades proven so generative for a particular type of religious militancy, and what does this fact indicate not merely about conditions "over there" but about those far closer to home?

These are not the terms through which we are usually encouraged to think about jihad. Instead of attending to the radical points of rupture that differentiate today's jihad from its earlier iterations—and likewise gesture at over-lapping social and political dynamics in the West—there is a tendency to stress, and even manufacture, continuity. Take David Cook's *Understanding Jihad*, a well-researched, almost encyclopedic examination of jihad throughout the centuries. Though he acknowledges that jihad has assumed many meanings throughout the history of Islam, he none-theless suggests that an essential thread runs through this long and varied history, such that the first step to under-standing al-Qaeda or Boko Haram is a detailed chapter on "the life and teachings of the Prophet Muhammad" and "the ramifications of the great Islamic conquests of the seventh and eighth century."[7] Moreover, while jihad is a suppos-edly consistent element of Islam through the ages, there are centuries-wide lulls (say, from the Crusades through the late eighteenth century) that are simply skipped over because they do not conform to this narrative.

Offering very little in the way of contextual analysis, Cook argues the impetus to wage jihad derives from "the need of the Muslim community to revive its domination in the world and to affirm its sense of superiority over nonbelievers."[8] Having decided that Muslims (All of them? Everywhere? At every time?) are animated by an urge to assert their superiority—an argument that is equal parts Orientalist scholar and pop psychologist—questions of context become utterly irrelevant. So too do differences *within* the history of jihad, as if the Muslim conquest of Spain was of the same essential character as the anti-Soviet war in Afghanistan or the 2005 attacks on London's Underground. Despite the genuine cleavages that separate groups like the Islamic State or Boko Haram from their predecessors, Islam is assumed in such analyses as a coherent thread that binds them all together. Not only is this an unsustainable view of religions, which ignores their existence as evolving, historically embedded phenomena, but it also causes us to miss points of connection that reach across religious and cultural lines.

For instance, one might rather make a stronger case for analyzing present-day jihadist groups in the framework of twentieth-century revolutionaries and insurgents, particularly given their proclivity for adopting strategies from these sources. In a similar vein, Faisal Devji has argued that al-Qaeda borrows both in rhetoric and concept from global humanitarian and environmental movements. "Given that militants today routinely invoke the plight of suffering

Muslims in exactly the same way that humanitarians do of victims in general, the identification of Islam with humanitarianism is hardly surprising."[9] More recently, Olivier Roy has argued that jihad occupies the same role that used to be filled by the radical left, and that absent any compelling, universal political vision from the latter, the young and discontented are increasingly pulled into the former's nihilist orbit.[10] In short, there is much to recommend a more differentiated treatment than is usually offered, one that is attentive to the uniqueness of contemporary jihadi movements within Islamic history and to what links them to developments that are truly global in scale.

Making those points of connection clear is of the utmost importance, even if it means putting "our" violence and "theirs" in uncomfortable proximity. Whether it be examples like Omar Mateen—who blurred the line between terrorist violence (which Americans will sacrifice everything to combat) and homegrown mass shootings (which Americans will continue to treat as the natural order of the universe) —or the growing number of private military companies working in conflict zones, or even the way the Islamic State reports on its activities, there is something elemental and seismic happening the world over that is changing humanity's relationship to violence. But we cannot tell that story if we assume that it is only about Islam.

"The Qur'an Made Me Do It" and Other Stories

Over the last two decades, hundreds of books have offered explanations for the resurgence of religious violence in general—and jihad in particular—at the dawn of the twenty-first century. These accounts differ dramatically in quality, from insightful scholarly works to crass polemics. The most simplistic might be described as "Scripturalist" in nature. Proponents of this view claim that contemporary jihad stems directly from the Qur'an and that Islam's intrinsically violent nature is self-evident to anyone who can pick up and read its central text. The general approach is no doubt familiar to anyone who has had to suffer through Bill Maher quoting Qur'anic verses. Glenn Beck is another public figure who has embraced this methodology, explaining in his polemical screed *It IS about Islam* that Muslims' "own words" prove that Islam is uniquely prone to violence and fanaticism and, consequently, incompatible with liberal ideals of freedom or democracy:

> We're going to quote straight from the Quran, Islam's most holy book, so you can see what it really says. We're going to quote straight from the Hadith, the collected deeds and sayings of Allah's prophet Muhammad, which form one of the primary bases of Islamic law. And we're also going to expose the foolish, naïve, and, as we'll learn in some cases, intentionally deceptive views of Islam apologists in the United States who have worked hard to convince everyone that there is nothing to see here. That there isn't something inherently wrong with the way millions of people are practicing the Islamic religion. That Islam has nothing to do with the fact that so many people want us dead.[11]

The problems here are manifold, but three in particular deserve attention. As many critics have noted, many religious texts contain passages that denigrate nonbelievers and that call for violence. Surely the Qur'an does not have a monopoly on such problematic content. Those who favor theological explanations are also unable to provide an account for the sudden proliferation of militant groups and insurgencies over the last four decades. If Islam is the problem, shouldn't it always have been a problem? If contemporary violence stems from certain Qur'anic verses that incite believers, how are we to understand the long periods in Islamic history that were not characterized by such militancy? Are we supposed to believe that Muslims did not have Qur'ans back in Olden Times? In short, explanations that are built around a trans-historical, essentialist conception of Islam are of little use to explaining the sudden, and in many ways unprecedented, resurgence of a particular type of jihad in the late twentieth century. Political and historical questions cannot be answered by recourse to theology alone because while religious texts (mostly) stay the same, their interpretations do not.

The final problem worth highlighting within a Scripturalist approach is more complicated, but arguably even more essential. Many people living in Western countries have come to think that religions function in essentially Protestant fashion. So ingrained is this as a normative model that we have to defamiliarize many of its assumptions in order to see how particular they actually are. For instance, it might seem ordinary for individuals to read the Bible alone, look for various meanings in its stories, and derive different spiritual and ethical benefit from this exercise. The Bible is largely regarded as a stand-alone text—one that you can make sense of without any other body of religious literature—that since its publication in vernacular languages beginning in the sixteenth century, laymen and women can access outside of a communal framework. Indeed, this was very much the goal of Martin Luther's Reformation, which sought to eliminate the role of clergy as intermediaries between the believer and the Word of God. All of this might seem quite unremarkable, so it is all the more important to underscore that this religious framework is *not* a universal one.

In contrast, Islam is a highly legalistic religion and the Qur'an has almost always been interpreted through a large body of supplementary texts. These include the traditions (aḥādīth, singular: ḥadīth) that record the sayings and deeds of the Prophet as well as voluminous commentaries and rulings of later scholars and jurists, resulting in a complex, century-spanning legal and exegetical literature. Like other religious texts, the Qur'an contains many passages that are ambiguous, allegorical, or simply contradictory. Some commands are considered limited in duration while others are eternal; some verses overrule others, and there is no consensus on which fall into which category. It has historically been the role of a specialized class of scholars and jurists (the ulema) to sort it all out, leaning on their own interpretive positions to mediate between the sacred text and everyday life. While Islam does not support a clerical infrastructure akin to the Catholic Church—there is no pope among Sunni Muslims to deliver declarative rulings, and scholars are a notably argumentative bunch—interpretation is also not a wholly democratic practice in which all views are considered valid. As the Qur'an states in an oft-quoted verse regarding the virtues of knowledge, "Are they equal, those who know and those who do not?" (Surah al-Zumar, 9). As we will see, one of the great ironies is that Western Islamophobes actually have something in common with many of the radicals they despise: namely, they read the Qur'an like good Protestants, casting aside much of this legal culture in favor of the "purity" of Islam's foundational texts.

To the extent that we can apply the term "fundamentalist" to the Islamic context, it is because of this fixation on origins, "the belief," to borrow from Michel Foucault, "that things are most precious and essential at the moment of birth."[12] Yet, as a term that originated to describe a new movement in American Protestantism a century ago, "fundamentalism" does not map easily onto the Islamic context. Debates that have animated modern Christian communities—about biblical literalism, for instance—do not exist in the same form within Islam, whose exegetes have long engaged in robust discussions about the allegorical or esoteric meanings of certain Qur'an verses while still assuming the authenticity of Muhammad's message. Moreover, in popular discourse, fundamentalism is used to connote a whole host of attitudes and behaviors—from extreme piety to exclusionary communal practices and a hostile view toward the outside world—that make it a rather imprecise label. What *is* useful about this term is its relatively recent vintage, a fact that gestures toward a more relevant point: fundamentalism is not the uncorrupted core of religious truth, miraculously preserved against the onslaught of modernity, a sort of time capsule from past centuries. Fundamentalist movements are the byproducts of modernity, reconstructions that are no less innovative than their liberal or reformist rivals. It is rather the denial of this fact that sets them apart.

It is through this lens that I approach Salafi* Islam, a revivalist movement that emerged as an attempt to reform by going back to the sources—in this case the Qur'an and Sunna, the ways of the Prophet Muhammad as recounted by his immediate companions. The intervening centuries are likewise regarded as times of decline and degradation, as the Muslim community drifted from the Prophet's model both politically and morally, adopting all sorts of syncretic religious practices that corrupted the faith. Thus, inherited traditions and local customs are cast aside in favor of a "true" Islam that is dictated by text rather than social practice. But the attempt to reconstruct a religious community along such lines is a fraught exercise, almost always leading to the narrowing of interpretive possibilities and to practices that are at odds with the surrounding culture. It is also a decidedly modern impulse, one that betrays itself in the self-conscious posturing of being "traditional." While most Salafis are not interested in today's jihad—and are rather regarded as "quietest" in the way one might have characterized Christian evangelicals in the United States prior to the 1970s—numerous militant groups (including al-Qaeda and the Islamic State) profess a broadly Salafi orientation with regard to questions of doctrine and legal interpretation. This shared ideological approach is one reason why attempts to

---

* Salafi is a term denoting *al-salaf al-sālih*, the pious forefathers who lived during the first three generations of Islam. Salafis claim that most foundational questions were decidedly settled during this early period and that the proper orientation is imitative rather than evolutionary.

distinguish between "good" Salafis (like Saudi Arabia, an important ally in the war on terror) and militant groups like the Islamic State have proved so difficult.

Yet there is a different mode of religiosity altogether—one that is oriented to the reality of diversity of practice, constant interpretation, and change. Institutionally, it is embedded in Islam's rich tradition of legal reasoning, which is accretive and arguably richer with time. This vision of Islam is no less authentic than the Salafi orientation, though the latter is often regarded as the original from which all others depart. This is a fiction. Salafi Islam is a modern invention, no less so than Islamic feminism. I belabor this point because it can help clarify an important method-ological question. Far too many words have already been uttered in furtherance of deciding whether the Islamic State is "really" religious or not. Did the group grow out of the inherently violent and fanatical nature of Islam? Or was it a consequence of material and political conditions, in this case, the regional instability and power vacuums left in the wake of the disastrous invasion of Iraq? For instance, President Obama tried to reassure Americans that the Islamic State was not "really" Islamic. "No religion condones the killing of innocents, and the vast majority of ISIL's victims have been Muslim."[13] Rather than a state imbued with a theolog-ical mission, the president argued that ISIL (his preferred acronym, referring to Islamic State of Iraq and the Levant) was little more than a band of terrorists. Critics had a field day with this attempt at nuance, indicating that the mere presence of "Islamic" in the group's name was proof enough of its religious credentials.

This debate has found its way into many academic accounts as well and often comes with the suggestion that viewing jihad as the byproduct of material forces means ignoring or misreading the importance of religious conviction. In the words of David Cook:

> The number of apologists who claim that jihad and terrorist activities carried out by radical Muslims have nothing to do with Islam or are solely the result of poverty or colonialism or other Western evils is still depressingly high. There is no lack of observers who will ask in bewilderment, "What was the cause of this?," even as an attacker says that his or her primary motivation stems directly from the Qur'an.[14]

As Roxanne Euben argued in an important work nearly twenty years ago, it is important to consider how individuals drawn to jihad explain their views and actions rather than brushing such accounts aside in favor of the material or political conditions that supposedly really matter.[15] But doing so requires a great deal of nuance: on the one hand, the ideology in question is not stable over time, but shifts radically in ways that cannot be explained purely with recourse to theology. Moreover, we need to understand why such interpretations gain purchase at certain moments and not others lest we fall back into inane pathologizing wherein the problem is "evil."

A Different Path

Historicizing jihad or contextualizing its appeal does not mean ignoring the clear declarations of its practitioners or casting their own professed motivations aside as false consciousness. The theoretical face-off between materialist and theological orientations is both unnecessary and unhelpful. We can sidestep it entirely if we view religions not as abstract essences that float through space in an unembodied fashion, but as contested, historically shifting, socially embedded phenomena. Religions are never just one thing. They change in relation to material conditions and evolve in dialectical relationship with real-life questions. People fight about what they mean in each generation. This fact does not make them less "authentic." It is rather part and parcel of how they function and why they are able to continue to claim a place of relevance within the lives of their practitioners. Change is less an aberration than the norm. Fundamentalists might deny this fact, but I see no reason why scholars need to join their choir.

With regard to contemporary jihad, this orientation allows us to treat it as one manifestation of Islam today, neither its essence nor its negation, and to similarly chart how this particular vision of religiosity has evolved. The present work takes up this approach in accounting for the rise and continued salience of the Islamic State against the backdrop of state fragmentation, crises of legitimation, and emergent configurations of sovereign and nonsovereign power. By moving the analysis to this plane, we can ask a different set of questions than those usually in circulation: What type of subject does the Islamic State envision, and what mode of politics are they invited to enact? How do constructions of identity and difference work within the global Caliphate? What is the relationship between today's jihad and different types

of governance? What should we make of violence targeting civilians? Thinking about contemporary jihad in these
terms also enables us to see parallels in more familiar quarters, from the reactionary fixation on "fake news" to mass
shootings and increasingly exclusionary forms of political
identity.

These questions remain relevant even as the Islamic State
has lost most of its territorial base, I argue, because they
ultimately reveal dynamics that are felt far beyond the con-
fines of the Caliphate. Even from a narrow national security
point of view, the notion that the group requires a safe haven
in order to inflict harm reflects outdated assumptions about
the relationship between territory and politics in a fully
globalized, and digitized, age. But more centrally to this
work, the Islamic State is worth studying not because it is
a threat to "us" but because its appeal, ideological pillars,
and operational rationale has much to teach about political
and social crises the world over. In this sense, I regard the
Islamic State as a microcosm that highlights the tensions and
limitations inherent within neoliberalism—a response that
both mimics and negates its underlying rationale. Thus, the
individual is central even as individual rights are ridiculed,
the community is both theoretically universal and exclusionary in practice, and sovereignty is punitive at the same time
that it is disavowed. Perhaps most importantly, examining
jihad alongside contemporary social and political formations in the West underscores a common nihilist thread, one
characterized by the inability to imagine a different sort of
life here on Earth. From this perspective, the apocalypse
and the end of history appear less like oppositional projects

than different symptoms of a common, and wholly modern, malaise.

Attending to this set of concerns enables us to see what is otherwise obscured in treatments that regard jihad as something foreign to the world that "we" inhabit. The chapters that follow take up this task in different ways, examining in turn ideas about agency, community, governance, violence, and political transformation that have emerged among mujahideen today. I should state that this is not a general history of jihad, even within the modern period, but a series of suggestions as to how we might consider "exotic" or "barbaric" phenomena not as historical aberrations, but as examples that expose that which is latent within the political and social forms we take for granted. As much as many want the Islamic State to belong to some other world—either the Islamic one or the medieval one—the more vital task is to ask what it reveals about the one we share.

1

A New Age of Private Violence

In the aftermath of September 11, 2001, President George W. Bush appeared before Congress—and millions of American viewers—to declare a war on terror. In a speech that announced the formation of the Department of Homeland Security and delivered an ultimatum to the Taliban, the President explained that the task was not merely the defeat of a group called al-Qaeda. "Our war on terror begins with al-Qaeda, but it does not end there. It will not end until every terrorist group of global reach has been found, stopped and defeated." Perhaps sensing the impossibility of fighting such an elusive enemy through conventional means—not to mention the endless duration that such a task implied—he cautioned his audience that this war would not resemble those of the past:

> This war will not be like the war against Iraq a decade ago, with a decisive liberation of territory and a swift conclusion. It will not look like the air war above Kosovo two years ago, where no ground troops were used and not a single American was lost in combat.

Our response involves far more than instant retaliation and isolated strikes. Americans should not expect one battle, but a lengthy campaign, unlike any other we have ever seen. It may include dramatic strikes, visible on TV, and covert operations, secret even in success. We will starve terrorists of funding, turn them one against another, drive them from place to place, until there is no refuge or no rest. And we will pursue nations that provide aid or safe haven to terrorism. Every nation, in every region, now has a decision to make. Either you are with us, or you are with the terrorists. From this day forward, any nation that continues to harbor or support terrorism will be regarded by the United States as a hostile regime.[1]

In theory the power to declare war rests with Congress, but such conventions had already been rendered obsolete by the extended "conflicts" in Korea and Vietnam—to say nothing of covert operations in Iran, Latin America, or Afghanistan during the Cold War. Despite the various campaigns undertaken by the US military in the last seventy years, Congress has not formally declared war since 1942. This fact attests not only to the concentration of power in the executive branch, but to the changing nature of the wars that the United States has fought: our foes are no longer other countries, but factions, non-state actors, or—as in the war on terror—abstractions.

The corollary is that so-called "conventional wars" (meaning those that nineteenth-century military theorists had in mind) seem to have gone out of fashion almost everywhere. In lieu of national armies facing off on the battlefield, conflicts involving several rival factions have torn apart Afghanistan, Iraq, Syria, Sudan, Somalia, Yemen, and Libya in recent years, and we are only a generation away from genocides in Rwanda and Bosnia. The implosion of states is the new normal. The great national wars that shaped the twentieth century likewise seem like ancient history, while the purposeful targeting of civilians has become so commonplace as to be constitutive of this new way of fighting. The resurrection of jihad over the last forty years belongs to this history as well—not as an example of failed modernization, but rather as a trailblazer. Almost everywhere we look we find that violence is less tied to states, a phenomenon that includes not only Islamic militant groups that contest the legitimacy of governments, but a wide range of what political scientists have come to call "non-state actors." This term encompasses many different types of nonsovereign entities that come to exercise power, from insurgent groups and NGOs to multinational corporations, private military companies (PMCs), and militias operating in conflict zones around the world—which as of this writing include several US cities.

A century ago the sociologist Max Weber defined the state as the "human community that (successfully) claims the monopoly of the legitimate use of violence within a given territory."[2] Modern European states developed through a lengthy process that involved wresting the power to use force from many other contenders, such as the Catholic Church and feudal lords who had their own private armies. It was a process that culminated in the systems of law and order many take for granted—that, for instance, if your home is broken into, you will likely call the police rather than try to track down the culprit yourself. Weber highlighted that this accord rested on a necessary link between political legitimacy and force: absent the former, there was no way to effectively concentrate the latter in the state's hands. Today many states fall short of this criterion: the government lacks the legitimacy required to monopolize violence or the capacities needed to enforce the law. In such cases, you might not trust government officers any more than you trust the person who harmed you. Consequently, disputes bring other players into the mix, from tribal councils to charities, community organizations, militias, and mercenary forces.

Concentrating violence in the hands of the state is not an inherent good. Past and present experiences with totalitarianism make it clear that modern states are capable of inflicting violence on an unprecedented scale. The only thing laudable about restricting the use of violence to states has been the possibility of exerting democratic control over it. The oft-repeated observation that democracies do not go to war with one another is built around the presumption that popular majorities will eschew warfare and that such conflicts are less likely if the burden of war—from military service to taxation—is evenly distributed throughout society. We would likewise expect that the undermining of democratic control over warfare accompanies the triumph of factional interests over the public good. It is no strange coincidence that US forces are currently embroiled in more than a dozen conflicts worldwide about which the public knows very little and that the growth of such wars under neoliberal auspices has been accompanied by attempts to undermine democratic governance—from Citizens United to outright voter suppression. Of crucial importance, the waning of democratic control over violence does not mean that states become less coercive. On the contrary, as they become less responsive to the needs of their citizenry, they also rely more on brute force to sustain prevailing political and economic conditions—something that became painfully apparent in the government response to the 2020 anti-racism protests in the United States.

Neoliberalism is a notoriously difficult phenomenon to define, connoting both a distinctive approach to markets and governance as well as the varied ideological forms—for example, individualism—that support its underlying structural assumptions. While often characterized as a *laissez-faire* style of economic management in which the government intervenes as little as possible in the private sector, it is more accurately described as a process of institutional capture wherein the state, including its regulatory agencies, is recalibrated and redeployed to serve the needs of capital.[3] The goal is no longer the public good, but the maximalization of corporate profitability, which generations of business leaders and their acolytes have argued is synonymous with broad-based well-being and prosperity.

The most common view is that neoliberalism emerged as a response to the growth crises of the 1970s, in which the rate of return on capital fell on account of a variety of factors, ranging from oil shocks to increased competition from emerging markets.[4] Ideas that were once regarded as fringe by economists began to move to the center of universities and think tanks and from there to government agencies—not because they were widely accepted, but because they had the weight of cold hard cash behind them. For instance,

Friedrich Hayek secured his influential post at the University of Chicago through the external funding provided by the William Volker Fund, a right-wing foundation dedicated to disseminating free market ideas. Similarly, a generation earlier the American Enterprise Institute emerged as part of the millionaire backlash to the New Deal—in which the state assumed an active role not just in regulating business, but in trying to provide some minimal safety net for its citizens—counting executives from many of the country's largest corporations among its founders.

As a style of governance, neoliberalism aspires toward the selective hollowing out of the state: its champions view the provision of basic human needs, from education to health care and housing, as best secured through the private market rather than through the state. Its hallmarks are lower rates of taxation—supported, incredulously at this point, by the claim that such reductions lead to greater levels of investment—attacks on organized labor, and the dismantling of publicly funded social services. All this in the name of "freedom" of a particular type. We need to stress that the dismantling of the state under neoliberalism is decidedly uneven: while budgets evaporate for public schooling or drug treatment programs, there is no such shortfall for police, prisons, and the military. In this too we can find parallels from colonial contexts, wherein spending on "security"—the police, prisons, and soldiers required to pacify public opposition to imperial control—accounted for a large percentage of government budgets, while few resources remained for public goods such as education.[5] Decades of such spending prioritization has produced an increasingly precarious social reality in the

United States today, one that is maintained largely through the tools of coercion, criminalization, and incarceration.

As a tool to shield the wealth of individuals and corporations from the sort of redistributive projects that built the American middle class, neoliberalism has been spectacularly successful. One need only consider that income tax rates on the top bracket hovered between 70 and 94 percent from 1936 to 1980, whereas in 2018 billionaires paid only 23 percent of their income in state, local, and federal taxes, compared to an average of 28 percent for working class people.[6] But neoliberalism has just as spectacularly failed to provide broad-based prosperity, leading rather to record levels of economic inequality, declining developmental indexes, and what Ruth Wilson Gilmore has termed the "organized abandonment" of black, brown, and poor communities. Above all, the neoliberal state provides few public checks on capital accumulation; instead it promotes a form of market freedom that even its champions recognize is at odds with democracy. Senator Mike Lee from Utah was explicit in this regard, writing on Twitter, "Democracy isn't the objective; liberty, peace, and prospefity [sic] are. We want the human condition to flourish. Rank democracy can thwart that." Indeed, from increased disregard to the human costs of pollution to the rollback of workplace safety laws and attacks on public education, the social and political effects of neoliberalism in the West are beginning to resemble those more typically associated with colonial and postcolonial states of the Global South. And why not, given that it was in these latter contexts that the modern state was notoriously honed as a vehicle to maximize commercial profitability by suppressing democratic demands.

In short, if the process of modern state formation involved the concentration of force in public institutions, an uneven and difficult process to say the least, we seem to be living through the reverse mechanism. A number of states in the Global South are actively fragmenting, while those in the West are eagerly getting "out of the way" of the market. (The lack of a coordinated response from the US federal government to Covid-19 has resulted in a mortality rate 40 percent higher than in other G-7 nations.)[7] Neither trajectory appears very favorable to democratic governance, a fact that will almost certainly lead to further shifts in the use of violence both within states and without. This does not indicate that the world is moving backward in time, because whatever model of sovereign or nonsovereign power supplants the international state system is bound to differ in substantive ways from the old feudal or imperial orders. But it does suggest that we are hurtling toward a new age of private violence, one whose traces can be found not merely in conflict zones, but in the heart of the West, and whose makings are fundamentally antidemocratic. As Ajay Singh Chaudhary has argued, "States do not drown in seas of democracy; they dissolve or are diminished by private power."[8]

Placing the recent history of jihad within this global context should spur us to ask: What is the relationship between today's religious militancy and the state? Posing the question in such terms shifts the analytic field away from the tightly bounded world of "Islamic violence" to suggest other, more productive points of comparison. It allows us to finally relinquish any notion of jihad as an unbroken chain and likewise to abandon the fruitless quest to locate roots of contemporary militancy in Qur'anic verses or medieval fatwas. Rather than regarding today's mujahideen as heirs to seventh-century warriors, we can instead consider them alongside more compelling corollaries, however strange these bedfellows might initially seem.[9] In short, by looking across cultural and geographic lines, it is possible to discern a new constellation of violence emerging.

War and Terror, Revisited

At face value it seems like a substantial gulf separates terrorism from war, which might suggest images as disparate as the Twin Towers collapsing on the one hand and the D-Day invasion on the other. Yet the moral distinction conjured up in such contrasts—terrorism, cowardly and evil; war, unfortunate but necessary—has become increasingly difficult to sustain for a number of reasons. Take the widespread notion that terrorism targets civilians whereas wars are chiefly between armies. Although civilian casualties are accepted as collateral damage, noncombatants are supposedly not primary targets. Yet the targeting of civilian populations has been a fixture of modern warfare since the early twentieth century. World War II—"the good war"—included numerous such instances, from the fire-bombing of Dresden to the atomic attacks on Hiroshima and Nagasaki. Elaborating on these difficulties, Virginia Held has noted some of the logical pitfalls that one must stumble into if we hold that the intentional targeting of civilians is the mark of terrorism. Is it sound to conclude, for instance, that al-Qaeda's attack on the Twin Towers was terrorism, whereas

their simultaneous attack on the Pentagon—an undoubtedly military target—was not?[10] The slippery logic at play
in upholding the civilian/combatant criteria has led many to
abandon it entirely, which is not to say we should treat war
and terror in a totally undifferentiated fashion.

Rather, the most compelling logical distinction remains
the most unsatisfactory ethical one: war is the purview of
states, whereas terrorism is violence undertaken by non-state
actors. This definition was taken for granted for many centuries, seeming self-evident to Jean Jacques Rousseau, for
instance, when he wrote that "War is not ... a relationship
between one man and another, but a relationship between
one state and another."[11] The distinction lies not in tactics or
the justice of the cause, but in the nature of the entity wield-
ing force. Not surprisingly, this is the definition favored by
governments who "characteristically define 'terrorism' as
something only their opponents can commit."[12] Notwithstanding the growing body of theoretical literature on "state
terror," the idea remains a contradiction in terms for most
policy analysts and government officials wedded to the idea
that state violence alone is legitimate—a proposition that at
times bleeds into the notion that all state violence is legitimate. Non-state actors can launch insurrections or terrorize
populations, but they cannot wage war in the formal sense.

In a similar vein, Muslim jurists writing about jihad largely
took the state for granted. While there is a tendency to regard
jihad as an utterly foreign phenomenon—either in the guise
of "holy war" or terrorism—much of the mystique falls
away when one understands it as a mode of warfare, directed
by Muslim rulers and bearing its own rules of engagement.

Browsing through the vast juridical literature on jihad helps lift the fog of exoticism, as the issues tackled therein are of quite practical nature: Who has the authority to declare war, and on whom? How should the believer conduct himself in battle? How should fighters treat noncombatants? Should places of worship be guarded? What weapons can be used? These far more quotidian questions constitute the majority of the vast theological and legal discussions regarding jihad. As Faisal Devji has clarified:

> The debate on jihad in the Muslim tradition is largely juridical in nature, concentrating upon attempts to define legitimate occasions for holy war, permitted rules of engagement and the like. There is for instance the distinction between the offensive war to spread Islam and the defensive one to protect it, as well as that between the greater or spiritual jihad against one's own evil impulses and the lesser or military jihad against an internal enemy. For our purposes, however, what is of chief interest is the fact that this debate, like every legal discussion, is concerned primarily with the privileges of authority—in this case with *reserving the jihad's military function for the properly constituted authority of a state.*[13]

The legal literature around jihad developed in earnest during the Umayyad and Abbasid Caliphates and often in clear conversation with the imperatives of governance. The Umayyad Caliphate ruled from its base in Damascus over Arabia and the Levant from 661–750 CE/41–132 AH, whereas its successor, the Abbasid Caliphate, ruled from Baghdad over an even larger territory until the Mongol invasion of 1258 CE/656 AH. These were formative years in the history of Islam, corresponding not merely to the geo-graphic expansion of Islamic empires but also to a period of extraordinary scientific, philosophical, and artistic pro-duction. This was also a period of intense doctrinal conflict, negotiation, and eventual crystallization in which the four Sunni law schools emerged, hadith collections were for-malized, and scholars established the principles of Islamic jurisprudence. That extended treatments of jihad seemed to flourish near the seats of political power merely underscores the essential relationship between war and the state.[14]

Indeed, and despite their other points of disagreement, the jurists by and large agreed that jihad could only be waged under the direction of a legitimate ruler. In Khaled Abou El Fadl's words, "the jurists seemed to relegate the decision to make war or peace to political authorities," and conse-quently, literature on "the conditions that warrant a jihad is sparse. It is not that the classical jurists believed that war is always justified or appropriate; rather, they seemed to assume that the decision to wage war is fundamentally polit-ical."[15] This makes intuitive sense and in fact corresponds to how Western political philosophers viewed the question of war. Writing in the medieval Christian context, Thomas Aquinas stated, "A private person does not have the right to make war... But since the responsibility for the common-wealth has been entrusted to rulers it is their responsibility to defend the city or kingdom."[16] Individuals can—and often must—participate in a war as soldiers, but they cannot wage one on their own. This is why the law regards someone who kills out of their own volition as a murderer but does not extend this judgment to the soldier who kills in battle. That is, a declaration of war by a recognized authority serves as a legal device that renders violence permissible. For the most part, mujahideen prior to the twentieth century were conscripts rather than insurgents or vigilantes.[17]

We find another reflection of this fact in the way that Muslim jurists understood the obligation to engage in jihad. One of the principle distinctions of shariʿa is that between individual (*fard ʿayn*) and collective obligations (*fard kifāya*). In general, individual obligations include those like fasting, prayer, and pilgrimage, which one must perform for oneself. They are of a different legal status than commandments that rest upon the community as a whole, such as the obligation to bury the dead. In the latter case, some members of the community can fulfill the obligation for all. Most Sunni jurists in the early period "consistently asserted that it was the caliph alone who possessed the right and prerogative to call for jihad and that the people were under no personal obligation to wage jihad until the caliph summoned them to it."[18] Jihad was, accordingly, viewed as a communal obligation (*fard kifāya*) that was fulfilled on a collective basis, much as individuals might be drafted in wartime. Under extraordinary circumstances, jihad could become a personal obligation in matters of defense—for instance, upon Muslims facing invasion or those in their immediate vicinity.[19]

Nevertheless, the legal tradition still took it for granted that individuals did not declare jihad on their own, no more so than European peasants were in a position to declare war upon a neighboring kingdom. But on the heels of the vast social and political upheavals of modernity, a number of urgent questions appeared on the horizon that would definitively transform this tradition: How could the Muslim community discharge its obligation to engage in jihad absent political autonomy? What if there was no legitimate ruler to lead the faithful in battle? Could one declare jihad against a Muslim ruler? It was in the context of democratization and a critique of absolutism that thinkers started asking questions in this vein, which arguably could not have been formulated were it not for seismic shifts in ideas about governance, leadership, and subjectivity. Indeed, it is not hard to trace the theoretical seeds behind this realignment back to liberal sentiments, both with regard to how political authority is legitimated and the elevation of the individual as primary political subject.

Thus, and not surprisingly given the overall transformation of warfare in the last century, jihad has shifted in fundamental ways and today bears only fleeting resemblance to premodern iterations—to say nothing of theoretical formulations in classical texts. That most people have come to associate it not with war but with terror is itself very telling. However, even as modern manifestations of jihad depend on certain shared conceptual shifts, we must be cautious to avoid treating them as a singular phenomenon. For instance, despite all the international solidarity they mobilized, the wars waged by mujahideen in Afghanistan and Bosnia in the final decades of the twentieth century remained within the operational logic of the nation-state. Independence was their goal even if, as in Bosnia, it was tied to a secular government.[20] Al-Qaeda offered a different model entirely— detached from any particular territory or cultural formation, with an operating structure that, as characterized by Philip

Bobbitt, "more greatly resemble[s] VISA or Mastercard organization charts" than "the centralized, hierarchical structures of nation state governmental organizations."[21] So too, the Islamic State has advanced an alternative vision, trying to reestablish political authority over the practice of jihad while maintaining al-Qaeda's global vision of both Muslim identity and the field of operations. Each of these formations bear their own marks of distinction, but none of them can be understood outside of the modernity that produced them.

Attending to the seismic shifts that undergird the history of modern jihad compels us to raise a new set of questions. If today's jihad does not look much like its earlier iterations, what does it resemble? As I argue throughout, tracing these points of connection has much to teach us about a world held in common.

The New Face of War

One pathway into this subject is to contextualize contemporary jihad within the broader experience of twenty-first century warfare and to note how far afield this reality is from classical theories. Few of us, for instance, would be satisfied with the idea that Bashar al-Asad's forces were fighting a war in Syria while opposition groups were roving gangs of terrorists.[22] Taking stock of this conceptual ambiguity, the political scientist Mary Kaldor has argued that the contemporary era is characterized by a new type of warfare altogether, one that requires us to scrap the lexicon of earlier centuries and attend more systematically to the ways that such violence operates in the present. Whereas conventional wars sought "the capture of territory by military means," Kaldor argues that new wars involve exerting control over civilian populations by sowing fear and hatred:

> The aim is to control the population by getting rid of everyone of a different identity (and indeed of a different opinion) and by instilling terror. Hence the strategic goal of these wars is to mobilize extremist politics based on fear and hatred. This often involves population expulsion through various means such as mass killings and forcible resettlement, as well as a range of political, psychological and economic techniques of intimidation. This is why all these wars are characterized by high levels of refugees and displaced persons, and why most violence is directed against civilians. Behavior that was proscribed according to the classical rules of warfare and codified in the laws of war in the late nineteenth century and early twentieth century, such as atrocities against non-combatants, sieges, destruction of historic monuments, etc., constitutes an essential component of the strategies of the new mode of warfare.[23]

Kaldor's immediate case study was the war in Bosnia-Herzegovina, but elements of her analysis are clearly visible in other conflict zones, from the South Sudan to Islamic State–controlled Syria and Iraq. The fact that all of these countries were engaged in civil wars is far from incidental; the contestation of political authority—the robustness of which is supposed to help us distinguish war from terror—is built into their DNA. Taking Kaldor's lead, it is far more productive to consider certain manifestations of contemporary jihad alongside other "new war" factions than to regard them as the unwelcome resurrection of medieval fanaticism.

Take the case of Iraq, for instance, where a number of insurgent groups began to emerge over the summer of 2003 to challenge the US occupation. Some were explicitly secular and nationalist—such as the Popular Resistance for the Liberation of Iraq or the Ba'thist Fedayeen Saddam—while others readily deployed Islamic frameworks to mobilize their forces. Among the latter we could look to the 1920 Revolution Brigades, Sunni militias operating out of Anbar province, or Muqtada al-Sadr's Madhi Army. Finally, the chaos of postwar Iraq offered al-Qaeda a new foothold in the region, from which it managed to foment a sectarian war between Sunni and Shi'a communities and spawn the Islamic State. Despite their substantive differences in opinion with regard to what an independent Iraq should look like, all of these groups undertook guerrilla operations against US forces and their allies that were characterized as terrorism. Most targeted civilians and participated in the effective ethnic cleansing of Iraq that occurred between 2006 and 2008. Cities and villages in which Sunni and Shi'a populations had long lived alongside one another became homogenized in the matter of months as each group retreated to their respective strongholds; those living on the "wrong" side were forced out (or worse). The violence drove the number of refugees to 4.7 million by 2008 according to the United Nations High Commissioner for Refugees.[24] The use of death squads and torture was widespread, including among government forces, some of whom were also members of Shi'a militias. Where do the lines of demarcation between resistance, terrorism, civil war, and jihad actually lie? The difficulty we face in trying to sort Iraq's numerous insurgent groups along such lines underscores that far from being stuck in the past, jihadist groups are right at home in the new wars of this century.

Moreover, however much Americans were cast as the new Mongols, the resulting insurgency and interfactional fighting looked less like thirteenth-century Baghdad than contemporary civil wars elsewhere. Consider, for instance, the war that broke out in South Sudan in 2013, two years after its recognition as an independent state. President Salva Kiir Mayardit accused his former deputy, Riek Machar, of attempting a coup d'état, and the struggle quickly descended into a struggle for primacy between two ethnic groups, the Dinka and Nuer. Government forces, dominated by ethnic Dinkas and supported by a number of irregular militias—including the President's private army, Mathiang Anyoor—began killing ethnic Nuers in the capital of Juba shortly after the war began, going door to door in what has been described as a pogrom, and killing hundreds more in the police station. The final report of an African Union commission of inquiry found that, in the oil-rich Unity State, "government forces destroyed almost everything, killed civilians, burned houses and farms, killed cattle, committed sexual violence, and killed children and teenagers despite the cessation of [a] hostility agreement signed in Addis Ababa."[25] The opposition's forces were blamed for the 2014 massacres in Bentiu, in which ethnic Dinkas were targeted. Assailants reportedly went into traditional places of refuge—churches, hospitals, and the Kali-Bellee mosque—and separated people based on ethnicity before killing hundreds of them. Rape has been weaponized by all factions, including government forces. According to UN estimates nearly 2.3 million South Sudanese have fled to neighboring countries, while another 1.87 million remain displaced internally.[26]

South Sudan is a predominately Christian country with only a small Muslim minority (approximately 6 percent according to a 2012 estimate),[27] and the fault lines of the civil war have been largely ethnic and political. There is no recourse to jihad to explain gratuitous—and quite often, grotesque—violence like raping women before burning them alive, as one UN report detailed.[28] As has too often been the case over the last century, people who lived side-by-side for generations showed themselves all too willing to commit atrocities for the sake of "their" communities. (That ethnic or religious identity should trump all other forms of community does not reflect the natural state of affairs but is rather the outcome of shifting calculations.) Indeed, South Sudan has all the characteristics of a new war that Kaldor noted decades before in Bosnia: state fragmentation, private militias, the criminalization of the economy, widespread atrocities against civilians including sexual violence, and ethnic cleansing, resulting in an extreme refugee crisis. Jihadi factions are not among the partisans, but they have far more in common with South Sudanese militias than medieval Muslim warriors.

Like other insurgents, Islamic militant groups—from the Islamic State to Hay'at Tahrir al-Sham in Syria and al-Shabaab in Somalia—flourish where states are fragmented and political authority is contested. In each of these conflicts we can see the telltale signs of a new war: the dissolution of the combatant-civilian distinction and the purposeful targeting of the latter; ethnic cleansing; the targeting of places of worship and other sanctuary sites that classical rules of warfare (including Islamic sources) proscribed; the development of a war economy built around extortion, looting, and struggles to control valuable natural resources; and the disappearance of any separation between the battlefield and the home front. A lengthy pamphlet released in 2007 to announce the birth of the Islamic State in Iraq demonstrated just how well the group grasped the changing nature of warfare and what this fact implied for its own aspirations. Tackling the naysayers who would dispute its formation based on the fact that it lacked territorial consolidation or genuine sovereignty, the pamphlet writers advanced the argument that such traditional markers of statehood mattered less and less in the modern world. So too the traditional concept of war required rethinking to match this emergent reality, in which "the classical style of conducting battles through open fronts and orderly lines does not reflect the reality of the current battle."[29]

The case for thinking about jihad in the new war framework is likewise strengthened by the proclivity of borrowing strategies from an earlier generation of revolutionaries and insurgents. One of the best examples of this is the compilation of writings published online in 2004 under the title *The Management of Savagery*, which has become something of a how-to guide for militant groups. As scholar Steve Niva has argued, the text is representative of the field of "jihadi security studies," which arose in response to Ayman Zawahiri's call for new strategic thinking after the fall of al-Qaeda's safe haven in Afghanistan. While the ideological orientation is Salafi, the text's "core assertions primarily draw upon the strategic doctrines of communist and leftist insurgents such as Mao, Che and Western theorists of insurgent warfare, the most consistently cited of which is Robert Taber's *The War of the Flea.*"[30] Even ideas by the heterodox US military thinkers William S. Lind and Thomas X. Hammes make an appearance. A summary version of the strategy—in the form of a five-point flow chart—even appeared in the very first issue of *Dabiq*, the Islamic State's short-lived English language magazine. First comes migration (*hijra*), then congregation with like-minded individuals (*jamāʿa*), who work together to destabilize existing regimes, consolidate their control over territory (*tamkīn*), and finally resurrect the Caliphate (see figure below).

Invoking Abu Musʿab al-Zarqawi, who rose to prominence as the leader of al-Qaeda Iraq following the US invasion, the feature stresses the dependence of this strategy on crumbling states: as governments lose control over different areas, their territories become bases for jihad. Such references illustrate the centrality of the Iraq war to the emergence of new practices and understandings of jihad—in other words, the "eternal" religious command seems to have undergone substantive revision in response to the material reality of war and occupation. As an article in *Dabiq*'s inaugural issue explained:

How to achieve the Caliphate in five easy steps:
a flow-chart from the first issue of Dabiq.

The *jama'ah* [sic] would then take advantage of the situation by increasing the chaos to a point leading to the complete collapse of the *taghut** regime in entire areas, a situation some refer to as "*tawahhush*" ("mayhem"). The next step would be to fill the vacuum by managing the state of affairs to the point of developing into a full-fledged state, and continuing expansion into territory still under control of the *taghut*.[31]

---

* *Taghut/ṭāghūt* (pl. *tawāghīt*) is an Arabic term that means "idol" in classical usage and is used by contemporary militants to refer to tyrannical rulers, playing off the word's theological associations. The tyrant is one who elevates himself above the status of other men, thereby denying their fundamental equality, which itself constitutes an act of idolatry. For the sake of ease, I will use the Anglicized "taghut" and "tawaghit" throughout.

It was in its attempt to construct an alternative political structure that the Islamic State most differed from its militant predecessors and contemporary peers. While accepting the legal recategorization of jihad as a personal obligation, explored in depth in Chapter 2, the Islamic State nonetheless rejected the previous generation's assertion that waging it could be done without a leader. A pamphlet released early in the group's formation, *Informing the People about the Birth of the Islamic State of Iraq*, emphasized the obligation to bind together and create a state, as many core religious duties could occur only under its umbrella. This applied to jihad as well, the authors argued, such that "there is no jihad without a commander and leader, an Imam."[32] This emphasis on the leader's centrality departs from an earlier generation of idealogues like Abdallah Azzam, who "aimed to empower individuals to ignore the teaching of religious, political, and familial figures in order to do jihad on their own volition."[33] In this sense, we can regard the Islamic State as an attempt to reroot jihad in the authority of the state after decades of use as an insurgent tactic. Yet, as we shall see, the nature of this "state" has evolved considerably, and it advances a different view of the relationship between territory, population, and violence than the one Max Weber identified a century ago.

The demonstrable link between new wars and state fragmentation also explains the ease with which the Islamic State has established, or absorbed, franchises in other conflict zones. As of this writing, the Islamic State claims affiliates in Central and West Africa, the Sinai Peninsula, Iraq, Syria, Yemen, Libya, Central Asia, and Southeast Asia (including the Philippines, Indonesia, and Malaysia). The situation in each of these countries possesses its own complexities, which are too great to survey here. The great uniting factor, if one can be said to exist, is the weakness and perceived illegitimacy of central governments and the associated turn toward factionalized violence. Perhaps needless to say, deploying the vast resources of American Empire to equip armies and police forces is not enough to stabilize states in the throes of legitimation crises. Success in this regard would seem to require far more expansive—and in many instances oppositional—thinking about the meaning of security than has heretofore circulated among policy makers.

Back to the Future

Twitter has never been my medium of choice, but it is occasionally useful in bringing the subtext to the fore. After sharing a fairly bland article about the lack of cost savings associated with outsourcing key military functions, I was surprised to receive a sharply worded message in response:

> The military can not [sic] and will not ever take on a task like Boko Haram. In America—it is not within their scope. I am here to explain this to you. Private military contenders are the only ones who can fight those kind of wars.

Coming from someone claiming to be a veteran of Blackwater and DynCorp—two of the United States's largest private military contractors—the comment succinctly underscored the antidemocratic nature of current US wars. Indeed, the United States is engaged in a dozen conflicts across the world about which the public is largely in the dark ("those kind of wars") and which private security contractors increasingly fight on our behalf—for a tidy fee, of course. DynCorp, for example, has provided police training in both Afghanistan and Iraq, and it currently has contracts to support the Saudi Arabian National Guard and Royal Air Force as well as US and NATO forces in Afghanistan. The vast majority of the company's annual revenue (just over $2 billion in 2018) comes from the US federal government, though this is only a drop in a bucket when you consider that total government spending on such services tops $200 billion annually. Private contractors have consistently outnumbered regular US forces in both Iraq and Afghanistan, and often by huge margins.[34] In 2020, for instance, there were over 22,000 contractors working in Afghanistan as compared with approximately 4,000 US troops.[35] It is also significant to note that in 2017 the Department of Defense stopped reporting the number of US military personnel in Afghanistan, Iraq, and Syria, accentuating the attempt to undermine democratic oversight of these wars. The privatization of violence did not spring up suddenly from the primordial ether. In the context of the neoliberal turn described above, wherein many core functions of the state have been turned over to private hands, security too is "no longer seen as exclusively provided by the state, but rather as something to be bought from a marketplace," as Rita Abrahamsen and Michael Williams have noted. "The state is merely one of many potential providers, and not necessarily the most efficient and reliable one."[36]

The embrace of PMCs was ostensibly in response to the force reductions brought about by the end of the Cold War but was equally a product of the move toward market-based solutions tout court. Among the first was Executive Outcomes, which was founded in 1989 by a former lieutenant colonel in the South African army, Eeben Barlow, who had previously worked as a commander in one of the apartheid government's death squads (incredulously named the Civil Cooperation Bureau). Once described as "the world's first fully equipped corporate army," Executive Outcomes played a pivotal role in civil wars in both Angola and Sierra Leone while also servicing corporate clients in the oil industry. While the privatization of the US military began in earnest in the 1990s, it received a boon from Donald Rumsfeld's appointment as Secretary of Defense. On September 10, 2001, Rumsfeld declared war on the Pentagon's bureaucracy and promised to leverage the private sector's spirit of competition and innovation to create a leaner war machine. One of the firms that stood to gain enormously from this shift was Blackwater (now Academi), which was founded in 1996 by former Navy seal Erik Prince, who hails from a wealthy Michigan family of conservative powerbrokers. (Prince's sister Betsy DeVos, who served as Secretary of Education during the Trump administration, pursued the privatization of US schooling with the same gusto.)

Much has been said about the privatization of the US military, and we need not rehash it all here. What is most significant for our purposes is that the use of PMCs enables leaders to bypass public oversight of warfare. In the words of John F. Sopko, the US special inspector general for Afghanistan reconstruction, "The only people who don't know what's going on and how good or bad a job we're doing are the people paying for it—the American taxpayers."[37] PMCs are consequently perfectly matched for waging wars without democratic consent. Perhaps the most insidious lesson of the Vietnam experience—communicated by anti-war protestors and draft dodgers alike—was that deeply unpopular wars cannot be sustained through conscription. It has proved much easier to fund an ever-increasing defense budget (few candidates for office want to appear "soft" on defense) through taxation and outsource the fighting to the private sector. Particularly as the nature of armed conflict has evolved, the private military sector has argued that it is more nimble, creative, and thus better equipped to deal with nontraditional adversaries.

The growth of the private security industry continues mostly unabated despite numerous reports linking companies to misconduct and human rights violations. These range from the abuse of migrants in detention facilities to clashes with local communities over land use and mining rights (particularly relevant for contractors hired by extractive industries) and instances of sexual harassment and assault by workers within this "highly male-dominated and traditionally masculine industry."[38] US readers might recall that over half the interrogators working at the notorious Abu Ghraib prison were employees of CACI International, while contractors employed by Blackwater killed fourteen Iraqi civilians and injured twenty more when they opened fire on Nisour Square in 2007. Despite such grave misconduct, the use of private security contractors continues to increase for reasons having very much to do with the unpopularity of current US military engagements. In the words of one report, "Because contractors operate in the shadows, without effective public oversight, they allow policymakers to have their cake and eat it too—by appearing to withdraw, while keeping proxy forces in theater."[39] Criticism from watchdog organizations has led to a greater push for government oversight of PMCs, though few states have established anything close to adequate protections. Pressure to regulate such entities offers a prime example of neoliberal logic in action: public funds are now required to oversee the private contractors who were supposedly saving taxpayer dollars by doing the job better and more efficiently. Yet even researchers from the libertarian Cato Institute have questioned whether private military contractors save the US government any money, noting that "despite all the claims of its advocates the free market ideology has hardly been confirmed by the evidence."[40]

Significant as they have become, PMCs are only part of the ever-growing market for private security services, which is projected to reach $420 billion by 2029.[41] This is likely an underestimate: "It is difficult to determine the full size of the private security market due to a large number of providers working within grey and black markets."[42] Encompassing not only the new mercenaries, this vast industry also includes companies hired to guard retail stores, schools, places of worship, and the homes of wealthy clients. According to *The Guardian*, "More than 40 countries—including the US, China, Canada, Australia and the UK—have more workers hired to protect specific people, places and things than police officers with a mandate to protect the public at large."[43] Private security guards are particularly prevalent in countries with extreme levels of economic inequality, such as India (an estimated 7 million private officers vs. 1.4 million state police), South Africa (487,000 private vs. 195,000 public), and Brazil (where private officers outnumber police 5:1).[44] In many instances private security workers are literally tasked with keeping the poor masses away from gated compounds and luxury hotels, serving as the violent enforcers of a highly stratified social order. Long a mainstay of elite life in the Global South, private security services are expanding rapidly in Western countries as well, perhaps not surprisingly given the overall uptick in economic inequality.

In a 2019 report co-authored by the Geneva Centre for Security Sector Governance and the Danish Institute for Human Rights, researchers noted the interrelation between the growth of private military and security services on the one hand and neoliberal reforms that undermine the effectiveness of states on the other.

> Due to a real or perceived increase in insecurity, security functions that were traditionally considered a State prerogative are increasingly undertaken by a range of private actors, especially where the demand cannot be met by public forces … This has occurred against the backdrop of a general trend towards privatization of public services, which includes decreased budget and personnel for armed forces and public security in many States.[45]

The factors driving the growth of private security services likewise gesture toward the link between the pursuit (and preservation) of profit and the weakness of states, including "high levels of foreign investment, in particular the presence of extractive industries; situations of recent or current armed conflict; or weak public governance, leading to a lack of trust in public security institutions."[46] In short, the existence of a luxury class of security services both reflects diminished public capacities and exacerbates them, undermining a sense of common civic experience. Security is no longer regarded as a basic function of the state, but something only available to those who can pay a premium.

A particularly jarring example of this trend came during the 2018 California wildfires, which ripped through nearly 1.9 million acres. Thousands of homes were lost to the blazes, which were the deadliest and most severe ever reported at that time. The $60 million mansion of Kim Kardashian and Kanye West was not among them—not because it was spared by geography or wind patterns, but because a team of private firefighters had been hired to protect the property. Increasingly used by insurance companies with large assets to protect—AIG reportedly has its own "Wildfire Protection Unit" while other insurers contract with Wildfire Defense Systems, a Montana based company—private firefighting offers a perfect example of the tiered access to public services that is fast becoming one of neoliberalism's trademarks.[47] "Rich people don't get their own 'better' firefighters, or at least they aren't supposed to," one writer quipped in exasperation.[48] Examples like this suggest that the United States is hurtling toward a sort of neofeudalism, characterized by extremely high levels of inequality, the ceding of public power to private entities, the dismantling of the social and the political as fields of democratic intervention, and gated access not merely to wealth or status, but to basic security and social services.

More recently, the US federal government's response to the Covid-19 pandemic—looking to the private market to volunteer solutions, rejecting national coordination, and only belatedly using the powers of the state to secure essential, life-saving supplies—has often seemed like an exercise in voluntary delegitimization. Who can possibly come away from this experience with a greater faith in the power of government to solve collective problems? "It might seem hyperbolic to compare the U.S. government to a failed state that cannot project its authority or adequately ensure the safety of its population," one journalist recently noted amidst the ongoing Covid-19 crisis. "But for much of the past month, the White House has shown an inability to do either."[49] While relying on spontaneous, unfettered market activity is an ill-suited strategy for battling a pandemic, it is not a "mishandling." It rather represents an extremely successful exercise in undermining public faith in government as a vehicle for creating a society that is just, fair, or decent.

This is another face of private violence, both miles away from the new wars terrain just surveyed and yet largely compatible with its rules of engagement. It is amid this broader reconfiguration of state and market forces, and the intertwined production of both security and precarity, that we need to situate our discussion about contemporary violence, jihad included. If every economic period has its corresponding forms of political community and culture of violence, neoliberalism finds its match in states that no longer impede private interests, and indeed, facilitate those interests at the expense of the public good. The fragmentation of states is not tangential to this history but core to its governing logic. That the effects of this anti-statist and anti-social logic are politically destabilizing, even in advanced democracies, has become painfully obvious. What I am suggesting is that far from standing apart from this drama, jihad plays a starring role.

The Periphery at the Center

The idea of placing contemporary jihad within the broader history of neoliberalism's triumph might seem counterintuitive. After all, how can a militant group like the Islamic State, which grew out of the US invasion of Iraq, have anything in common with private security guards in London or military contractors in Afghanistan? This question underscores the need for a theoretical orientation that is attuned to the ways in which common underlying forces can be experienced in radically different ways. Here too we can find a way forward by looking to the Global South.

One of the insights developed by historians of colonialism is that the experience of the "periphery" is inextricably intertwined with that of the center, regardless of how distinct they might appear. For instance, the way that colonies were integrated into the world market—not as independent entities, but as auxiliaries designed to fulfill specific needs of the imperial economy—ensured both European progress and the colonies' own underdevelopment. Thus, Indian textile manufacturing declined precipitously in the nineteenth century, as the British wanted raw materials that they could manufacture domestically and sell on the world market, not competition from their subjects. Technologies that could have rationalized Indian textile manufacturing—as they had done in Manchester—were purposefully kept out of the subcontinent, while tariffs were put in place in England to protect domestic manufacturing. In the English case, colonial economic integration helped fuel a massive expansion of nineteenth-century manufacturing, and with it, a wave of urbanization and the development of a working class. By the late nineteenth century, the political effects of these changes were being felt in the expansion of franchise rights and the introduction of state-funded compulsory education. India, by way of contrast, was living through the Great Famine of 1876–78, in which draught conditions were badly exacerbated by colonial policies. (During the famine, a record 320,000 tons of grain was exported to England.) Living standards actually seem to have declined for much of the nineteenth century and scant provision was made for public education, leaving literacy rates in the low single digits. These are not different histories, but different experiences of the same set of political and economic forces.

The challenge with understanding contemporary violence is to maintain this sense of simultaneity as we examine its different expressions. I have argued that we might begin by situating contemporary jihad in the new wars framework —thinking about it as an instance of violence that rivals that of the state, yet appeals to a different political rationale. Against this background it becomes possible to discern a broad continuum of violence that is no longer grounded in the nation-state, from PMCs to multinational corporations and even Islamic militant groups. The point is not that the Islamic State and Blackwater are essentially the same, but that they are two different manifestations of the same phenomenon, experienced—like other effects of capital—unevenly.

Moreover, we should note that many of the states at the center of this study share a common trajectory in their postindependence years that is intimately bound to the advance of neoliberalism. Pakistan, Syria, Iraq, Nigeria, Algeria, Egypt, and Libya each experienced tremendous pressure to liberalize their economies beginning in the late 1970s and extending to the first decade of the twenty-first century, with the attendant directives to reduce public subsidies and trim government spending on housing, health care, and education. Reading policy papers written in the 1990s—many of which assumed that political liberalization would follow closely on the heels of its economic cousin—is an unwelcome reminder of the hollow thinking at the heart of the Washington Consensus. The empirical results of the neoliberal experiment are in: increased rates of poverty and unemployment on one hand, and rising concentration of wealth in the hands of the ruling elite on the other.[50] None of these policies did much to support democracy or combat corruption, which rather grew as authoritarian governments guarded the pathways to private wealth accumulation. As Stephen J. King has shown, rather than undermining state patronage networks, liberal economic reforms gave authoritarian regimes a new lease on life. "With weak to nonexistent regulation of the privatization of state assets, regimes have discretionary power over these very resources and have utilized them to create new forms of rent-seeking behaviors."[51] Even the "success" stories—Syria in the first decade of this century, for instance, during which time its GDP more than tripled—contained clear seeds of the current disaster.[52] When accounting for the rise of Islamist movements in the 1980s and 1990s—many of which, like the Muslim Brotherhood, emerged to fill the social service gaps left by the contracting state—we must remember this shift toward "reform" and austerity. Finally, it is worth noting that many of the chief ideologues of contemporary jihad matured in the streets and prisons of the Middle East's autocratic regimes—and in particular those states (Jordan, Egypt, and Saudi Arabia) that became US aid recipients during the Cold War and that have historically served as cornerstones in the quest for "regional stability."

The colony has always been a theatre for experimentation, and many of the darkest innovations associated with modernity developed in colonial settings before coming home to roost. From the concentration camp (first used by the British in South Africa) to Orwellian systems of surveillance, the Global South has proved a fruitful laboratory to try things out. In terms of violence and warfare, developments in the "periphery" may again point toward the future. Far from failing to catch up, the Global South might have lapped those of us living in advanced democracies. Though it may seem counterintuitive, I will argue that examining the Islamic State's ideas about individual agency, community, governance, and political action allows us to see in high relief what is latent in the West's own political and social crises. Far from being a blast from the past, the Islamic State belongs to a possible future.

2
The Triumph of the Individual

This war is every Muslim's war.

—Abu Bakr al-Baghdadi

"Why did you join the Islamic State?" In recent years journalists and researchers have posed this question hundreds of
times to current and former members of the militant group.[1]
The answers vary—with foreign fighters often expressing a
degree of idealism out of step with the more pragmatic concerns of local Iraqis and Syrians attracted to the prospect of
a regular salary. Yet one common thread that runs through
many testimonies is the allure of being part of something
bigger than oneself, of fighting for something that truly
mattered. "Honestly, they gave the impression that they'll
help people and that they're the good against the evil ... and
I thought maybe I'll become a hero." In the words of one
NATO report:

Daesh [Islamic State] propaganda products are designed to create
the feeling that it is the organization that best understands what is
missing in their lives. Not only do they provide a path forward to
improving their lives, but they also provide a purpose larger than
the individual, the excitement that comes from doing something
valuable.[2]

If today's jihad offers atomized individuals a path to
community and self-fulfillment, that should be enough to
signal that this is no longer the same conceptual universe
as that inhabited by medieval or even early twentieth-
century Muslims. By contrast, even among the patriotically
inclined, we do not find Ottoman Muslims speaking of their
World War I service in terms of self-actualization. Peasant
farmers do not need a war to make their lives meaningful.
Fighting for the preservation of the empire, the protection
of Islam, the defense of the homeland, or simply because
they were forced to were more common motivations among
those who answered the call—to say nothing of those who
actively avoided conscription. It is not that today's jihad
totally eschews this type of collective vision, but that it
refracts it through a discourse that centers the individual
as the primary agent of change. How do we explain this
shift, and in what ways is it meaningful in accounting for
contemporary jihad?

It is a central premise of this book that jihad became
unmoored from its traditional keeper, the state, over the
course of the last century. In this chapter I argue that a new
ideological scaffolding has emerged to match this reality, one
in which individuals—as believers, soldiers, and martyrs

—have moved center stage. This shift clearly parallels the growth of private violence examined in Chapter 1, and indeed it would be strange if the broader transformation of warfare left jihad unscathed. On the contrary, the primacy of the individual in both moral and political terms reflects something novel within militant thought: namely, a sense of disenchantment with both politics as usual and established forms of collective resistance. This is one reason that the Islamic State considers Islamists like the Muslim Brotherhood apostates, as they seek to reform the existing political order rather than destroy it. That the ideological reconfiguration of modern jihad has taken place against the backdrop of diminished faith in the state and a corresponding pivot to a discourse of individual responsibility is not, I believe, a strange coincidence. In this, it bears traces of the moralizing turn we have seen in the West, in which every collective problem is presented as an individual ethical choice. Sure, you might not be able to stop climate change, but you can carry reusable shopping bags and buy beauty products made of natural dyes! The inadequacy of this focus on individual conduct in the face of systemic crises is readily apparent, but the governing logic of neoliberalism still propels us to think in such terms. What the new jihad offers, I would like to suggest, is the apparition of personal agency amid an ever-growing sense of collective futility.

This chapter examines the forms of individualism embraced by militant groups like al-Qaeda and the Islamic State (who approach this issue quite differently, as we will see) and ask what they might have to do with the world at large. Who is the modern *mujahid* as a political subject? How

does he, or she, exercise personal agency? How does today's
jihad provide a path for individuation and self-actualization?
How do we account for a political system that centers individuals as agents even as it deprives them of rights? And in
what ways are these dynamics part of a common political
condition, apparent not merely in the Caliphate's authoritarian dictates, but within expressions of right populism that
are ascendent in the West? In what follows, I will trace the
mechanics by which the individual moved to the center of
jihad in both ideological and material terms and suggest that
here too it is possible to discern traces of shifts felt around
the globe.

The Reformation Will Be Televised

In the years since the attacks of September 11, 2001, public
figures like Thomas Friedman and Salman Rushdie have
argued either that an Islamic Reformation is needed or,
more hopefully, is in the process of occurring. Just as the
Protestant Reformation is widely (if somewhat erroneously)
believed to have paved the way for a less literal relationship
with the Bible, advocates imagine an Islamic Reformation as
a sort of silver bullet. If only Muslims could muster it, they
too might gain all that came in Martin Luther's wake: liberalism, secularism, and the ultimate triumph of the market over
irrational forces—resulting in a political and social system
that privileges individuals and their freedom, in terms of
both conscience and commerce.

Unfortunately for such partisans, there is a strong case to
be made that an Islamic Reformation has already happened

and that—far from resulting in some sort of liberal utopia—contemporary jihad is one of its byproducts. Take, for instance, the case of Ruhul Amin (whose *nom de guerre* was Abu Bara' al-Hindi), a British Muslim of Bangladeshi descent who appeared in a 2014 Islamic State recruiting video:

> Oh brothers and sisters, open the Qur'an ... and everything will become clear to you ... All the scholars telling you: "Oh this is *fard* [a legal obligation], this is not *fard*, this is not time to do jihad"... forget everyone, read the Qur'an, read the book of Allah, the instruction of life, and you'll find out what is jihad and if you're meant to do jihad or not.[3]

Traditionally speaking, determining the conditions under which individuals are obliged to engage in jihad is a fairly complicated exercise: Was it declared by a legitimate ruler? Do you live in the vicinity of the battle? Did you get permission from your parents? But these legal questions were of no interest to our young fighter. He rather viewed the Qur'an as a stand-alone text that could be understood by the average person apart from the accompanying body of legal commentary.

Prior to the twentieth century, few Muslims thought to approach the Qur'an in this way. At the very least, most would have lacked the literacy required to read the Qur'an in good solitary fashion, though many did commit it to memory. The communal recitation of the holy word was far more common, and with it came communal frameworks for determining meaning. It was by sifting through the Sunna (which records the words and conduct of the Prophet), the opinions of early commentators, and the voluminous body of latter rulings that one could determine what the Qur'an actually intended to communicate or demanded from the believer. Because the Qur'an, like other scriptures, contains verses that seem to contradict one another, interpretation involves acts of textual reconciliation that go far beyond the apparent meaning of a single verse. When looking at a Qur'anic passage, for example, a scholar would have to consider the issue of abrogation, for instance, in which certain verses are understood to overrule others; whether the verse in question was *muḥkam* (clear) or *mutashābih* (ambiguous, esoteric, or allegorical) or historically bounded or eternally valid (and there is no central database that determines any of these questions definitively). It has traditionally fallen to jurists, working within their distinct traditions, to issue rulings as particular cases present themselves.

This inherent legal pluralism makes shariʻa, as an ongoing interpretive process, quite different than "law" in the popular sense of the term. Take the so-called "sword verse" (Qur'an 9:5), which is often invoked by Islamophobes and militants alike:

> But when the forbidden months are past then fight
> The polytheists wherever you find them and seize them,
> Beleaguer them, and lie in wait for them in ambush,
> But if they repent and establish regular prayers,
> And practice regular charity then the way is open for them:
> For Allah is Oft-Forgiving, Most Merciful.

How should one understand this directive given the presence of other verses that command mercy? The very next verse in the sequence (9:6) states: "If one of the polytheists asks thee for asylum, grant it to him, so that he may hear the word of Allah and then escort him to where he can be secure." Which should take precedence, 9:5 or 9:6? Unending hostility or tolerance? Who falls within the category of polytheists? And were these verses intended only for Muhammad's immediate context, or were they valid for all times and places?

Within the classical tradition, there were some who interpreted 9:5 as unrestricted in duration and more powerful than other verses commanding tolerance (such as al-Hasan al-Basri, d. 110AH/728 CE). Still other prominent figures, including ibn Ishaq and al-Tabari, understood the verse as counseling Muhammad to allow polytheists who might be interested in Islam the ability to hear his message and then return to their lands in safety regardless of whether they accepted it. In the late nineteenth century, the Egyptian reformer Muhammad 'Abduh argued that 9:5 was limited to the Prophet's immediate context in which he battled recalcitrant pagan tribes around Mecca (who are referred to in the prior verse, 9:4). More recently, the Syrian scholar Muhammad Said Ramadan al-Bouti argued that partisans who believe that 9:6 (the verse commanding toleration) is abrogated by 9:5 are ignoring the foundational principle that later verses typically abrogate earlier ones, and not the other way around. Truly diving into the legal complexities would also mean contending with who the "polytheists" might be, and here too we would encounter divergent opinions. While some interpret "polytheists" to mean all non-Muslims, others (including Hassan al-Banna, the Muslim Brotherhood founder) held that this category clearly does not include "People of the Book," that is, Jews and Christians.

We have barely scratched the surface of the scholarly debate, but it is already clear that what began as a seemingly simple exercise is incredibly complicated in practice. Any attempt to pretend otherwise marks a clear rejection of Islam's hermeneutic tradition, one that is a byproduct of modernity rather than a holdover from the past. As this fact suggests, for most of Islamic history, legal interpretation was not a practice undertaken by the masses, but rather the province of a scholarly class, the ulema, who had attained specialized training in exegesis and jurisprudence. This is not to say the ulema constituted an entrenched elite class. The doors of the madrasa were open to those who showed promise, even if they came from poor or provincial families. In this sense, there was a democratic aspect to Islamic learning as a mode of social advancement. We need to differentiate this, however, from the idea that anyone, regardless of their education or training, is able to derive authoritative rulings. The latter is an attack not merely on the traditional centers of institutional power, but on the knowledge that circulates within them. This distinction might seem incidental at first, but actually helps us differentiate between various "populist" critiques of elite power that are apparent in the West as well.

One of the pitfalls of viewing Islam as a monolith is that it obscures the extent to which contemporary jihad represents a radical challenge to dominant modes of religious, political, and social life: to Islam's complex legal culture and its traditional practitioners, to governments and the ruling class more broadly, and to family and immediate community as arbiters of meaning. It is not that militants reject this accord in full, but that they rework each of its components —interpretation, authority, community—in substantive ways. In particular, they have embraced a type of religious hermeneutics that rejects the authority of traditional elites and places individual interpretation at the center of the "authentic" Muslim experience. And while they do advance their own version of community—which I examine in more depth in Chapter 3—it is altogether different than the ones they grew up in, even among those from religious families. Indeed, as Oliver Roy has argued based on his own data set of individuals who took part in terrorist attacks in the West, the pathways to radicalization are more likely to include MMA gyms than the local mosque.

This is one reason that the rebuke of militant groups by mainstream Muslim scholars and clergy is often ineffectual. Take for instance the Open Letter to Abu Bakr al-Baghdadi, signed by hundreds of scholars and community leaders from Egypt, Uzbekistan, Morocco, the United States, Indonesia, and many other countries.[4] Published in September 2014, the letter to Baghdadi was neither grounded in a liberal discourse of universal human rights nor a misguided attempt to distinguish between ISIS and "real" Islam. Rather, the letter was written in the legal language of Islamic jurisprudence, and its refutations stemmed from the logic and precedents of this tradition. Endorsed by many prominent Sunni religious figures—including the Grand Mufti of Egypt, the head of the Nigerian National Supreme Council for Islamic

Affairs, the Chairman of the Indonesian Council of the Ulema, and numerous senior scholars from a wide range of educational institutions—the list of signatories reads like a "who's who" of the Sunni establishment. Alas, however laudatory the attempt to refute the Islamic State from within, such rebuttals land like a report by climate scientists at a Trump rally. Appeals to the authority of an entrenched religious establishment and its requisite forms of elite training are unconvincing to a generation with little knowledge of Shari'a or respect for its traditional practitioners. Indeed, according to a cache of Islamic State documents captured in 2016, recruits were well educated as a whole (the majority had completed high school and many had university degrees), but 71 percent of foreign fighters listed their level of religious knowledge as basic.[5]

Hewing to the customary position, the letter specified that jihad as a form of warfare commanded by states was entirely different than that taken up by individuals: "Jihad without legitimate cause, legitimate goals, legitimate purpose, legitimate methodology and legitimate intention is not jihad at all, but rather, warmongering and criminality." So too, the scholars took time to specifically rebuke Ruhul Amin's DIY approach to Islamic jurisprudence:

> It is not permissible to constantly speak of "simplifying matters," or to cherry-pick an extract from the Qur'an without understanding it within its full context. It is also not permissible to say: "Islam is simple, and the Prophet and his noble Companions were simple, why complicate Islam?" This is precisely what Abu Al-Baraa' Al-Hindi did in his online video.[6]

How did it come to pass that dozens of esteemed scholars and clerics the world over were forced to debate the nature of jihad with Amin, a twenty-five-year-old with limited Arabic language skills, no formal legal training, and a reported penchant (before his radicalization) for football, drinking, and night clubs? This was certainly not the intent of the groups of reformers who, beginning in the late nineteenth century, set in motion a series of shifts that helped erode the traditional bases of religious authority. The intellectuals associated with the Islamic Modernist movement were spread from North Africa to India, but a particularly important cluster of scholars lived and worked in Egypt, including Jamal al-Din al-Afghani, Muhammad 'Abduh, and Muhammad Rashid Rida. These reformers argued that a return to the foundational sources of Islam, chiefly the Qur'an and Sunna, was necessary to harmonize religious life with the demands of economic and political modernity. Reform would revitalize Islam and thereby better equip Muslims to fend off the political, economic, and cultural encroachment of European empires.

Muslim modernists displayed great concern over stagnation, arguing that centuries of imitating the legal rulings of earlier times (not to mention the "yoke" of Ottoman rule) had led to the decline of Islamic societies. They rather advocated a return to *ijtihād*—independent legal reasoning —based on direct access to Islam's foundational sources. In a strike at the inherited authority of his own scholarly cohort, 'Abduh argued that the "gates of *ijtihād*" remained open to anyone who developed the requisite knowledge to walk through them. At a minimum, this meant would-be interpreters must be sane, able to read Arabic, and in possession of at least a moderate level of religious education.[7] He certainly could not have envisioned that *ijtihād* would become the prerogative of the common man (or still less, woman) lacking in even rudimentary Islamic education, or that the upending of judicial precedence might spell chaos in a religious tradition anchored in material practice rather than faith alone. Yet the dangers were apparent to 'Abduh's traditionalist rivals, and it is hard not to give credence to at least some of their concerns. As one scholar summarizes these critiques:

> *Taqlīd* [imitation, that is, judicial precedence] was the foundation of the rule of law within Islamic societies. If, as these reformers suggested, it was replaced with *ijtihād* as independent legal reasoning, judges would no longer be constrained to give similar rulings for similar legal cases, and petitioners for legal advice could go from one mufti to another until they received a ruling they liked. Furthermore, since the reformers saw *ijtihād* as something all individuals could do for themselves, they would theoretically be able to resolve their own legal questions. Legal authority on religious questions would no longer reside in the hands of the scholars, but would be possessed by ordinary individuals.[8]

Imagine, for a moment, if Americans decided to start resolving legal questions based on the text of the US Constitution alone, casting aside both judicial precedent and indeed the judges themselves. Though this might sound like utopia within certain circles, it would also likely result in a great amount of chaos as the established structures of authority crumbled and new ones competed for dominance. Analogies are never precise, but it is hard to understand contemporary jihad without taking account of the authority vacuum that has grown, over the last century, from this pivot toward the individual as the arbiter of religious meaning.

Battles over the proper approach to Islam's legal culture might seem a world away from life in Western countries, but I believe this contest between jihadists and "the establishment" bears traces of some more familiar dynamics. Indeed, if the Islamic State's call to reject the learned opinions of an expert class has a familiar ring to it, that is because it exemplifies a form of right-wing populism that is everywhere ascendant. Much commentary about populism comes from self-identified centrists who equate right and left populism and find them both equally dangerous (the Bari Weiss school of "here I sit nobly in the center speaking truth to power"). But the theoretical foundations between right and left populism do in fact differ in fundamental ways. Chief among them is that right populism often manifests as a critique of knowledge rather than of power structures. Indeed, the problem with power is that it is not sufficiently concentrated in the proper hands. Right-wing populists therefore aim not at the democratization of power or the deconstruction of privilege, but the replacement of an entrenched elite with new and even more autocratic one. Disdain for expertise— and the elite class that lays claim to it—is baked into the pie.

By way of contrast, the Islamic Modernist position was not that anyone could act as an interpreter of shari'a, but that anyone who acquired the requisite knowledge could offer new insights on new (and old) problems. This stance is not to be confused with an anti-intellectual posture that would assert that such specialized knowledge is itself unnecessary or somehow corrupting. Legalistic religions are accretive, a fact that has not traditionally been viewed as a liability. It is rather through the continual act of reinterpretation that sacred texts find new meaning for each generation. In that sense, they are not dissimilar to other bodies of knowledge that build off earlier contributions without any notion that doing so undermines some kind of original conceptual purity. In contrast, Indira Falk Gesink has argued that the original-ist position embraced by many radicals represents nothing less than a "disinheritance of the hermeneutic tradition," one with clear consequences. "Shukri Mustafa, leader of the militant group that assassinated President Anwar al-Sadat of Egypt in 1981, once stated that the Qur'an was written in 'clear Arabic' and that anyone with a good dictionary could interpret it."[9] This is an assessment with which many experts would disagree, but we should note the primacy of the individual—as reader, interpreter, and actor—in such a framing. And here is the predecessor to Rahul Amin's invitation to "read the Qur'an," and of repeated appeals by militants to the simplicity of Islam. Perhaps more than its predecessors, what the Islamic State brought into focus was the rupture between the new mujahideen and the "establish-ment" legal tradition.[10] Yet, as we shall see, advocates of this split do not conjure up a democratic utopia. On the contrary, the Islamic State will have you believe that even though the world is quite simple, only they can truly understand it.

Beyond clarifying the relationship between the scholarly class and popular sentiment, contemporary jihad demon-

strates the formative role of new technologies in shaping
challenges to religious authority. We should remember that
while Luther's translation gave the masses unprecedented
access to the Bible in a vernacular language, it would have
been far less consequential without the spread of printing
presses throughout Western Europe in the late fifteenth and
early sixteenth centuries. By enabling individual reading of
the Bible on a large scale, the printing press helped foster an
entirely new way of being a Christian. This fact undercuts
the tendency to think about religious identity and behavior in ahistorical terms. Though the underlying texts may
(or may not, but that's a story for another time) remain the
same, little else about religions do—least of all the practices and subjectivities of their adherents. More recently, the
development of mass media in the form of newspapers, radio
stations, and television channels did not merely provide
additional outlets through which stable religious messages
could be disseminated. Rather, new media fundamentally
affects the nature of religious thought, belief, and practice.

In our own digital age, online platforms like YouTube,
Twitter, and Telegram have facilitated new expressions of
Islam, most of which do not manifest in the type of militancy that is at the heart of this study. As Gary Bunt has
described, many of these are quite mundane, from online
shopping for modest clothing to apps that calculate prayer
times, locate the direction for prayer, or allow young singles
to connect.[11] But proponents of jihad have also found in
the Internet a most efficient way to sidestep the traditional
gatekeepers of public opinion. This is part and parcel of the
democratic nature of online life, which offers new avenues

for both emancipatory and reactionary expression. Contrary to libertarian fantasies, the vast amount of information at our fingertips is not an uncontested good that necessarily makes humans freer. Rather, digital life also enables new forms of control by those bent on usurping the power of traditional elites, and indeed, reconstituting that power on an increasingly authoritarian basis. That this is all done in the name of everyday people is not ironic. It is an essential part of the appeal.

There is, in short, a strong antiestablishment thrust present within contemporary jihadi thought, one that ridicules the traditions and claims to authority of mainstream scholars and clerics. Elemental as this fact is, it is often overlooked by observers who associate religious scholars with shari'a and shari'a with ISIS. Yet the Islamic State's media products and public statements regularly reference the moral bankruptcy of mainstream scholars and clerics, who are condemned for needlessly complicating Islam. The underlying thrust of such critiques is that Islam is simple and its directives crystal clear; all this scholarly "knowledge" is just nonsense. Attending to these internal dynamics suggests we might more fruitfully consider the Islamic State as an instance of right populism rather than a washed-up remnant from the past. While contemporary jihad should not be regarded as a direct parallel to Western phenomena, there is danger in thinking that it dwells in cultural isolation. As the populist façade of contemporary jihad reveals, it is by understanding this story in its specificity that we can begin to glean insights with universal reverberations.

Sayyid Qutb and the Moral Quest

Few have done more to articulate the parameters of today's jihad than the Egyptian thinker and activist, Sayyid Qutb (1906–66). Along with Ibn Taymiyya, Qutb occupies a place of privilege in the jihadi pantheon, serving as a frequent pit stop on the path to radicalization. Though mostly known in the Western world as "the philosopher of Islamic terror," as the American writer Paul Berman once characterized him, this is an incredibly reductive view that ignores the originality and indeed, modernity, of his political imagination.[12] Writing largely from his prison cell—he was executed by the Nasser regime on trumped-up conspiracy charges—Qutb refashioned the concepts of freedom and sovereignty to accommodate a world in which Muslims everywhere seemed under attack and in which various secular political projects had failed to liberate them. As he wrote in the prologue to his most influential work, *Milestones*, Western democracy had proved infertile and Marxism was contrary to human needs. "All nationalistic and chauvinistic ideologies which have appeared in modern times, and all the movements and theories derived from them, have also lost their vitality. In short, all man-made individual or collective theories have proved to be failures."[13]

As this passage suggests, Qutb was deeply affected by the rapid transformation of political and social life in the heartlands of Islam. After the collapse of the Ottoman Empire following World War I, the empire's Arab provinces—encompassing present day Iraq, Jordan, Syria, Lebanon, Israel, and the Occupied Palestinian Territory—passed into French and British hands under the League of Nations Mandate system. They joined other Muslim majority countries that were already part of colonial empires—including Morocco, Libya, Algeria, Tunisia, and Egypt—as well as the crown of the British Empire, India, with its large Muslim minority (numbering approximately 90 million in 1940). With the exception of Palestine, each of these states achieved independence, sometimes after protracted battles, in the wave of decolonization that followed World War II.[14] Thus, in a rather short span of time, a number of new states emerged, all intent on reforming, modernizing, and remaking the nature of both political and social life in their territories. The descent of many postcolonial states into various forms of dictatorial, authoritarian, and autocratic rule is well documented. What deserves attention is the profound crisis that such disappointments engendered, because this formed the context for Qutb's arguments regarding political legitimacy, individual agency, and jihad. However much he invoked an idealized past, his work is not "premodern" in any way; rather it bears the traces of a failed modernity, a sense that man-made political solutions have been tried and found wanting. And paradoxically, the "return" that he called for bore many traces of the modernity he claimed to reject.

Like many Islamists, Qutb did not come from the traditional scholarly ranks, but he received the most modern and secular education available at his time. In lieu of the prestigious center of Sunni learning, al-Azhar, he attended Dar al-'Ulum, a teachers training college devised as a modernizing institution and whose alumni also included Hassan al-Banna. Qutb spent years working as a bureaucrat for the

Education Ministry in Egypt and even pursued graduate study in Colorado in the late 1940s. Not surprisingly given this trajectory, his works are characterized by a direct engagement with the Qur'an rather than with Islam's exegetical or legal traditions. This fact makes them far more accessible to the novice than contemporary works by classically trained scholars, which are written in a style of disputation that is geared toward other specialists. Though Qutb does cite select commentators from earlier periods, he joins other Islamists who "write *outside*, and often in conscious opposition to" traditional frameworks. In keeping with the pivot toward individual interpretation analyzed above, "the conversation is not with the earlier exegetes, but directly with God."[15] Indeed, it is worth noting that some of the most important Muslim leaders of the last century never received a conventional religious education, yet proffered solutions to all forms of modern malaise with Islam at the center: Ali Shariati (sociology), Khurshid Ahmad (economics), Hasan al-Turabi (law, at the Sorbonne), Osama Bin Laden (civil engineering), and his successor, Ayman al-Zawahiri (medicine). This trend continues among many rank and file mujahideen as well, like Ahmed Abousamra, a Boston-born computer scientist who edited the Islamic State's English-language glossy, *Dabiq*. A recent book by Diego Gambetta and Steffan Hertog has found that engineers are disproportionately represented in the ranks of mujahideen.[16]

In Qutb's hands jihad turned into something much more than the Muslim way in warfare; it became, rather, more akin to the individual's ultimate weapon in pursuit of social justice. His central contribution was offering the individual, lacking a customary political framework for collective action, the means to engage in jihad. Qutb took the modernist critique of absolutism largely for granted and started with the assertion that the supposed apostasy of contemporary rulers invalidated their claims to authority. Moreover, if Muslim political leaders were illegitimate on such grounds, they were also ineligible to lead the faithful in jihad. Fighting in the path of God rather devolved to each individual Muslim—that is, jihad became a personal obligation rather than a collective one. As discussed previously, jihad has traditionally been considered by the majority of Sunni jurists as a collective duty, a designation that makes intuitive sense if we recall the essential link between jihad and the state. Propelled by the quasi-democratic notion that rulers could not demand obedience purely because they occupied a position of power, Qutb laid the foundation for the pious rejection of a whole generation of Muslim leaders. Jihad would become the instrument for this rebellion.

Qutb's central idea was that contemporary Muslims were steeped in a new era of *jahiliyya*, a pejorative term used to refer to the "age of ignorance" prior to Islam.[17] Yet unlike in the ancient world when such ignorance stemmed from not yet knowing the true God, modern *jahiliyya* is "a conscious usurpation of God's sovereignty (*hakimiyya*)."[18] Most importantly, *jahiliyya* for Qutb is not an epoch but an existential state, and its antithesis is not "knowledge" per se but rather *hakimiyya*—the sovereignty of God. That is, you can either haphazardly organize life around rules rooted in human fallibility, or you can accept the already perfected divine legislation, the shari'a. This concept of divine sovereignty undergirded an essentially egalitarian argument about humanity and a corresponding critique of any rulers who would elevate themselves above the mass of their brethren. As he wrote in the preface to his last and most radical work, *Milestones*, "This *jahiliyah* is based on rebellion against God's sovereignty on earth. It transfers to man one of the greatest attributes of God, namely sovereignty, and makes some men lords over other."[19]

Insofar as it entails the creation of man-made laws, the act of ruling is an unlawful seizure of power. Because the divine law has already been given, all that remains is for a righteous leader to administer the state in accordance with its precepts.[20] Consequently, the leader has no right to oppress the people, nor any power in fact other than implementing the law.

> The ruler in Islamic law is not to be obeyed because of his own person; he is to be obeyed only by virtue of holding his position through the law of Allah and His Messenger; his right to obedience is derived from his observance of that law and from no other thing. If he departs from the law, he is no longer entitled to obedience, and his orders need no longer be obeyed.[21]

The importance of even a legitimate ruler is thus greatly reduced from lawgiver to middle management, a theme I examine in further detail in Chapter 4. The problem—unacknowledged by Qutb—is that shari'a is a process of legal reasoning, not a set of codified laws. It does not exist "out there" just waiting to be applied in some sort of pure, unadulterated fashion, but is in fact always mediated

by one's own position and interpretative priorities. Qutb
would never have admitted as much; rather, he saw his own
views as synonymous with Islam itself. In Roxanne Euben's
concise phrasing, "the denial that an interpretation is an
interpretation is a crucial characteristic of what it means to
be a 'fundamentalist'."[22]

Jihad, in this framework, was the only way to liberate
humanity from servitude to those unlawful rulers who had
usurped divine sovereignty. As such, Qutb posited freedom
rather than domination as its ultimate aim.

> The jihad of Islam is to secure complete freedom for every man
> throughout the world by releasing him from the servitude to other
> human beings so that he may serve his God, who is one and who
> has no associates.[23]

Thus, jihad aims to "eliminate all human kingships" and
to "abolish all those systems and governments which are
based on the rule of man over men and the servitude of one
human being to another."[24] In tracing how jihad made the
jump from conventional war to insurgent tactic, it is hard
to overstate the importance of Qutb's intervention. Indeed,
the revolutionary potential of his words was not lost on the
Egyptian government, whose prosecutors leaned heavily on
Milestones to build their sedition case.

Qutb's attack on the legitimacy of various political forces
thus marched hand in hand with his reconceptualization of
jihad as an individual duty, overturning the majority view
of Sunni jurists. Lacking a legitimate ruler to command the
forces of Islam, jihad had become a personal obligation in

the new age of ignorance. Qutb was also able to globalize jihad to a degree unimaginable prior to the age of modern communications and transportation, making it incumbent upon Muslims regardless of where or how they lived. The enemy was not, as in Ibn Taymiyya's time, the Mongol invaders threatening Damascus; the enemy was rather *disbelief* and its oppressive structures of authority and systems of thought, wherever and among whomever they might appear. In this he served as an important precursor to the Islamic State, which dismisses national and geographic boundaries in appealing to Muslims worldwide to join its cause.

It is worth considering this pivot toward individual jihad within a still broader context by noting that the flip side of Qutb's individual empowerment is a rather dim outlook toward the possibility of social or political change through traditional means. Disillusionment with politics as usual, and in particular with the state as a vehicle for advancing justice, is written into the turn toward individual action. His elevation of jihad to an essential personal obligation thus represents a moralizing turn—an attempt to delineate the agency that individuals still have in the face of systemic foes. Rather than depending on the state to lead, a group of pious individuals—the vanguard—should take up the mantle of jihad to work for the slow but steady reform of society. We should not, however, regard Qutb as forwarding an alternative political model so much as registering the bankruptcy of the status quo. The Caliphate was, in his mind, a remote goal rather than an immediate aspiration, which is perhaps one reason he had very little to say about the details of governance or institutions. Indeed, one of the enduring frustrations for both scholars and contemporary partisans is that Qutb left so little in the way of actual blueprints for how the ideal Islamic society should function.

As much as he was influenced by contemporary geopolitics, Sayyid Qutb also did not work in an intellectual vacuum. His thinking about jihad owes much to earlier Islamists like Hasan al-Banna and Abul A'la Maududi. Similarly, figures like Muhammad Abd al-Salam Faraj and Abu Mus'ab al-Zarqawi have made their own substantial contributions to jihad thinking in his wake. Yet it is hard to account for the surge of Islamic militancy in recent decades without considering the central ideological transformation that Qutb most cogently articulated: from jihad on behalf of the state to jihad *against* the state; from an army's jihad for the sake of Muslims to the individual's jihad for the sake of Islam. All militant groups operating today more or less take this conceptual turn for granted, though, as we shall see, the Islamic State has completed the dialectical circuit in its attempt to re-embed jihad in a structure of political authority—its own.

Qutb was executed in 1966, before he could see the full flowering of his intellectual efforts. But the 1980s provided fertile ground from which to engage with his call: the Soviet invasion of Afghanistan, an Islamist uprising in Syria, and the Iran–Iraq war—not to mention the introduction of economic liberalization and austerity measures that began reshaping the fragile social contract in many postcolonial states. The resulting challenges to governing elites and, in extreme cases, fragmentation of the state itself created ideal conditions for the growth of militant groups who would refashion Qutb's message for a new generation of the disenchanted.

Getting Off the Couch

Had the recalibration of jihad as an individual duty focused solely on revising musty legal categories, it is hard to imagine these deliberations making much of a dent in practice. Yet one of the innovations within this contemporary body of thought is the premise that jihad is not just possible for Muslims qua individuals but that it is fundamental to living an authentic religious life. "Jihad is the identity of the Muslim in his existence," the scholar Abu Qatadah once claimed.[25] Within such frameworks, jihad is not just something Muslims might be called upon to do, but something they should seek out. Indeed, the pursuit of death through suicide attacks only began in the 1980s, and the subject remains theologically dicey because of the clear prohibition on taking one's own life. The dialectical rendering of death as life, the annulment of living being its greatest affirmation, is central to the type of subjectivity modern jihad constructs. Beyond appreciating the novelty of this position, however, we need to ask why such arguments have found a receptive audience—however small—in the current age.

Writing a generation after Qutb, Muhammad Abd al-Salam Faraj—an electrical engineer, keeping with a theme —referred to jihad as "the neglected duty," in an influential pamphlet of the same name. Faraj served as one of the founders and key leaders of Egyptian Islamic Jihad (the group previously known as Tanzim al-Jihad or simply al-Jihad), which organized the assassination of President Anwar al-Sadat in 1981. *The Neglected Duty* opens by striking a double blow at the traditional structures of power: first at the ulema who have ignored jihad "despite their knowledge that it is the only way to return and erect the tower of Islam again"; and second, at "the tyrants (*tawaghit*) of this land" who will not absent their posts "except by power of the sword."[26] It is within this context of betrayal by religious and political leaders that the radical idea of jihad as Islam's "sixth pillar" has gained traction. Prayer, fasting, charity, pilgrimage, and the declaration of faith—Islam's canonical obligations—are all behaviors that individuals can perform on their own; tacking jihad onto this list is only possible if, following the discussion above, you reconceptualize it with the individual at the center.

More recently, the Syrian mujahid and thinker Mustafa bin ʿAbd al-Qadir al-Rifaʿi (better known as Abu Musʿab al-Suri) recalibrated the role of individuals within jihad following the destruction of al-Qaeda's territorial base in Afghanistan. Trained as a mechanical engineer, al-Suri joined up with the mujahideen in Peshawar in 1987 and returned to Afghanistan a decade later after stints in Spain and London. In his 2004 book, *The Call to Global Islamic Resistance*, al-Suri advanced the idea of a "jihad of individual terrorism" (*jihād al-irhāb al-fardi*), a type of warfare that individuals can take part in wherever they happen to find themselves. In the difficult circumstances of the present, he argued, it was incumbent upon Muslims to regard jihad as an open source practice rather than a struggle managed by al-Qaeda or any other central organization.[27] The decentralized view embraced by al-Suri is often credited with inspiring attacks by "lone wolves" in the West, who do not act upon any clear orders from a known militant group.

Within the individualist framework, normative behaviors become liabilities for the true believer, who is always seeking differentiation. Faraj, for instance, specifies that the usual requirement to secure one's parents' permission before engaging in jihad does not apply in the case that it is an individual obligation, *fard 'ayn*. This may seem like a somewhat tangential point, but viewed through the lens of ascendant individualism, the directive to disregard what your parents think becomes more legible. Even the construction of community—fashioned with the idea of loyalty and disavowal (*al-wala' wa-l-bara'*) at its core—is built upon the individual's principled rejection of all those who might compromise the true practice of religion. Jihad is not merely fighting but *becoming*, with all the hints of self-actualization this term implies. Here we might also remember that Osama bin Laden spoke of jihad as a sort of coming-of-age ceremony, best undertaken by people between fifteen and twenty-five who have "not yet been weighed down by the filth of the world."[28]

Many of these ideas converged in an Islamic State video featuring Abu Sohayb al-Faransi, who narrated his own personal journey toward jihad. Born into a Catholic family in France, he rejected the Church, withdrew from his studies, and eventually traveled the world, observing many different types of customs and peoples—an experience he describes as positive though it placed him in spiritual peril. "I was searching for something though I didn't know what, I was searching for truth all over the world. I found truth in the book of Allah." Soon after his conversion, he recounted visiting Algeria and feeling awed by the experience of being in a truly Islamic milieu. Yet the enchantment soon wore off after his encounter with various sheikhs, whom he realized were not worthy of the title. "Why? Because they corrupt the religion that I knew from the Qur'an and the Sunna. They distort the truth. How so? They do not speak about jihad, they do not speak about it clearly." He decided to challenge one of the sheikhs he encountered, asking, "We are commanded in the Qur'an to do jihad. So why don't we discuss it? Why don't we talk about it more?" only to be told, "Quiet! Don't talk about that."[29]

We can follow this ideological thread by looking at what the Islamic State offers to its prospective fighters and supporters. Whether we examine the triumphant videos recorded in the group's early years or its well-known magazines, it is noteworthy that its media stress perpetual motion. Here finally Muslims are *doing something*. The visual imagery is all action: buildings exploding, rockets being fired, pickups racing across the desert. Not only that, particularly when the group was expanding its territorial gains, media highlighted its state-building and social service operations: doctors delivering cancer treatments, orphans being educated, coins being minted. Likewise, the Islamic State juxtaposes this sense of productivity with the presumed passivity of supporters watching the action from afar. As one fighter implored in 2014, "You can be here in these golden times, fighting, or you can be on the sidelines commentating. It's your choice."

Echoing al-Qaeda before it, what the Islamic State holds out is the prospect of making a difference and of effecting meaningful change in the immediate term. It is a message custom made for an era characterized by "slacktivism" and an overwhelming sense of futility: Don't just sit there and lament—you too can make a difference! This is one reason that Islamic State media is littered with reference to hypocrisy (*nifāq*), which is nearly tantamount to the sin of disbelief. Thus our self-taught exegete, Abu Bara' al-Hindi, recounted, "With me, in the UK … I used to feel like a *munāfiq* [hypocrite], you know, when I used to read diaries of jihad because I wasn't doing nothing I felt like a *munāfiq*." Similarly, one article from *Dabiq* argues that

> abandoning *hijrah* [migration to Islamic State-controlled territory] —the path to jihad—is a dangerous matter. In effect, one is thereby deserting jihad and willingly accepting his tragic condition of being a hypocritical spectator. He lives in the West among the kuffar [infidels] for years, spends hours on the Internet, reads news and posts on forums.[30]

In each instance the individual is confronted with an enormous moral choice between action and sloth, jihad and business as usual. Such binaries play off the universal gap between what people might desire and what is actually achievable; the suggestion that there need be no separation between the two is the central act of seduction.

Hypocrisy functions on a larger scale as well: it is what all other governments do in positing a division of life between the private and the public, the spiritual and the material, the ethical and the worldly. Here too the Islamic State promises to close the gap. It is only as a "result of secularism pervading the people's intellects in our era" that Muslims have

grown to regard such wholeness as unnatural and imprac-
tical. They have rather become accustomed to "separating
between religion and state, and between the shari'a and
governance, and treating the Qur'an as a book of chanting
and recitation rather than a book of governance, legislation, and enforcement."[31] In lieu of ethical standards, we
are supposed to content ourselves with the amoral nature of
realpolitik and impersonal whims of the market. Expressions
of solidarity from Western governments—such as those
extended to New Zealand's Muslim community following
the 2019 attack on mosques in Christchurch—are likewise
denounced as "crocodile tears" given the number of civilians
killed by US drone strikes.[32] In contrast, the Islamic State
promises an alternative social and political order in which
there is no artificial division between what is felt in the heart
and done by the hand. "It is not the manner of the Islamic
State to throw empty, dry, and hypocritical words of condemnation and condolences like the Arab *tawaghit* do in the
UN and Arab League. Rather, its actions speak louder than
its words."[33]

Like al-Qaeda before it, the Islamic State mobilizes stories
of Muslim suffering to create a sense of moral outrage among
its audience, playing off the sense of unjustified disconnect
between the ethical ideal and the world as it stands. "Come,
O you who seek the freedom of your prisoners. Heal your
breasts! How often do they fill with rage and oppression, on
account of the oppression of the idolatrous rulers and their
followers?"[34] Images of dead children and harrowing tales
of the struggle for survival pepper the media mix and serve
to convey a sense of urgency: the world is on fire, what are

you doing about it? As Faisal Devji has argued, the structure of this affective appeal is not terribly different than that employed by NGOs that run commercials featuring photos of starving children.[35] At different scales, they both rely on the bundle of conflicting emotions felt by humans living within sprawling political and social systems. People are both outraged yet paralyzed; determined to change this terrible status quo, yet unsure where to start, what to do, or whether change is even possible. The Islamic State has geared its pitch to capitalize on these contradictions, affirming the capacity for individuals to take bold action in the face of systemic oppression. As opposed to the slowly grinding wheels of contemporary politics and the particular incrementalism of democracy, they will have you know that all is not futile after all.

It is within this context that the concept of death as life, with the glorification of martyrdom as its ideological lynchpin, comes to influence the construction of agency. Take for instance the frequent profiles of fighters killed in combat or who undertook suicide missions, like the series "Among the Believers are Men" from *Rumiya* magazine. These go far beyond standard hagiography, and often recount a story of personal growth and self-fulfillment achieved ultimately in death. For example, the profile of Abu 'Abdullah al-Britani recounts a young man raised in the United Kingdom, surrounded by "mischief and corruption," but who nonetheless prevailed amid these currents to choose the path of truth, learning more about Islam and eventually undertaking a journey to Syria. There too he encountered challenges, falling in with the wrong group, a so-called "Islamist" faction that "wasn't implementing the Shari'ah in the territories over which it had taken control." Disheartened and thrown about between different militias, our hero eventually found his way to the Islamic State where he took part in many battles. Like many others, he is said to have prayed for his own martyrdom. "During Ramadan, he made much du'a [prayer of supplication], asking Allah to grant him shahadah [martyrdom] in that blessed month, but he did not attain shahadah that year. Little did he know, however, that his du'a had been accepted."[36] Indeed, after requesting to be placed on the list of suicide operatives, he was blessed by a US drone strike in Raqqa during the following Ramadan, "attaining shahadah thereby in the blessed month for which he prayed." It's not quite a nineteenth-century novel, but the elements of *bildungsroman* are still apparent: through strength and perseverance, our hero finally achieves his goal.

Understanding this appeal to individual agency undercuts many accounts, both from polemicists and policy makers, that assume people join militant groups out of some sort of religious fanaticism or primordial bloodlust. The fact is that the Islamic State in particular has excelled at fashioning a more positive message built around the prospect of contributing in meaningful ways to the construction of a truly ethical political and social order. It also augments the findings of prior researchers who have disputed the notion that fighters are particularly impoverished, uneducated, or desperate to escape a miserable existence. In a pioneering study published in 2005, based on data from 315 suicide attacks from 1980 through 2003, the sociologist Robert Pape argued, "In general, suicide attackers are rarely socially isolated, clinically insane, or economically destitute individuals, but are most often educated, socially integrated, and highly capable people who could be expected to have a good future."[37] They tended to be better educated than those in their immediate surroundings and to come from the middle or even upper classes. More recently, Olivier Roy echoed this finding in his own survey of 140 individuals who have either taken part in terrorist attacks in Europe or left to join the Islamic State abroad, arguing "Above all, the jihadis' profiles show a large group of well-integrated and well-educated youths." Revolutionaries, he wryly notes, "almost never come from the suffering classes."[38]

In short, understanding why people join organizations like the Islamic State requires looking beyond essentialized constructions of religious fanaticism or individual privation. Though practical considerations—such as, Can I feed my family?—*did* compel some Iraqis or Syrians to join the group, such opportunistic motives apply far less to the bulk of foreign fighters. In the case of the latter, the allure of personal agency and the promise of solidarity play a foundational role in structuring the Islamic State's appeal. But shifting the analysis to this plane also generates the question as to why people feel so helpless to begin with, at which point it threatens to overflow the neat geography of the "Islamic world" altogether. Mary Kaldor, for instance, has described the "individualism and anomie that characterizes the current period" as creating a sort of political vacuum: "the sense that political action is futile given the enormity of current problems, the difficulty of controlling or influencing the web-like structure of power, the cultural fragmentation of both horizontal networks and particularistic loyalties."[39] In contrast, jihadist groups hold out the prospect of transformation in an age characterized by deep sighs of resignation.

This is one way to understand the sense of failure discernable in many contemporary calls to jihad, from Sayyid Qutb's writings down to the present day. Socialism, nationalism, secularism, communism, and liberalism have been tried and found wanting, each failing to create a truly just society. The militant embrace of Islam, with jihad as its mode of actualization, is one response to this shared sense of frustration, but there are certainly others. The problem, at least with regard to the Islamic State, is that the society to be built on the ruins of modernity's -isms holds little promise for genuine human flourishing. But this should not blind us to the fact that a widespread sense of despair exists today among many who had hoped for a better world and that movements that acknowledge this deep-seeded frustration are everywhere ascendent. That the solutions they proffer are poorly aligned to the very real grievances of the communities they claim to serve cannot, amid a new golden age of authoritarian populism, appear an anomaly.

In sum, the fact that an aspiring statelet found adherents during an age of mass demobilization is not a strange coincidence. Nothing about the rise and proliferation of militant groups at *this specific time* is preordained in the Qur'an or medieval commentaries, and indeed, their ideological organization around the individual marks them as wholly modern. What I am suggesting is that their emergence must be understood as a response to the sort of civic paralysis that is not just some unfortunate byproduct of neoliberalism, but truly its goal. Yet—and not unlike right populism more generally—the particular path down which frustrated individuals are asked to walk does not end with the utopian dream they've been promised, but with a new regime of power that is even more repressive than the last. This fact becomes readily apparent by examining the Islamic State's approach to governance, including its attempt to reestablish centralized political control over jihad.[40] But before tackling that subject, we must ask what type of community the Islamic State brought into being and where its points of demarcation lie, in both geographic and social terms. Chapter 3 will turn to these questions.

3

Making the *Umma* Great Again

In June 2014 the Islamic State released a promotional video that boasted of nothing less than redrawing the map of the Middle East. Featuring footage of a bulldozer destroying a portion of the border between Iraq and Syria, the video triumphantly announced the end the idolatrous Sykes-Picot line—that infamous mark of Western imperialism that, during the midst of World War I, parceled up the Ottoman Empire to France and Great Britain. Never mind that the region's national boundaries do not correspond precisely with the lines the two statesmen drew in Paris. The Sykes-Picot agreement lives on as a preeminent example of colonial hubris, a cautionary tale of what happens when a culturally and politically contiguous territory is divided into new nation-states in accordance with the needs of Empire. For the Islamic State, Sykes-Picot looms large not merely because of its imperial origins, but because of the artificiality of the borders it created. Identities shaped around these imposed boundaries—Lebanese, Jordanian, Iraqi, and so on—are

dangerous because they complicate the individual's complete identification with the one true Islamic community, the
umma. In an age in which identities are increasingly viewed
as fixed and singular, it should come as no surprise that the
Islamic State is a jealous God.

As with other tenets of its philosophy, the Islamic State
claims that eradicating the boundaries between nations is a
return to a more glorious past, the sloughing off of divisive
attachments in order to create a truly united community.
While it is certainly the case that the Middle East's contemporary borders, and associated national identities, are barely
a century old, destroying them does not necessarily constitute a return to something that existed in the past. On the
contrary, the Islamic State conceives of identity and community in a wholly modern, even hypermodern, fashion.
Ironically, while the Islamic State may claim to have done
away with the nationalist order, its own mode of thinking
about political identity and the political community reflects
the same exclusionary frameworks. These do not, I contend,
represent the continuation of "medieval" forms of Islamic
governance, but rather appear right at home alongside the
new nationalism, with its attendant obsession with defining
insiders vs. outsiders, prioritizing collective (rather than
individual) freedom, and dreaming of homogenization
through either forced or "voluntary" ethnic cleansing.

Rather than mining the distant Islamic past for precedents,
we should regard the Islamic State's vision of political community as an example of what the historian Eric Hobsbawm
called "the invention of tradition."[1] In casting around
for some semblance of legitimacy, Hobsbawm noted the

tendency of national movements to appeal to a "traditional" past that never was—either selectively appropriating bits of the past to justify a political and identarian project in the present, or sometimes just fabricating things outright. Positing a direct line of descent from the noble ancestors of the past to present peoples, such projects often depend on fictive claims of ethnic purity and have, as such, frequently been exclusionary by nature. On the surface, the Islamic State rejects such racialized frameworks, but its vision neither reenacts the Islamic past nor supports a more ecumenical view of the political community in the present. And why should this be at all surprising? Almost everywhere we turn, the discursive power of difference is accelerating, separating "authentic" members of communities from the hordes who are just pretending. As the inimitable Stuart Hall once observed regarding the social effects of neoliberalism, "You're left with the English as a tight little island somewhere around London with about 25 souls and the Thatcher government hovering over it."[2] Indeed, the narrow limits of the Islamic State's "real" *umma* finds a corollary in rising xenophobia in Western countries, where the insider/outsider discourse has become one of the Right's most effective mobilizing strategies. As much as political projects built upon such divisions depend, both logically and rhetorically, upon the legacy of nationalism, they also supplant it. Here too the Islamic State's hypermodern view of identity and political community—globalized, digitally mediated, and highly selective—has more to teach about the present and possible future than the past.

Dealing with Difference

It is often assumed that exclusionary political models—
you know, the ones that lurk behind the last century's grim
history of partition, ethnic cleansing, and genocide—are
remnants of a less civilized past. The reality is that it was
modernity and the age of nationalism in particular that
rendered the inevitable fact of human difference uniquely
threatening. Premodern empires regarded heterogene-
ity as the natural order of the universe. Difference needed
accommodation and often careful management, but not
eradication. The various Islamic empires that have existed
over the centuries (with noted points of exception, such as
the virulently fanatical Almohads of twelfth century North
Africa) largely ruled along such lines. Scholars as rightward-
leaning as Bernard Lewis have noted that because shari'a
provides a legal framework for ruling over non-Muslim
populations, "protected" peoples (*dhimmis*) were not subject
to arbitrary decrees like those inflicted on European Jews.
Second-class subjecthood (speaking of citizens would be an
anachronism) was not necessarily idyllic, but it was better
than living outside the law.

Two examples are particularly illustrative in this regard.
In an important study about conversion to Islam in its early
centuries, the historian Richard Bulliet noted that territories
conquered by the invading Arab-Islamic armies during the
seventh and eighth centuries CE remained predominantly
non-Muslim for hundreds of years.[3] Forced conversion was
an anathema, based on the verse "There is no compulsion
in religion" (Sura al-Baqarah, 256). Even in those early

times, then, we find that the Umayyad and Abbasid Caliphates ruled over peoples who were largely unlike them and
indeed developed religious and administrative laws that
reflected this reality. The second example is the more recent
Ottoman Empire, which controlled a growing swath of
the Middle East, North Africa, and southeast Europe from
the fourteenth to early twentieth century and was the seat
of the Caliphate until its abolition in 1924. The Ottoman
Empire's social diversity was often noted, combining a
plethora of different ethnic, linguistic, and religious groups
under a single imperial umbrella. When doing research for
my first book on Ottoman and Mandatory Palestine, I recall
feeling hopelessly inadequate when compared to some of my
sources who had not only mastered Arabic and Turkish, but
also spoke a smattering of French and English alongside their
native Ladino—a linguistic legacy of the empire's diverse
social reality. Nor were the Ottomans the only ones ruling
over heterogeneous populations, which for premodern states
was less the exception than the rule. Commentators who
have traced the Islamic State's extreme intolerance—for
nonbelievers certainly, but also for Shi'a, Sufi, and indeed
many of the world's Actually Existing Muslims—to something inherent within Islam must contend with a historical
record that is mostly at odds with this characterization.[4] Yet
on the other hand, and much as the Islamic State rejects
nationalism as idolatrous, its pursuit of homogeneity mirrors
modern nationalism's logic in fundamental ways.

In approaching this issue, it is useful to start by differentiating between terms that are often used interchangeably:
nation and state. I use the latter to mean the mechanism of

government, which can take several forms: the Ottoman state, the modern democratic French state, the feudal states of medieval Europe, and so on. States have existed for thousands of years, but only within the last few centuries have we seen the emergence of something called the nation-state. The nation is, broadly speaking, a community that claims some common unifying feature, be it ethnic, cultural, linguistic, religious, regional, or some combination thereof. Per Benedict Anderson's canonical study, the nation is largely an imagined community, one whose tenuous unity is the *product* of cultural and institutional development (for example, of a vernacular press, of public schooling, of nationalist histories recounting epic battles and great heroes, and so on) rather than a naturally existing phenomenon.[5]

Nationalism's chief innovation was to marry the nation to the state, and indeed, to argue that the levers of state power must be in the hands of "the people," however defined. In contrast, the kings and queens of premodern states did not claim to be of the same stock as the people they ruled—a fact that is abundantly clear if you have ever studied the intertwining family trees of European dynasties. In positing that the nation should control the state (which is how we arrive at the concept of popular sovereignty), and that the state should likewise work to advance the needs of a particular people, the nation-state encounters a formidable problem: How do you define this set of people, this nation? Does the nation include all who agree to abide by a particular set of laws and principles regardless of their religious, racial, or ethnic identities (as maintained in the still unrealized ideal of the American and French revolutions)? Or is the nation a particular people, bound together like the family through common ancestry, however fictitious ("pure" nations being anything but)? The latter is often called ethnonationalism for embracing a more restrictive and exclusionary vision of "the people," one that cannot accommodate any number of actual people living within a given state's territory. These "outsiders" thereby become threats to the integrity and sovereignty of the "real" nation. This is why the history of genocide and ethnic cleansing—from Armenia to India/Pakistan and the former Yugoslavia—is so bound up with the formation of modern nation-states. There are few large-scale precedents for this type of violence prior to the age of nationalism.

Nationalism did not create the logic of communal exclusion. But significantly, it did join the insider/outsider dichotomy to the state apparatus, thereby politicizing it in a novel fashion. As the historian Eugene Weber noted in his important study of French nationalism:

> Diversity had not bothered earlier centuries very much. It seemed part of the nature of things, whether from place to place or between one social group and another. But the Revolution had brought with it the concept of national unity as an integral and integrating ideal at all levels, and the ideal of oneness stirred concern about its shortcomings. Diversity became imperfection, injustice, failure, something to be noted and to be remedied.[6]

And indeed, the dawn of the national age brought with it the idea of difference as a liability. In the mind of the German thinker Johann Gottfried von Herder, such diversity represented a perversion of the natural social and political order. Writing in 1784 about the old imperial model, he stated:

> Nothing therefore seems more contradictory to the true end of governments than the endless expansion of states, the wild confusion of races and nations under one scepter. An empire made up of a hundred peoples and 120 provinces which have been forced together is a monstrosity, not a state-body.[7]

In contrast, Herder asserted that "the most natural state therefore is also one people, with a national character of its own."[8] In advancing such arguments, Herder laid the foundation for a form of blood-and-soil nationalism that regards multiple peoples living under a single state umbrella as a corruption of the "natural" order rather than a reflection of a widespread social and political reality. However commonplace such arguments have become, these "timeless" truths are no older than the spinning jenny.

At first glance, the Islamic State seems to offer a return to an era before this type of thinking became dominant.

> It is a state where the Arab and non-Arab, the white man and black man, the easterner and westerner are all brothers. It is a Khilafah [Caliphate] that gathered the Caucasian, Indian, Chinese, Shami [Levantine], Iraqi, Yemeni, Egyptian, Maghribi [North African], American, French, German, and Australian. Allah brought their hearts together, and thus, they became brothers.[9]

It was through these idealized terms that Abu Bakr al-Baghdadi described the social fabric of the Islamic State shortly after the proclamation of the Caliphate. The divisions of old, national and racial, are here cast aside in favor of a truly global community that purportedly knows no discrimination. And indeed, supporters have often touted the lack of racism within the Islamic State's ranks. These appeals are pitched in particular at Western Muslims raised in the shadows of the war on terror with all its legal and social ramifications—from police surveillance to discrimination and violent hate crimes.

The idea of radical equality among Muslims, regardless of race or ethnicity, finds ample theological support within Islam's foundational sources. The Qur'an and hadith collections include numerous sentiments that stress the equality among believers and suggest that it is individual merit— be it from learning, piety, or righteousness—that inspires divine favor. Equality in this sense is explicitly theological: all believers are equal before the overwhelming power of God, who alone can claim superiority. Yet the ontological equality of believers did not imply their political equality, and believers are likewise directed to obey those in positions of authority—an imperative that many classical jurists argued was almost absolute. One of the central contributions of Islamic Modernist and Islamist thought since the late nineteenth century has been to transpose this theological equality to the political stage and use it as a basis for attacking despotic rulers who elevate themselves over their subjects. These are, in contemporary jihadi lingo, the *tawaghit*, a term often translated as tyrants but that denotes idol worship in traditional theological texts. This is telling: despotism not only violates Islam's original vision of human equality, but it also constitutes an idolatrous act because it bestows upon human rulers a form of superiority that belongs only to God.

Another facet of this fundamental equality is that it renders mute any division or discrimination based on race or nationality. As Sayyid Qutb argued in one of his early works, "When it is thus denied that one individual can be intrinsically superior to another, it follows that there can be no race or people that is superior by reason of its origin or its nature."[10] In this, he wryly notes, "Islam was freed from the conflict of tribal and racial loyalties, and thus it achieved an equality which civilization in the West has not gained to this day."[11] Pointing out the deficiencies of Western societies is a tried and true Islamist trick—one that is most powerful with regard to racism because it is undeniably true. Osama bin Laden often used this tactic in his video addresses, in which he never missed a moment to remind Western observers that the history of genocide—from the near-eradication of the Native Americans to the Holocaust and the use of nuclear weapons in Hiroshima and Nagasaki—is *their* history, not Islam's.[12]

On the one hand, the Islamic State is heir to this critical Islamist tradition, and the social power of the Caliphate lies largely in its promise to bridge divides that had heretofore afflicted the world's Muslims. But in a fashion that makes little sense outside the history of nationalism, the Islamic State also conceives of ethnic, religious (speaking within Sunni Islam), and linguistic differences as hurdles to overcome. Thus, while its media often highlights the diverse national backgrounds of foreign fighters, this is done in order to demonstrate their obsolescence. It is the act of jihad that rendered this unifying service, as fighters stood "in a single trench, defending and guarding each other, and sacrificing themselves for one another. Their blood mixed and became one, under a single flag and goal, in one pavilion, enjoying this blessing, the blessing of faithful brotherhood."[13] The rhetoric of nationalism is here unmistakable, as is the political goal: transforming a motley crew into a unified and uniform social body, ready to serve the ends of the state. It is the same process that fueled the unification of Germany, the transformation of "peasants into Frenchmen," and the Zionist movement's creation of "Hebrews" out of Jews from the four corners of the Earth. Massimo d'Azeglio is famous for stating, "We have made Italy. Now we must make Italians."[14] This sentiment is largely consonant with the notion that most Muslims are not really practicing Islam, but that with careful training and direction, they might be brought within the fold.

Understanding the Islamic State's vision of political community must therefore begin by confronting a number of seeming contradictions: Radical equality and genuine comradery, but only among "true" believers; appeals to the suffering of the *umma*, all while casting much of it outside the boundaries of genuine Islam. The remainder of this chapter will examine two theological concepts that have proved particularly important to forging this new vision of community: *takfir*, excommunication, and *al-wala' wa-l-bara'*, roughly translated as loyalty and disavowal. They both date to the early days of Islam, but like much else within the Islamic conceptual repository, they have assumed new form and significance at the hands of militants over the past several decades. We cannot assume that contemporary ideologues employ them in the same way as the pious forefathers just because they say so. It is rather the ways in which reactionaries lean on "tradition" to rationalize their own innovations that deserves attention.

The Obedient Believer

One of the ironies present within contemporary invocations of "true Islam" is that the reformers at the helm of the Islamic Modernist movement had to work very hard to create it. The Egyptian scholar Muhammad 'Abduh, whose views on legal interpretation were discussed previously, was most influential in this regard. At the heart of 'Abduh's project lay a conception of Islam as inherently rational, a position most famously articulated by his teacher, Jamal al-Din al-Afghani. There could be no conflict, consequently, between Islam and other rational fields of inquiry such as the natural sciences. If Islam in 'Abduh's day seemed to be associated with all sorts of superstition and anti-intellectual stances, that was because syncretic practices and local customs had cut most off from true Islam. As he is purported to have said after a European sojourn, "I went to the West and saw Islam, but no Muslims; I got back to the East and saw Muslims, but not Islam."[15] It was a sentiment that Abul A'la Maududi, the Indian-Pakistani thinker, shared as well, when he reported that "not more than .001% [of the people] knew what Islam actually was."[16] In promoting a view of Islam as an abstraction of which there could be true and false variants—and moreover, arguing that "true Islam" was something other than what the Muslim masses were practicing—these think-ers offered a logical precedent that has proved appealing to those promoting a radically different agenda today.

'Abduh may have distinguished between true and false Islam, but he did not believe these concepts should be expressed materially through excommunication—a practice which, in contrast, greatly informs constructions of com-munity among today's Islamic State ideologues. The literal translation of *takfīr* is "to make someone an unbeliever," or *kāfir*, though excommunication in a religion without a centralized hierarchy is a fairly subjective practice. *Takfīr* is most immediately associated with the extremist Kharijite sect (*Khawārij*), which revolted against the authority of the Caliph Ali in 37 AH/657 CE after he agreed to arbitration with his rival, thereby denying God an opportunity to choose a winner on the battlefield. The term pops up frequently in the contemporary jihadi world as a slur against oppos-ing militant groups: "We're not *Khawārij*, but those guys over there definitely are." (Nearly everyone is a moderate in their own eyes.) Recognizing the destabilizing potential of unrestricted *takfīr*, Muslim scholars have traditionally exercised great caution with regard to the practice based on a number of injunctions in the Qur'an and hadith. For example, Muhammad is reported to have said, "If a person says to his brother, oh unbeliever! Then surely one of them is such."[17] The medieval scholar al-Ghazali (d. 1111), widely considered among the most authoritative codifiers of Sunni orthodoxy, similarly cautioned against the practice, writing "the mistake of leaving a thousand unbelievers to go free is lesser than shedding the blood of a single Muslim."[18]

Commenting on this source, an American scholar asks, "This is the case of the wrongful killing of a single Muslim believer accused of apostasy. How much greater, then, is the case of those who declare whole cities, countries, and societies full of Muslims to be unbelievers?"[19] Such reluctance is even evident today among Salafi-jihadi theorists such as Abu Muhammad al-Maqdisi and Abu Basir al-Tartusi, both of whom have criticized the Islamic State's zeal for mass excommunication.

It was the thirteenth century jurist Ibn Taymiyya who offered the most notable exception to this general rule. Writing in the aftermath of the Mongol destruction of the Abbasid Caliphate, Ibn Taymiyya famously declared jihad against the invaders from Central Asia. Although the Mongols had embraced Islam, he did not consider them genuinely Muslim on account of their hybrid legal system, which combined shari'a with elements of tribal law. Contemporary insurgents lean heavily on Ibn Taymiyya's example to create a precedent for fighting rulers who, though nominally Muslim, do not govern in accordance with shari'a. This selective use of Ibn Taymiyya is illustrative, as it suggests a clear link between *takfir* and political authority: *takfir* becomes a tool to legitimate rebellion rather than merely a means of demarcating and protecting the community of the faithful. In other words, *takfir* is the means by which it becomes permissible to kill other Muslims.

Rarely practiced in the centuries that followed the Mongol invasion, *takfir* resurged in the eighteenth century at the hands of the puritanical reformer, Muhammad bin Abd al-Wahhab.[20] The namesake of present-day "Wahhabism" whose alliance with Ibn Saud continues to shape life in Saudi Arabia, Ibn Abd al-Wahhab revitalized the practice in his attempt to rid the Arabian Peninsula of apostasy and disbelief. In this, his adversaries were not just non-Muslims, but popular forms of Islamic mysticism and the reigning ulema of the region, who enlisted the emir of Riyadh to oppose him.[21] The Islamic State treats both Ibn Taymiyya and Ibn Abd al-Wahhab in a reverential way that is particularly noteworthy given their disdain for many contemporary scholars, and one finds laudatory mention of both men sprinkled liberally throughout their public statements. Indeed, the group claims to be picking up where Ibn Abd al-Wahhab left off, leading to an abundance of public feuds with Saudi-backed scholars over who is the rightful heir to the Wahhabi project.

Much as contemporary militants invoke this legacy, the Salafi-jihadi use of *takfir* as a political tool to "explicitly delineate the boundaries of faith, creating an 'in-group' of rightful adherents while also identifying an 'out-group' of heretics," dates only to the 1980s, and it only crystalized into a coherent idea following the 2003 invasion of Iraq.[22] One of the most significant innovations in this regard is to generalize Ibn Taymiyya's logic and apply it to state institutions or even whole societies. There is an enormous theoretical leap between declaring an individual ruler an apostate and extending this judgment to anyone who supports the state, votes in elections, or works a government job. The latter impulse cannot, by definition, abide by the directive to consider each person's individual conduct and circumstances—indeed, al-Qaeda leader Ayman al-Zawahiri explicitly declared that pausing to do so was both impossible and ultimately unnecessary.[23] In recent years al-Qaeda has arguably become more cautious in this regard, in part because of widespread condemnation of their attacks on fellow Muslims and no doubt in part to differentiate themselves from the Islamic State. Indeed, the latter's zeal for excommunication was one of the chief factors that broke the alliance between the two militant groups.

It is within the ranks of the latter that excommunication has been most fully linked not merely to communal identity but also to political obedience. *Takfir* in the hands of the Islamic State is potentially universal in scope: not just directed against certain rulers (that is, to justify a revolt) or groups deemed heretical, but against anyone who resists the Caliphate's claim to authority. "Indeed, it is an incredibly disturbing phenomena we are witnessing that an entire country and all of its Muslim citizens are declared to be apostates and heinous violence is justified against them."[24] Much has been made of the fervor with which the Islamic State has embraced *takfir*, but it is usually cast in a theological light rather than a political or identarian one. I'm not suggesting that the lines between the three are distinct; quite the opposite is true. With regard to the Caliphate, determining who is part of the "real" Muslim community is integral to the group's attempt to establish itself as the only legitimate political *or* religious authority in the Islamic world today. This has naturally come with a large helping of disdain for its ideological and political rivals, from the state-friendly Wahhabi Islam of Saudi scholars to other insurgents like the "murtadd (apostate) nationalist Taliban" and "Jabhat al-Ridda" (apostasy)—a play on Jabhat al-Nusra (aka the

Nusra Front), the al-Qaeda affiliated militant group that operated in Syria during the early years of the civil war.

This emphasis on *takfir* found expression in a textbook authored by the radical scholar Turki al-Bin'ali for use in Islamic State training camps. The book spends an inordinate amount of time parsing the different categories of disbelief and the conditions under which the true believer is obliged to make *takfir* on other Muslims. Perhaps most incredulously given the traditional caution of scholars mentioned above, the text states, "The 'ulama—may God have mercy on them —have explained that one who has not denounced the disbeliever as a disbeliever or doubted his disbelief is himself one who disbelieves."[25] If you can follow the logical turns here, the argument is that it is not sufficient to live piously oneself; you must also denounce disbelief and those associated with it, otherwise your *own* belief is compromised. So too it was telling that the Delegated Committee of the Islamic State published a lengthy fatwa in May 2017 that identified *takfir* as "among the principles of true religion," stating, "knowledge of it must precede knowledge of prayer and the remainder of obligations that are known of religion by necessity."[26] Though the fatwa was later retracted because of the uproar it caused, the Islamic State's effort to make excommunication the foundation of what it means to be a Muslim offers us a glimpse at something truly novel in the history of Islam.

But we would be missing half the story if we view this heightened concern with the boundaries of faith as stemming from doctrinal conviction alone. Looking at the fatwa mentioned above, for instance, it is noteworthy that its final pages were not about excommunication at all but rather dealt with the absolute obedience owed to the Islamic State. Here the Delegated Committee leaned heavily on the same tradition of political quietism that radical figures have otherwise denounced, citing classical statements including: "Whoever is kind to Allah's authority, Allah is kind to him"; "Whoever obeys me has surely obeyed Allah, and whoever disobeys me has surely disobeyed Allah. And whoever obeys my emir has surely obeyed me, and whoever disobeys my emir has surely disobeyed me"; and, "If the imam is just then he receives a reward and you must be grateful. And if he is a tyrant then he bears the burden and you must be patient." As the author summarizes these sources, the "*ahl al-sunna* [an honorific reference to the "people of tradition," i.e. the true Muslims] are patient with those in authority over them, being sincere and admonishing them secretly, not instigating the rabble and masses against them, nor being helpful to the unbelievers against their state and those in authority over them."[27] Thus, the Islamic State came full circle to embrace the justifications for absolutism that have long been questioned by radicals—including those like Qutb that are often regarded as its ideological forefathers. I will have more to say about this in Chapter 4, but here it is worth noting the essential link the fatwa reflects between excommunication and political authority. The true Muslim is not just he who believes, but he who obeys.

It has been through these sorts of theoretical gymnastics that the Islamic State justifies its killing of (in no particular order) Muslim soldiers serving in national armies, the Shi'a and other "deviant" sects, tribes associated with the US-backed Sunni Awakening, towns that have resisted the Islamic

State's expansion, and Sunni religious scholars who refused to pledge their allegiance. Among the latter was Muhammad al-Mansuri, the imam of Mosul's Great Mosque of al-Nuri—from whose pulpit Abu Bakr al-Baghdadi announced the renewal of the Caliphate—who was killed along with twelve other ulema shortly after the city was occupied in 2014. By way of justification, the Islamic State has repeatedly stressed that it does not care—as many Salafi scholars implore—to consider people's individual circumstances before casting them outside the bounds of true Islam. Apostasy thereby becomes a collective act, removing the burden of differentiation. "The Shaykh [Abu Mus'ab al-Zarqawi] explained that the people of *tawḥīd* (monotheism, here meaning the true Islamic community i.e. ISIS) do not distinguish in their disavowal (*bara'tihim*) between polytheism and its people, between a tyrant (*taghut*) and his worshipers, between leaders and their followers and helpers."[28]

Statements like these, which help legitimate generalized pronouncements of *takfīr*, are certainly historical novelties. They are incomprehensible outside a modern conceptual matrix that assumes a base level of liability of people for the conduct of their rulers—a notion that would have made little sense to medieval Muslims. Indeed, as Faisal Devji astutely noted in his important study of al-Qaeda, there is a quasi-democratic impulse present within such condemnations, which mirrors those directed at Western targets. For instance, al-Qaeda has long disputed the characterization of its attacks as being directed at innocent civilians, arguing that as democratic subjects, civilians are complicit in the actions of their governments. "In playing this role," al-Zawahiri stated,

> the western countries were backed by their peoples, who were free
> in their decisions ... they cast their votes in the elections to choose
> the governments that they want, pay taxes to fund their policy, and
> hold them accountable about how this money was spent.[29]

Indeed, it seems that the voluminous body of rulings and commentary issued by al-Qaeda to justify attacks on Western civilians during the early twentieth century has blown back to Muslim communities at the hands of the Islamic State.

Looking beyond its sheer destructiveness, it is crucial to note just how well this ideological reconfiguration of excommunication fits within the new wars framework described in Chapter 1. At the strategic level, the Islamic State's use of *takfir* creates a means of rendering the distinction between civilians and combatants—which is central to classical legal debates regarding jihad—obsolete. In the words of one scholar who has thrown his lot behind the Caliphate, Abu Mariya al-Shami, "It is time to scrap from our dictionary in Syria the expression[s] 'civilians' and 'combatants' from the Nusayri (Alawi) sect ... except if it is confirmed that this civilian has condemned the regime and has joined the Sunnis."[30] As we have seen in other instances of ethnic cleansing, "guilt" in such frameworks stems primarily from membership in a particular community.

It is difficult, if not impossible, to account for the Islamic State's campaign of terror against civilians in Iraq and Syria by recourse to Islamic theology or classical legal debates alone. But such conduct is wholly consistent with that displayed by other partisans who have dreamt of demographic homogeneity—from Bosnia to East Timor, Myanmar, or

South Sudan. Here we can also clearly see how civil wars in particular have proved fruitful to the theological refinement of these exclusionary concepts. The mere fact that the homogeneity the Islamic State aspires toward is ideological rather than ethnic does not render the point moot, as the political and social logic of the insider/outsider division can accommodate a variety of criteria.

In short, the Islamic State's vision of an exclusionary, homogenized community is hardly traditional at all, in either theological or historical terms. Still, questions remain. Why should an aspiring Caliphate display such harshness toward the very people it claims to defend? Why is the act of exclusion so foundational within the political community the Islamic State hopes to build? And what does this political logic teach us about the outside world?

Community by Choice

When Abu Bakr al-Baghdadi declared the return of the Caliphate on June 29, 2014, he assumed the name Caliph Ibrahim. Though purportedly al-Baghdadi's given name, this choice undoubtedly reflected a far loftier association: the Prophet Ibrahim (Abraham), forefather of three religions, who was exemplary in his commitment to monotheism despite being surrounded by polytheism. In turning away from the idol worship that was prevalent in his time and professing the unity of God, Ibrahim is said to have exemplified true piety in the face of overwhelming opposition. As retold in the Islamic State magazine, *Dabiq*, it is the path (*millah*) of Ibrahim that has "quenched a thirst" within the soul of the young fighter and "restored his confidence in his religion and creed, especially with respect to the issue of openly disassociating oneself from the *kuffar* [nonbelievers] and *mushrikin* (polytheists)."[31] Ibrahim in such telling is not merely a model of piety, but of purification. The story might be an old one, but the uses to which it is put today are wholly anchored in the present.

The figure of Ibrahim looms large in Islamic State discourse on account of the importance that militants attach to the concept of *al-wala' wa-l-bara'* (loyalty and disavowal). Ibrahim is said to have exhibited both qualities in spades, first by reconstructing the *ka'ba* and preaching the unity of God (his *wala'*), and second by destroying the idols that surrounded it and disavowing polytheism (his *bara'*). Much like *takfir*, *al-wala' wa-l-bara'* offer an excellent example of the ways in which contemporary militants put old theological concepts to new uses. In particular, the concept has evolved into a model for both social purification and political confrontation with allegedly un-Islamic forces—be they people, practices, or institutions—and as such is central to the Islamic State's construction of community.

The application of *al-wala' wa-l-bara'* to an explicitly political field is of relatively recent vintage, dating back no further than the eighteenth century alliance between Ibn Saud and Muhammad bin Abd al-Wahhab. It was in the context of the wars between Ibn Saud and his political rivals that loyalty and disavowal evolved from an individual ethical precept into a collective one. Faced with an uprising in the Arabian Peninsula, the Ottoman Empire dispatched Muhammad 'Ali Pasha to fight Ibn Saud. Theologians cast

in the Wahhabi mold argued that the principle of *al-wala'
wa-l-bara'* forbade tribes from allying themselves with the
Ottomans, whom they considered polytheists. In the words
of one scholar, "Anyone who befriends a *mushrik* [polythe-
ist] is a *mushrik*; anyone who befriends a *kafir* (unbeliever)
is a *kafir*."[32] It was guilt by association taken to its extreme
conclusion.

Novel as the Wahhabi use of *al-wala' wa-l-bara'* was, the
concept has evolved further at the hands of contemporary
ideologues of jihad, who view it as an obligation to disavow
all that is not considered properly Islamic: institutions, states
and their laws, but also communities and popular religious
practices. *Bara'* thus becomes a mode of individual purification from the corrupting influences of the world, but does
not dictate—as in some Christian fundamentalist circles—
a retreat from that world. Rather, as the Salafi scholar Abu
Muhammad al-Maqdisi (another engineer, in the event
you're keeping track) argued in an influential work, *Millat
Ibrahim*, *bara'* requires active confrontation with that which
you disavow.

Written in the 1980s during his sojourn with the Afghan
mujahideen, al-Maqdisi's treatise is steeped in his own political context: references abound to the *tawaghit* who replace
the law of God with their manmade and often arbitrary
edicts. In his hands, the concept evolved into a "muscular and
aggressive" doctrine that required an offensive approach, a
type of individualized purge. It was, for instance, no longer
sufficient to perform *bara'* by shunning an unjust ruler;
one must challenge him directly.[33] In this sense the practice
gained a positive political content in a way that parallels

Sayyid Qutb's arguments about sovereignty and obedience. As the latter argued:

> This tradition indicates the necessity of getting rid of a ruler who abandons the law by deed or by word … This is another necessary step beyond the mere withholding of obedience, which is in itself a purely negative measure.[34]

Al-Maqdisi's innovation was in tying this adversarial political stance to the theological concept of *bara'*, which was not the way Qutb chose to frame the issue. Not surprisingly, it is the Wahhabi revitalization of *takfir* that al-Maqdisi cites as a model for *bara'*—rendered here as enmity toward all that is based on polytheism. Given the expansive definition of polytheism he employs—encompassing any political, legal, or social system not based on shari'a, including those of nominally Islamic governments—there are no shortage of things and people to disavow. In a recent book, Shiraz Maher notes how this iteration of *bara'* has become "a particularly powerful tool of mobilization for sub-state actors looking to undermine established institutions of power. It demands a withdrawal of support from the government, delegitimizes the judiciary and police, and undermines the legitimacy of state-sanctioned scholars."[35]

The contemporary sense of *bara'* also requires a reconfiguration of the true believer's social interactions and community. It is this aspect that speaks most directly to the seeming contradiction mentioned above: the Islamic State touts its sense of comradery and communal warmth while simultaneously condemning many of the world's actual

Muslims. Particularly in the early years of the Caliphate, videos often celebrated this sense of community: "Brothers" embrace, hands clasped together. Next they appear side-by-side, laughing with their weapons draped casually across their laps, and fighting as one in the field. But belonging does not come without a price, and is often accessible only by rejecting the communities in which one was raised. As Olivier Roy has argued, one consequence of this type of rebellion is that the Islamic State, even at its territorial highpoint, was remarkably detached from any particular cultural formation. Having abandoned the "culturally rooted religion of their parents," radicals rather "piece together a religion without any social and cultural grounding."[36] The "real" *umma* is not the one you grew up in, no matter where you were raised. It exists rather as a past fantasy and future hope, the germ of which the Caliphate claims to represent in the present.

The break with one's past thus serves as a manifestation of *bara'* par excellence, one that ideally concludes in migrating to Islamic State–held territory. Videos highlighting these individual journeys are, ironically, highly formulaic. The standard script paints the decision to relinquish the creature comforts of home as the ultimate triumph of personal will over social inertia. "Are your wives and children the reason that you're prevented from jihad? Are your homes, businesses, and wealth, more beloved to you than Allah, His Messenger, and jihad in His path?"[37] One video featured the Australian fighter, Abu Khalid al-Kambudi, who recounted his journey to Islam in terms of the intentional rejection of his natal community: "A brother said to me ...

'Why are you following the religion of Buddhism?' I said, because my family is. [And he said] 'That's not a reason to stay somewhere. You should keep searching'."[38] Stories like Abu Khalid's are typical, and the Islamic State often chooses to highlight the stories of converts as examples of individuals who have most fully disassociated from their prior lives.

Even as the Islamic State dismisses the notion of individual liberty (discussed at length in Chapter 4), tales of the mujahid's principled and heroic disavowal of his former life are central to these profiles in courage. It is in this context that we should situate the group's frequent celebration of independence from the familial and social bonds to which Islam has traditionally ascribed great importance.

> Today we are beginning to witness with our eyes and hear with our ears the wonder of wonders among the children of Mesopotamia ... this father kills his son the spy with his own hand—this tribe disavows its son, the Maliki (i.e. working for the Iraqi government) policeman—and the wondrous and astonishing [thing] that a woman leaves her husband and escapes his guardianship because he supports the Maliki government and his party.[39]

There are no doubt examples of such conduct—which the fatwa cites approvingly—from the early days of Islam, when believers turned away from pagan tribes to follow the Prophet. But in the jihadi redux, disavowal is cast as a necessary practice *within* the Islamic community, overturning the duty of fathers to care for their children and wives to obey their husbands. The Islamic State community is thus intentional rather than natural, chosen rather than given.

In *Holy Ignorance*, Olivier Roy has suggested that this transformation of the religious community is one outgrowth, ironically, of secularization. As religions have become less culturally embedded in everyday life, with all its messy realities, they have been reconstructed based on sacred texts alone—"purified" of any sullying material influence. This process is consequential for a number of reasons: by effectively breaking the link between faith and culture, it creates the possibility of a truly universal religion, shorn of anything that might suggest social accommodation or regional difference.[40] We see this manifest in the Salafi world more broadly through the renunciation of local customs and the rejection of Sunni Islam's four different schools of law—the very existence of which reflected the reality of diversity *within* the *umma*.

On the contrary, the community gathered under the Caliphate's umbrella thrives on the prospect of homogenization. Images of fighters burning their passports serve to convey the renunciation of their old, particular identities. From here on out they are Muslims alone—shorn of any adjectives. The fact that this newly adopted identity is *also* a particular one must be vociferously denied, of course, as the force of its social appeal stems from this claim to neutrality —not another version of Islam, but the thing itself. Identity in such terms is necessarily singular. The reality of multiple, overlapping, or complementary identities—a noted feature of social life under the Ottoman Empire, for example—is here dissolved in favor of something far more exclusive.[41] The idea that one might be an Egyptian *and* a Muslim, or an Iraqi *and* a Muslim, and so forth, is here dissolved in favor of a new universal.[42]

And therein lies the rub: much as the Islamic State claims to be "postnational," it is difficult to account for the exclusionary nature of its political logic without considering the ideological influence of modern nationalism. It has been under the shadow of nationalist thinking that composite identities became acutely problematic in an unprecedented fashion and that the heterogeneous nature of political and social space became a liability. This is an impulse that manifests not merely among the right-wing, anti-immigrant, and xenophobic. For instance, some political scientists have argued that European social democracies were successful in the post–World War II period because they were largely homogenous, thanks in no small part to the extermination of "problematic" populations. Meanwhile contemporary champions of nationalism—both liberal and authoritarian —link the smooth functioning of states to their ethnic or national uniformity, registering both a large degree of historical amnesia and an inability to imagine the boundaries of political community around any basis other than bloodlines. The nation-state form is uniquely unable to accommodate difference—which is why it is so often implicated in ethnic cleansing—but it is not the state's only possible form, past, present, or future.[43] Yet the Caliphate's conception of politics as neither a means to hash out differences between competing interest groups nor a site of intercommunal cooperation fits well within the logic of the new nationalism. Because politics is more akin to management—I will return to this point in Chapter 4—it requires a certain level of homogenization at the outset. This naturally requires purging the community of "undesirable" elements. In this sense, the

Islamic State's vision of community is informed by an exclusionary logic whose closest political corollaries come from the new nationalism, which also dreams of identity in black and white terms rather than the unruly mess of technicolor.

Yet, in keeping with the thesis that today's jihad is charting the future rather than reviving the past, the Islamic State's vision of community pushes this exclusionary logic in a new direction by globalizing the insider/outsider dichotomy—borrowing from modern nationalism but also superseding it. We need to consider the mechanics of such identification, and their implications, in greater detail.

The *Umma* at Large

> On the 17th of Muharram 1436 [November 10, 2014], the world heard announcements from the mujahideen of the Arabian Peninsula, Yemen, Sinai, Libya, and Algeria, pronouncing their *bay'at* [oaths of allegiance] to the Khalifah [Caliph] of the Muslims, Abu Bakr al-Husayni al-Baghdadi.[44]

So the Islamic State announced the creation of several franchises around the globe. As of this writing, the Caliphate claims provinces in Pakistan and Afghanistan, the Democratic Republic of Congo, Niger, Kashmir, Bangladesh, Sri Lanka, the Egyptian Sinai, Libya, Yemen, and Mali. Particularly after losing most of its territorial base in Iraq and Syria, these provinces have proved centrally important to maintaining a sense of active struggle and are often featured in Islamic State media. In April 2019, in one of Abu Bakr al-Baghdadi's few video appearances, the Caliph clutched dossiers presumably containing information on his various provinces, much like a chief executive surveying his global operations. As any multinational corporation could tell you, being able to claim branches (no matter how small) in regions across the world projects a sense of vibrancy. You're either growing or dying, as the old adage goes.

The custom of giving *bay'a* to the Caliph has assumed outsized importance within the Islamic State, as such pledges lend credibility to its claims to operate on a global scale. Historically, the practice is said to stem from an Arab tribal custom that involved clasping of the hands to indicate the election of and submission to a new leader. It was later adopted as a means of swearing allegiance to the Prophet and after him, the caliphs. "The *bay'a* of a caliph thus constituted a contract in which not only the latter was involved as a person receiving fealty, but also those voluntarily expressing the wish to obey their leader."[45] Early Muslim scholars disagreed (naturally) on how many participants were necessary to legitimize the caliph's rule, with opinions ranging from all "upright men" to a single official within the court. In practice, the institution of *bay'a* eventually evolved into a process of rubber-stamping the heir apparent, and was adopted in this form by modern states looking to legitimize themselves.[46]

This long tradition of *bay'a* should not blind us to the novelty of its usage by the Islamic State. At the most basic level, these oaths of allegiance—from groups in Afghanistan and Pakistan, Libya, the Sinai, West Africa, the Philippines and Bangladesh, to individuals carrying out solo attacks in the United States—are quite literally discursive events that become meaningful only to the extent to which they are known. "Gather people in the masajid [mosques], Islamic centers, and Islamic organizations, for example, and make public announcements of bay'ah. Try to record these bay'at [pl.] and then distribute them through all forms of media including the Internet."[47] Doing so would, it was hoped, trigger a domino effect such that various groups will "abandon their partisanship and also announce their bay'ah to the Khalifah Ibrahim."[48] Those living within "police states" should still broadcast their allegiance to the world, but through anonymous means.

The fact that the practice of *bay'a* has been widely embraced by militant groups invites us to pause and consider what kind of power is being recognized in such instances. On the ground in Iraq and Syria, *bay'at* functioned in a more traditional sense as recognizing and submitting to the ruler of a territory. Thus, we find the radical scholar Abu Mundhir al-Shinqiti calling on other militant groups operating in the region to pledge their allegiance to the Caliphate, arguing that they were duty-bound to do so.[49] On the other hand we find militants and even individuals in far-flung regions pledging their allegiance as well. Videos of these ceremonies are almost all the same: a few dozen fighters stand at attention as someone reads a script declaring the group's loyalty to the Islamic State and its Caliph, the "leader of the faithful." The fighters join hands and yell excitedly for a few minutes, and ... scene. Affiliates might be previously independent militant organizations like Boko Haram or newly constituted franchises. Many provinces can claim only a few hundred fighters, yet they constitute a networked diaspora of true believers. Citing a hadith, the Islamic State asserts that Muslims have been divided into seventy-three distinct factions, all of which are misguided with the exception of the one that "proceeds upon the prophetic methodology," which (you guessed it) is none other but itself.[50] Moreover, the Caliphate has forwarded the novel argument that obedience is only obligatory toward this rightly guided faction regardless of where in the world you reside. Pledging *bay'a* extends an opportunity to join this elite group from afar—much as you might an online fan club—and contribute to the cause without migrating to Iraq or Syria. In this way the Islamic State creates a parallel political and social structure of networked hubs, a vision of community as both selective and dispersed: the genuine *umma* is everywhere existent even if, in technical terms, it is nowhere sovereign.

How should we think about this form of political community? We might start by clarifying what it is not. This model is neither the imperial order nor the more modern one represented by nation-states, both of which necessitate genuine control over territory.[51] Nor is it an older diasporic one: Jews in Salonika did not exempt themselves from obeying the commands of local authorities on account of their communal connection to Jews in Baghdad. Rather, if we have to locate the Islamic State's networked version of political community within known models, it is the modern corporation that yields the most family resemblance. For the sake of comparison, consider an entity like Glencore, "one of the world's largest globally diversified natural resource companies." Headquartered in Switzerland, Glencore boasts of operations in more than 150 sites in over thirty-five countries, staffed by approximately 160,000 employees and contractors. As we will see in Chapter 5, the Islamic State regularly issues updates that look as if they could have been lifted from Glencore's annual report, deftly employing the same infographics to detail its operations in each province.

But for a short span of years in which it controlled a territory the size of England, the Islamic State has been more of an idea than concrete reality. Having been routed in their territorial strongholds and only present among pockets of insurgents in conflict zones worldwide, one might rightfully ask: Where does the Caliphate exist? Looking for answers in the traditional realm of geography suggests we do not understand the changing stakes of the game. The closest parallels to the Islamic State Caliphate are not those dynasties of centuries past who ruled from bases in Damascus or Baghdad, but affinity groups or corporations that lean on globalized media and communications to construct a transnational identity that is largely detached from territory. This is one way to contextualize certain radical scholars' claims that the Caliphate is legitimate even though it lacks *tamkin*, or territorial consolidation.[52] Oaths of allegiance from near and far put weight behind the otherwise incredulous claim that the *umma* appointed al-Baghdadi as the Commander of the Faithful. But perhaps more importantly, as an organizing principle, collecting *bay'at* from around the world gestures toward an emerging power structure in which nation-states are not the arbiters of identity or politics. In this sense, the Islamic State is not resurrecting a past political model but rather forging ahead with a hypermodern one that fractures the longstanding notion of correspondence between geography and identity. Importantly, it is only by utilizing the latest digital technologies that this parallel community in dispersion becomes possible—connecting militants in the Sahel to insurgents in the Southern Philippines to "lone wolves" in Western cities. It doesn't matter that you will never visit the Islamic State; it can come to you.

We would search the annals of history in vain for a past Caliphate that functioned along such lines, but there is no shortage of contemporary examples to draw on. The following chapter will look more closely at what this type of communal structure indicates about the changing nature of power and sovereignty worldwide.

4

The Democratic Foil

Is Islam compatible with democracy? The subject of count-less policy conferences and research papers since the turn of the last century, this question does not age well. Assuming a monolithic abstract called "Islam" that is either for or against democracy—here meaning Western liberalism, which as I write is itself facing its own internal crises—this question conveniently overlooks what actual Muslims think or do about questions of liberty, sovereignty, and govern-ance. Perhaps there is no better indicator of how unhelpful such framing is than to consider the historical fact that a mere century ago, on the heels of what is called the Islamic Modernist movement, you would encounter no shortage of learned scholars, budding journalists, educators, and politicians each arguing that "true Islam" was essentially democratic—grounded in the freedom and fundamental equality of humanity. Fast-forward to the present, and again a faction has emerged claiming the mantle of "true Islam"— but this time the argument has been inverted: democratic governance, in the mainstream Salafi view, violates God's sovereignty by placing human laws alongside divine ones. The Islamic State goes even further in regarding democracy as a form of polytheism that must be virulently and violently opposed. Which Islam are we talking about when considering its relation to democracy?

This chapter will take up the matter from a different angle by exploring how the contemporary Salafi-jihadi position has developed in dialectical tension to both the promises and limitations of democracy itself. Rather than existing from time immemorial, we should note that current views of divine sovereignty have emerged in conversation with modern democratic (and antidemocratic) movements. So too, we might wonder how militants' rather dim view of democracy intersects with the waning faith in that system in the West. Finally, what might the Islamic State's approach to governance have to teach us about the changing nature of political life more broadly?

The Dialectic of "True Islam"

"Oh you who believe, obey Allah and obey the Messenger and those in authority among you" (Sura al-Nisa', 59). This verse sits at the basis of what is often referred to as Islam's tradition of political quietism, a theological argument for obedience to those in power that persists to this day (and indeed, remains the dominant impulse among Salafis). Many textual sources from Islam's first centuries stressed the virtues of obedience, indicating a strong preference among early jurists for order and stability. Fearful of the anarchic effects associated with civil strife, jurists argued that even a usurper could be regarded as a legitimate ruler. They further stressed that the caliph need not be the most virtuous or pious, as long as he didn't prevent subjects from practicing the faith or commit clear and public apostasy. Even tyrants guarded the frontiers and preserved law and order, which was broadly viewed as a prerequisite to safeguarding religious practice. As the late Albert Hourani characterized it, "even an unjust ruler was ... better than none at all."[1]

In truth, political authority in premodern Muslim states (or sultanates) was never as absolute as imagined by western Orientalists. Rebellions were certainly not unknown in Islamic history, and the treatment of rebels by classical scholars is notably forgiving.[2] At the very least, as Wael Hallaq has argued, the existence of shari'a as a body of communal law distinct from the law of the state—and to which the ruler himself was theoretically subject—mitigated against the arbitrary abuse of power.[3] But much like Christian monarchs who leaned on Paul's Letter to the Romans—"Let every person be subject to the governing authorities; for there is no authority except from God, and those authorities that exist have been instituted by God"—Muslim rulers had a number of sources at their disposal to justify their position. Jurists attached to the state also took it upon themselves to make the case for obedience. As one such figure who served the court of the Abbasid Caliph Harun al-Rashid (d. 193 AH/809 CE) wrote in an administrative treatise:

> Do not abuse rulers, for if they treat you well, they will be rewarded
> and you must be grateful, but if they treat you badly, theirs is the

burden and you must be patient. They are a punishment by which God punishes whom He wishes; therefore, do not receive God's punishment with heat and anger, but with calm and humility.[4]

This classical accord was already on life support long before the new republic of Turkey abolished the Caliphate in 1924. Cracks had begun to appear in the early half of the nineteenth century, as intellectuals began rethinking the nature of Islamic governance in light of contemporary political philosophy. It accelerated toward the end of the century as more and more Muslims found themselves living under European political and cultural domination, often in clear dialogue with these challenges. Thinkers working within and alongside the Islamic Modernist movement were particularly influential in this regard. Much in the same way that reformers of this era held that "true Islam" was innately compatible with rationality and the modern sciences, they held that it was also essentially democratic. They argued that the Qur'an contained the seeds of democratic governance in ordering Muhammad to consult with the people (3:159), and that moreover, one could attribute the waning power of Muslim peoples compared with the West to a long chain of despots who had disregarded this directive. Within the Ottoman Empire, the period of "Hamidian despotism" (during the rule of Sultan Abdul Hamid II, 1876–1909) proved particularly fruitful to thinkers looking to slough off the tradition of political quietism.[5] For instance, Khayr al-Din al-Tunisi (d. 1307 AH/1890)—who briefly advised the Sultan—refashioned the Islamic practice of consultation into a call for parliamentary government. Jamal al-Din al-Afghani made the case against absolutism even more explicit, arguing for the right to revolt against and even depose an unjust ruler. Not surprisingly, both thinkers ran afoul of the Ottoman Sultan and, in al-Afghani's case, his counterparts elsewhere.

In short, by the turn of the twentieth century, a growing choir of modernists was asserting that unconditional deference toward political authority was emblematic of the moral decay Muslims had suffered as a result of their alienation from religious truth. The idea of consultation, *shura*, as the engine of Islamic democracy took root among a broad swath of progressive thinkers during this era and even worked its way into school curricula. Thus we find a secondary school textbook published in Egypt in 1930 that states, "Allah made *shura* the basis of governance in Islam and commanded his Prophet (the blessings of God be upon him), saying, 'And consult them in the matter'." In contrast to actually existing Islamic states, it was Western democracies that were most in accord with this Islamic ideal, according to the textbook:

> Look at the most advanced states in the current era and [see] their strength is found in their laws being based on consultation and that the will of their people is respected. This is the secret of their greatness, happiness, and progress.[6]

Reformers of this ilk might seem to represent the absolute antithesis of the punitive and reactionary version of Islam associated with the Islamic State. Yet thinking in these terms—which can often morph into a simplistic binary between "good" liberals and "bad" extremists—obscures some important points of overlap. First among them is that the type of democratic protest latent in the modernists' denunciation of absolutism paved the way for radical militant thinking regarding the illegitimacy of contemporary states and rulers. Once "true Islam" had been defined in opposition to despotism, the door opened to building an ideological alternative to the tradition of political quietism. A ruler who was not governing in accordance with genuine Islamic principles, however defined, was a ruler who had no rightful claim to power.

One can trace some of the connective tissue between these two reformist poles through Muhammad 'Abduh's student, Muhammad Rashid Rida (d. 1354 AH/1935), an early Islamist who developed a political theory of the Caliphate. Significantly for our purposes, Rida also led an all-out assault on the legitimacy of the political and religious elite, arguing that the former were tyrants and the latter were unimaginative traditionalists. This antiestablishment critique became sharper as the century progressed—taking aim not only at Muslim leaders but at the religious scholars who supported them. Whereas ulema in previous eras served as intermediaries between the government and the populations they ruled, the Islamic legal scholar Khaled Abou El Fadl has argued that their absorption into state bureaucracies effectively rendered them court priests. As he writes, "The emergence of highly centralized, despotic and often corrupt governments, and the nationalization of the institutions of religious learning undermined the mediating role of jurists in Muslim societies."[7] For instance, in 1961 the Egyptian government of Gamal Abdel Nasser brought al-Azhar—long considered

Sunni Islam's most prestigious educational institution—under state control. Though its scholars are still regarded as more independent than the state's official shari'a council, Dar al-Ifta, the fact that the head of al-Azhar is a presidential appointee (and indeed, these appointees often come from Dar al-Ifta) does not endear it to large parts of the population. As Nathan Brown has argued:

> Islamists outside the institution—sometimes within the [Muslim] Brotherhood and quite frequently in Salafi ranks—make clear that the institution has been partly co-opted and rendered subservient to high political officials; they often take a particularly skeptical view of the shaykh [head of al-Azhar], perceiving the holder of the position as a political appointee.[8]

In short, as more and more clerics have become government functionaries charged with propagating a state-friendly Islam, they have consequently sunk in popular esteem. As such, mainstream ulema are in no position to offer a compelling alternative to the radical vision offered by militants who place jihad at the center of religious practice. What they do offer is legitimation for a status quo that many find, not unreasonably, unbearable. With the effective disappearance of left-wing challengers over the past forty years (in Margaret Thatcher's infamous formulation, "There is no alternative") it is hardly surprising that religious militants have harnessed popular discontent to fuel their own reactionary ideals. Importantly, the break with "the establishment"—in this case meaning both the *tawaghit* and the scholars and other functionaries who legitimize and facilitate their rule—is central to their self-fashioning and integral to their appeal.

Thus, Islamic State media and public statements almost never fail to mention the moral bankruptcy of mainstream scholars and clerics, who are condemned for refusing to recognize the legitimacy of the Caliphate, all the while providing theological support to oppressive regimes. The Caliphate has been "opposed and forsaken by 'the wise ones,' the 'theorizers,' and 'the elders,' who labeled them as being Khawarij [Kharajites]." Such is the substance of frequent attacks on prominent Sunni clerics like 'Abd al-Aziz al-Sheikh (the Grand Mufti of Saudi Arabia) and Sheikh al-Azhar, Ahmad al-Tayyib, both of whom have issued denunciations of the Islamic State. Even more independent and radically minded members of the Sunni ulema—for instance, Yusuf al-Qaradawi, who infamously condoned suicide bombing against Israeli civilians—are viewed as apostates on account of their willingness to work within existing political and social structures or, as in al-Qaradawi's case, desire to reform them. A 2017 audio message drove the point home by calling upon supporters to assassinate prominent members of the ulema living in Egypt and other Arab countries.

Using an elite class that is widely viewed as corrupt and self-serving as its rhetorical, and in some cases physical, punching bag, the Islamic State poses as the liberator of the masses from business as usual. Yet unlike al-Qaeda, which shares in this antipathy toward Muslim rulers and their scholarly henchmen, the Islamic State actually erected a competing political authority. Within this changed landscape, it was no longer enough to rebel against leaders or attack the organs of existing states. It was also obligatory to submit to the Caliphate in all matters, temporal and spiritual; indeed, the very first issue of *Dabiq* devotes much space to arguing that the correct understanding of leadership includes both political and religious authority. This self-conscious presentation is important, as it gestures at how this all-encompassing view of governance has developed as the mirror image of the West's much-touted secular ideal. Asserting that there is no division between religion and politics is a self-consciously modern move. There is nothing like it among premodern Muslims, even those who arguably *did* create a separate political office, that of the Sultan, to administer worldly affairs. It is the indelible mark of a modernity that is disavowed.

The same article also makes the case for obedience as a doctrinal necessity. "There is no Islam except with jama'ah (congregation), and no jama'ah except with imarah (leadership), and no imarah except with ta'ah (obedience)."[9] This saying, attributed to 'Umar Ibn al-Khattab (a close companion of the Prophet and the second Caliph), appears at the end of the feature in large, modern font, as if begging to be hung alongside other inspirational posters in the Islamic State boardroom. Indeed, for all its claims to liberate the *umma* from their oppressors—both Western and homegrown—it is clear that the sort of freedom on offer is of a particular sort. It is certainly not democratic, either in terms of content or procedure. Rather, the Islamic State seeks to replace an elite ruling class with itself—to swap establishment despotism for a nimbler variety. Yet however counterintuitive, the militant rejection of governing elites as apostates is the contemporary heir to progressive reformers who argued that "true Islam" was incompatible with blind obedience. The Islamic State has completed the dialectical loop by harnessing the old theological arguments for absolutism to a new cart.

The effective capture and redeployment of popular discontent by the Islamic State in particular offers yet another reason to consider the Caliphate as a form of authoritarian populism and to situate its views on democracy and governance alongside other reactionary movements. The final goal of this rebellion against "establishment" leaders and traditional bodies of expertise is to position the individual in a submissive relationship to another authority figure who demands nothing short of total allegiance. The problem, as anyone tracking the presidency of Donald Trump could tell you, is that such "populists" do not actually have any solutions to the collective woes that propel them into power. They offer a violent negation of the status quo that, as I examine in later chapters, falls far short of a genuine alternative.

The Sovereign Challenge

If the notion that "true Islam" requires war on democratic governance—both in its legislative and procedural elements—is largely a creation of the twentieth century, it is important to note that this antidemocratic stance has evolved in relation to the object of its derision. The general outlines of the argument are as follows: only God can truly claim to be sovereign, and such sovereignty necessarily encompasses all aspects of life, whether spiritual or material. Moreover, God has already given a complete law code, the shari'a, essentially obviating any guesswork. This fact renders democratic sovereignty both unnecessary and idolatrous. Any attempt to place man-made laws alongside divine ones is akin to ascribing partners to God, a form of polytheism that elevates human creations to the status of the almighty. The result is a paradox: the Islamic state (speaking not strictly of the Islamic State Caliphate but in theoretical terms) must always disavow that which defines the state—namely sovereignty.[10] As I argue below, this denial is not merely a paradox but also the embodiment of a particular form of power. But let us come down from the theoretical heavens for a moment to examine the earthly machinations that led us here.

The idea of sovereignty now in vogue can be traced to the South Asian thinker and political activist, Abul A'la Maududi, who began life a subject of the British Raj and died as a citizen of Pakistan. As Vali Nasr has shown in his biography, Maududi's own view of divine sovereignty developed in concert with his growing fear of popular sovereignty. Like many educated middle and upper-class Muslims, Maududi originally supported the anti-colonial independence movement coordinated under the umbrella of the Indian National Congress. But as the nationalist movement became increasingly tied to Hindu identity under Gandhi's leadership, Maududi grew fearful that a democratic India would merely entail a new vehicle for Hindu domination. India's Muslims, though representing about one-quarter of the total population, would be hopelessly outnumbered by the sheer logic of demography. The logical outcome of this conundrum—the same one Zionists in Palestine were contemporaneously arriving at—was that "democracy ... could be a viable option for Muslims only if the majority of Indians were Muslim."[11] And as in British Palestine, partition and ethnic cleansing, resulting in the new states of India and Pakistan, became the prerequisites for democratic governance.

It was against this background that Maududi developed his highly original reading of divine sovereignty, *hakimiyya*, yet it is important to note that he did not dismiss democracy entirely. Rather, he was often at pains to demonstrate that his proposed Islamic state would be democratic, governed by elected officials who were bound by the same (divine) law as everyone else. It would represent a mash up of divine legislation with human administration—a "theodemocracy" or "democratic Caliphate."[12] In this sense, Maududi paved the way for Islamists who adopted the procedural elements of democracy without recognizing the validity of popular sovereignty. His views also left a particularly influential mark on Sayyid Qutb, who built his own argument against secular strongmen atop Maududi's condemnation of man-made laws as idolatrous. Indeed, it was Maududi who seems to have originally argued for a more expansive interpretation of *taghut*, which in classical usage meant "idol." In Irfan Ahmad's words:

> Maududi contended that Allah must also be the "Ruler, Dictator (*amir*), and Legislator" of the political domain. Consequently, if someone claimed to be the ruler of a country, then his statement would be equivalent to claiming to be God in the metaphysical

realm ... Thus, to share political power with someone who disregards the laws of Allah, Maududi declared, would be polytheism in the same sense as someone who worships an idol ... Thus *taghut*, another Qur'anic word, does not just mean Satan or idol but also means a political order not based on Allah's sovereignty. Maududi chided the ulema for reducing the meaning of *taghut* to mean, literally, an idol. For Maududi, the Qur'anic injunction to worship Allah and shun *taghut* meant securing a sharia state and rejecting a non-Islamic polity.[13]

Qutb largely adopted Maududi's framework, if not his political pragmatism. Rather, *hakimiyya* became essentially adversarial in Qutb's thinking, facing off in an endless dual against human pretense. And much like Maududi, though reasoning against a different set of political preoccupations, Qutb's divine sovereignty was envisioned as a check on human sovereignty—this time not on the democratic masses but on the autocratic leaders of the postcolonial order:

Every government that is based on the principle that *hakimiyyah* (absolute sovereignty) belongs to none but Allah and then implements the shari'ah, is an Islamic government. Every government that is not based on this principle and does not implement the shari'ah, cannot be called Islamic, even if the government is run by official religious organizations. The obedience of the people is to be given only if, and as long as, the government recognizes that *hakimiyyah* belongs to Allah alone and then implements the shari'ah without any qualification other than justice and obedience.[14]

Qutb also envisioned at least procedural democracy within his idealized Islamic state. "No ruler has any religious authority direct from Heaven, as had some rulers in ancient times; he occupies his position only by the completely and absolutely free choice of all Muslims."[15] That is, even if one holds that the law is already given and even perfected, there is no reason that people cannot choose those who will administer it and hold them accountable for their shortcomings. Importantly—and much in contrast to those who governed states during Qutb's lifetime—shari'a was a body of law to which rulers would also be subject, effectively serving to restrain them from the arbitrary pursuit of their own private whims. A utopian vision perhaps, but one shaped against the very real backdrop of the postcolonial state.

The specter of democracy as the tyranny of the majority was also highly influential in shaping Abu Mus'ab al-Zarqawi's strategic logic during the early years of the Iraq War. Largely dismissive of the US forces—whose heavy losses would one day send them packing, he predicted—al-Zarqawi argued in a 2004 communiqué to al-Qaeda's leadership that the only possible road to victory was stoking a sectarian war between Iraq's Sunni and Shi'a populations. Identifying the latter as the major enemy, al-Zarqawi argued that extreme, spectacular violence would be necessary to drive Iraqi Sunnis into the jihadi camp—a destination many had proven reluctant to visit. Timing was of the essence, as the reconstitution of Iraq as a democracy would, given the demographics, lead to Shi'a political domination. The fight against the democratic path was thus not only about theology, but about a minority population's fear of majoritarian rule.

While Maududi and Zarqawi were preoccupied by demographics and Qutb by dictators, al-Qaeda stands out for joining its critique of democracy to that of capitalism. Take, for instance, Osama bin Laden's 2007 video address, "The Solution." Addressed to the American people, the video offers a remarkable explanation for al-Qaeda's rejection of democracy—seen not as the guarantor of rights and freedoms, but as the engine of the most coercive force in human history, namely capitalism:

> This greatest of plagues and most dangerous of threats to the lives of humans is taking place in an accelerating fashion as the world is being dominated by the democratic system, which confirms its massive failure to protect humans and their interests from the greed and avarice of the major corporations and their representatives. And despite this brazen attack on the people, the leaders of the West—especially Bush, Blair, Sarkozy and Brown—still talk about freedom and human rights with a flagrant disregard for the intellects of human beings. So is there a form of terrorism stronger, clearer, and more dangerous than this?
>
> This is why I tell you: as you liberated yourselves before from the slavery of monks, kings and feudalism, you should today liberate yourselves from the deception, shackles and attrition of the capitalist system. If you were to ponder it well, you would find that in the end, it is a system harsher and fiercer than your systems in the Middle Ages.[16]

It is uncanny to see Bin Laden describe the symptoms of neoliberalism's failings, from "the burden of interest-related debts" to "global warming and its woes" and "the abject poverty and tragic hunger in Africa." Nor would many leftists disagree that "the capitalist system seeks to turn the entire world into a fiefdom of the major corporations." Where we might differ is of his diagnosis of the underlying illness. Because for Bin Laden, the unbounded nature of contemporary capitalism under globalization exists "in order to protect democracy." It is democracy, rather than capitalism, that is to blame for this sordid state of affairs. He sees no possibility that the two might exist in tension or that democracy might even restrain the neofeudal drift. In truth, speaking before the global financial crisis of 2008, at a time when the Washington Consensus still touted the necessary link between capitalism and democracy, Bin Laden was echoing the establishment view.

More recently, the Islamic State has advanced a somewhat different, and ultimately sharper, critique of democracy. On the one hand, the group espouses the broader Salafi view of democracy as an affront to divine unity and sovereignty, stressing the expansive meaning of *taghut* advanced by Maududi:

Taghut linguistically is from the Arabic root tagha, meaning to transgress the limits. This limit—in the context of the Quran and Sunna—is Allah's tawhid (oneness), the taghut thus being anyone and anything by which Allah's unique attributes and sole right to be worshiped are transgressed upon. From the pillars of Allah's tawhid is that He alone has the right to legislate … Accordingly, human legislators, manmade laws, modern constitutions, judges who rule thereby, and rulers who enforce such upon others are all tawaghit whom the Muslim must disassociate from and disbelieve in.[17]

Genuine disavowal (*bara'*) therefore demands the aggressive confrontation with modern-day idol worship and the destruction of its domes "whether they be over graves or over the councils of parliament."[18] As this statement suggests, the Islamic State has driven the critique of democracy to a fevered pitch, even outstripping other jihadist organizations. This is no doubt attributable to the fact that, unlike al-Qaeda, governance was central to the Caliphate's claims to authority: it not only attacked apostate regimes, but also tried to erect a rival one. Doing so necessitated a different mode of legitimation and a more robust concept of antidemocratic subjectivity. Moreover, I believe it is telling that it is democracy—not capitalism or even Western imperialism—that has become the principle target of a militant organization that has matured under neoliberal auspices. It is to the outlines of this system that we now turn.

Piety from Above

> From amongst the polluted ideologies that have afflicted people the entire world over through out [sic] the course of the tyranny carried out by the forces of kufr (disbelief), is the notion that the people can choose whether to follow the truth or to embark upon falsehood ... They went to the extent of attributing this "methodology of free choice" to the religion of Allah ta'ala [the Almighty], and to the call of the prophets, peace be upon them.[19]

Taken from an article about the prophet Noah, this particular piece of Islamic State writing offers a remarkable glimpse into the Caliphate's attempt to envision a new kind of political subject to compete with democracy's liberated citizen. When Noah warned people about the impending flood, the article continues, he did not cordially invite them to repent and join him if it suited their fancy. No, it is "either me or the flood," the Caliphate or damnation. The authors utilize this prophetic tale to argue that free will is not an essential good, but can only be offered to individuals who already reside within a genuinely ethical order. No one is free to choose falsehood.

Suffice it to say that this argument is at odds with much of Islamic theology, as the effective eradication of free will undermines the entire structure of divine reward and punishment. Abul A'la Maududi advanced a seemingly similar thesis decades prior—holding that salvation did not depend on knowledge of God but rather absolute obedience—which was, notably, rejected by one of the leading scholars of his day.[20] The Islamic State redux, however, is not chiefly concerned with submission to the Almighty, but submission to itself. That these are claimed to be one and the same is of course one of the group's chief contentions and gestures at its particular understanding of the relationship between Islam and the state. By way of contrast, we should recall that Maududi remained incredibly suspicious of the state of Pakistan and forbade his followers from swearing an oath of allegiance to it.

This degradation of individual choice also differentiates the Islamic State from previous ideologues like Sayyid Qutb, who argued that human emancipation was the ultimate aim of jihad.

It [Islam] has the right to destroy all obstacles in the form of institutions and traditions which limit man's freedom of choice. It does
not attack individuals nor does it force them to accept its beliefs;
it attacks institutions and traditions to release human beings from
their poisonous influences, which distort human nature and which
curtail human freedom.[21]

Ever mindful of the Qur'anic injunction that "there is no
compulsion in religion" (2:256), Qutb envisioned a world in
which people were free to choose to embrace Islam or not,
noting that "In an Islamic system there is room for all kinds
of people to follow their own beliefs, while obeying the laws
of the country which are themselves based on the Divine
authority."[22] In practice, as many commentators have noted,
there is a domineering streak within this concern for human
freedom, which is predicated on the destruction of all those
institutions that restricted the practice of "true Islam."[23] Yet
in contrast to the Islamic State, Qutb still regarded the latter
as something actual humans wanted to live in accordance
with, rather than an external system of constraint that must
be enforced from above.

The antidemocratic ethos of the current Caliphate is
difficult to account for merely by revisiting the annals of
twentieth century Islamism or the birth of the modern jihadist movement. It is routinely celebrated and boasted of by
fighters, who express something of pity for those poor fools
still chasing after popular sovereignty. As the Islamic State
argued in a long feature released prior to the 2016 election, there is no real difference between George W. Bush
and Barack Obama, Hilary Clinton and Donald Trump, all

of whom are committed to waging war against Islam. The allure of democratic choice is thus also a form of deception. There is no virtue in choosing "the lesser of two evils" when the whole system is rotten. Therefore, anyone who participates in such a system, in whatever capacity, stands outside the bounds of true Islam.

> Whoever votes in the democratic system—whether or not he himself is a candidate or nominee—has made himself a *taghut*, a rival to Allah in rule and legislation. Whoever does this, is an apostate whether he is an open secularist or an alleged "Islamist" … Accordingly, the person does not disassociate from the *taghut* of democracy—the "people"—and disbelieve in it if he has not abandoned the democratic vote.[24]

In lieu of democratic choice or other manifestations of individual freedom, the Caliphate offers an alternate goal for its subjects: collective well-being, which is secured not through the exercise of individual choice but through submission.

Like good Hegelians, the Islamic State claims that the Caliphate is the vehicle for the realization of the divine will on earth, and thus the proper aim for individuals is not free choice, but alignment with the state. This vision of the modern state stems in part from Maududi's flirtation with Western philosophy and political thought prior to devoting himself to Islamic studies. Irfan Ahmad notes that Maududi publicly chided the ulema of his time for ignoring the Western philosophical tradition, and himself wrote (in 1939) a long article titled "The Philosophy of History of Hegel and Marx." He seemed particularly taken with the former (Marx's avowed atheism was a bridge too far) and with Hegelian dialectics in particular.[25] Maududi's concern for organic unity between the individual and the state echoed German romanticism's tendency to define "citizenship in the context of its need to foster homogeneity in its ethnonational community and, in turn, limited the scope of civil, political, and even social rights."[26] As Hegel wrote in the *Introduction to the Philosophy of History*, "A state is well constituted and internally strong if the private interest of the citizens is united with the universal goal of the state, so that each finds its fulfillment and realization in the other."[27]

It is fascinating to find contemporary far-right thinkers, the new nationalists for instance, advancing a parallel argument that collective freedom, rather than individual liberty, is paramount. Yoram Hazony's *The Virtue of Nationalism*, which has gone further than most in providing a theoretical scaffolding for an emerging illiberal order, also stresses the centrality of obedience to his idealized political order. This position stems from his belief that the political community is an extension of the "strong bonds of mutual loyalty" of the natal family rather than deliberate choice or rational calculation. People do not form a state because they are committed to the same civic order (as liberals think), but because they share blood, tradition, language, religion, and culture. Because it is the family, not the social contract, that is the true basis of political community, liberal virtues like individual freedom, rational calculation, and public deliberation are wholly out of place. Rather, the family (and by extension, the state) requires its members to practice "loyalty, devotion, and constraint."[28] A political order held together by an extended vision of the patriarchal family need not be democratic, of course, because nothing hinges on a shared civic pact. This is why there is a strong antidemocratic impulse within the new blood-and-soil nationalism, one which substitutes a commitment to individual freedom with the prospect of communal belonging and domination.

It is against this background that we should situate the Islamic State's contention that the Caliphate is not just desirable, as prior generations have held, but absolutely necessary for both individual salvation and collective flourishing. Only the coercive power of the state can tame those "private interests and passions" that stand in the way of a genuinely Islamic order—the latter defined very much in opposition to how most Muslims actually live. Though Maududi also advocated something of this position, he notably combined his regard for state power with a push for organic social reform, holding that the moral order he envisioned could only come into being gradually and after a long period of education. The Islamic State, on the contrary, has sought to enforce a rapid religious reorientation of the populations it governs from the outset. The centrality of the state as a means of enforcement thus turns the customary "flow of Islamicity" (to borrow a turn of phrase from Veli Nasr) on its head. It is no longer individual piety and communal practice that produces a moral social and political order, but the top-down directives of the state.

It is in this context that we need to approach the Islamic State's notorious zeal for shari'a enforcement. The Caliphate's *ḥisba* police force, modeled on a similar institution in Saudi Arabia (the Committee for the Promotion of Virtue and the Prevention of Vice), was tasked with ensuring compliance with legal rulings encompassing everything from taxes to beard length. There was no clearer sign of its punitive approach to religiosity than the rush to implement *ḥudud* (singular: *ḥadd*), those corporal punishments like amputation and flogging that have become synonymous with "Islamic law" for many a Western pundit. As much as *ḥudud* seem lifted out of medieval times (or Disney's *Aladdin*), scholars have shown that they were rarely implemented in past centuries because the burden of proof to establish guilt was so high.[29] With regard to theft, for example, the offense is defined as "taking the property of another by stealth from a place of custody." This meant, as Mark Cammack has argued:

> a thief who enters through an unlocked door is not punished with the *ḥadd* penalty because the unlocked door means the property was not in a place of custody. The property must be of a minimum value, and theft of property that is forbidden for a Muslim to own does not qualify. Nor is a poor person who steals food out of need punishable with the *ḥadd* penalty, and the *ḥadd* penalty does not apply if there is any doubt as to whether the thief had any ownership interest in the property.[30]

Moreover, stringent and highly technical proof requirements seem custom-made to never be met, including a confession of the accused or direct eyewitness testimony from upstanding persons. In the case of an adultery charge, the latter entails four trustworthy male witnesses who must all appear in the same court session to testify, in extreme detail and in unambiguous language, that they saw the couple engage in sexual activity and that the man penetrated the woman to the extent that "his penis has entirely disappeared from sight."[31]

Nor is circumstantial evidence permitted to establish guilt, while "the law provides various means by which apparently guilty persons can nevertheless escape punishment."[32] As these cases indicate, the customs that grew up around Islamic jurisprudence historically served as a type of buffer between the literal dictates of the sacred text and actual practice, a situation that finds analogues in other traditions as well. We could, for instance, point to the Talmudic sages who were clearly uncomfortable with the bare-faced logic of certain biblical directives, like the command to stone the rebellious son (*ben sorer u-moreh*). In turn, they applied so many legal restrictions so as to guarantee that the punishment described could never actually be carried out, so much so that later commentators asserted that the law "never was nor will it ever come to be."[33]

The desire to transform shari'a from a cacophonous and highly variable style of legal interpretation into a codified body of law—one that is standardized so as to be usable by the modern state—fundamentally altered both its structure and the purpose. Wael Hallaq has argued that for most of Islamic history, shari'a served as the law of the community rather than that of the state. As such it did not reside "above" the people, but was hashed out in dialectical fashion between the written sources of tradition and their actual needs.[34] What we see of "shari'a law" today is not, he contends, representative of how this system functioned prior to being standardized and subsumed within the modern state's disciplinary apparatus. Indeed, the historian Jessica Marglin has shown that Jews and Christians living in Islamic lands often turned to shari'a courts to litigate disputes that could have been addressed within their own communities—something that is inexplicable if we believe this style of justice was merely cruel or arbitrary.[35]

Needless to say, the Islamic State has displayed a very different approach to shari'a, one that is almost exclusively focused on punishment. This is not surprising given their disdain for traditionalist ulema, who are said to corrupt "true Islam" through the type of legal wrangling detailed above. While it may be tempting to attribute this fact to medieval barbarism, it is in fact more consonant with the punitive nature of the modern state, with its attendant concerns for surveillance and discipline, and use of technology to gain visibility into all domains of life.[36] We also find a great deal of continuity with the systems of intimidation, detention, and torture that are a feature of modern authoritarian states, and in particular, Iraq and Syria. According to interviews with former detainees in Islamic State prisons, the group adopted the practices of Bashar al-Asad and Saddam Hussein's security forces, including extreme forms of torture.[37] This became particularly true after the summer of 2016, when the Islamic State pivoted from attempting to win the "hearts and minds" of those in conquered areas to ruling through fear and intimidation. In short, if we consider the morality apparatus that the Caliphate developed to regulate social life and punish offenders, it is the modern police state that springs to mind as the closest living relative.

The Triumph of Management

There remains yet another piece of the governance puzzle to unravel, one that gestures toward an uncanny point of overlap between contemporary jihad and shifts in political life more broadly. Stemming from an idea that shari'a is a ready-made system of law requiring little in the way of human interpretation, the Islamic State stands at the forefront of a trend that hopes to transform government into management—politics into mere administration. Walking through the logic needed to arrive at this view brings us into close proximity with some strange bedfellows indeed, most notably the neoliberal thinkers who aspire toward depoliticization by bringing every realm of human activity into the marketplace. In each instance, we encounter repeated claims that "this is just the way the system works," with the corresponding denial of human agency in creating the system itself. It is perhaps here most of all that contemporary jihad resembles the "enemy in the mirror."[38]

Here too we find that the idea of politics as management owes much to the contributions of Abul A'la Maududi and Sayyid Qutb. Maududi advanced a utopian vision of the true Islamic state, one in which the use of the divine law as the basis of the constitutional order would render much of political life obsolete. Here it is worth quoting scholar Vali Nasr at length:

The state was neither democratic nor authoritarian, for it had no need to govern in the Western sense of the term. Concern for that kind of government was generated by crises of governability and legitimacy, which were in turn generated by demands for political participation and mass mobilization and the need to manage the economy effectively. In a polity in which there were no grievances and both the government and the citizenry abided by the same infallible and inviolable divine law, there would be no problems with democratic rights and procedures. The question of democracy would not arise, for democracy and authoritarianism were defined as opposites. If the populace did not feel itself oppressed, it would not dream of democracy.[39]

Democracy within the Islamic polity could therefore function on a purely procedural level because the law had already been given. Maududi was still close enough to a traditionalist milieu to admit that human interpretation was required, but he clarified that legislators (who should be Islamic legal experts) were still more akin to law-finders than to lawmakers in the democratic sense.

It was Sayyid Qutb who pushed Maududi's utopian thinking into more familiar form by denying the centrality of human agency in determining the rulings of shari'a. If we recall, Qutb held that a ruler could only claim legitimacy by overseeing the direct application of shari'a, which he envisioned as a check on the power of the state. The problem, unacknowledged by Qutb, is that shari'a is a process of legal reasoning rather than an unambiguous set of codified laws. As the Islamic legal scholar Wael Hallaq has argued, "With the exception of a relatively few Qur'anic and Prophetic statements that were unambiguous and contained clear and specific normative rulings, the rest of the law was the product of *ijtihād*," or independent reasoning.[40] Much as Qutb disputed the idea that his own interpretation of the Qur'an was in fact an interpretation, he rejected the notion that the application of shari'a within a social setting required any input from mere mortals. It is against this ideological background that we need to understand the Islamic State's disavowal of its own sovereignty. Because God alone is the one true ruler, the Caliphate claims it is only administering the divine, and absolute, will. There is no positive function, within this schema, of politics as a mode of dealing with discord. The point is rather to eliminate difference so that the population can be managed, rather than governed.

A 2016 video on the structure of the Caliphate drove the point home, unveiling the Caliphate's organizational chart and detailing the activities of its different departments.

> The head of its affairs is Amir al-Mu'minin [the commander of the faithful], *hafithu Allah* [my God protect him], and he is the Khalifah. He upholds and spreads the religion, defends the homeland, and fortifies the fronts, he prepares the armies, implements the *hudud*, enforces the people's adherence to the shari'a rulings, and governs their worldly affairs.[41]

The work of communicating orders to the people and ensuring their execution is delegated to a select group of upstanding men with leadership skills, "as the Khalifa cannot personally carry out all the work of the state." This close group of advisors, the Delegated Committee, is tasked with overseeing the activities of the Islamic State's different provinces, fourteen government offices, and various committees, as represented in the figure below.

The *dawawin* include departments of health, agriculture, natural resources, and infrastructure, alongside the *hisba* police force and others dealing specifically with the needs of soldiers. Meanwhile, there are unique offices and committees dedicated to immigration, the affairs and families of martyrs, shari'a research, and public relations, among others. Above all, early Islamic State productions like these aimed to convey a sense of order, which—for a population that had lived through years of chaos and warfare—proved a not wholly unattractive option. Indeed, during the Islamic State's brief period of sovereign rule in Iraq and Syria, residents noted that the garbage was collected, the streets were clean, and the electricity flowed more regularly than when they lived under government control. We know from documents captured by journalists and researchers that a budding

The administrative structure of the Caliphate, according to a 2016 video

bureaucracy existed to support such services: receipts were issued, records were kept, fatwas numbered and ordered. Though less commented on than the spectacular and propagandistic use of violence, it was this ability to offer "less bad governance," as Mara Revkin has characterized it, that enabled the Caliphate to entrench itself.[42]

With duties and responsibilities so clearly demarcated, chains of command in place, and the law already given, there is nothing left to do but submit to the order within and battle the enemies without. This mode of governance is best regarded as an attempt to *depoliticize* civic life by minimizing the number of problems that require political—as opposed to administrative—solutions: the bureaucratic fix taken to its logical, antidemocratic end. As Faisal Devji has noted, early twentieth century Islamists often took their cues from anarchism and Bolshevism, with its theory of the "withering away of the state."

> In both anarchist and Bolshevik inflections of Islamism, government was reduced to governance, and the state deployed in an active role only in the beginning, to replace man's sovereignty by God's, just as Marxism's "dictatorship of the proletariat" was meant to displace the capitalist state before dissolving it entirely into Lenin's "administration of objects."[43]

More recently, he notes, some Islamists have turned to "a neoliberal model of social management by the market," which offers a different blueprint for depoliticization. As Milton Friedman argued in *Capitalism and Freedom*, "What the market does is to reduce greatly the range of issues that must be decided through political means, and thereby to minimize the extent to which government need participate directly in the game."[44] Indeed, however counterintuitive it may appear, the idea of Islam as an all-encompassing system of legislation is like a funhouse mirror that both reflects and negates the neoliberal attempt to bring all human activity —not just infrastructure, health care, or education, but our most intimate interpersonal relations as well—into the domain of the marketplace. "In each era," Philip Bobbit has argued, "terrorism derives its ideology in reaction to the raison d'être of the dominant constitutional order, at the same time negating and rejecting that form's unique ideology but mimicking the form's structural characteristics."[45] I may differ from Bobbit on the virtues he ascribes to the contemporary market state, but the simultaneous movement of negation and mimicry he describes is fundamentally sound.

Finally, the Islamic State also offers a case study in how the disavowal of sovereign responsibility serves to augment a particular type of power. The individuals who administer the Caliphate, including the Caliph himself, are said to be mere functionaries—the sieves through which the divine will flows. This idea grows naturally out of the one-dimensional view of shari'a discussed above, which must deny at every turn the foundational role of scholars and jurists in shaping what the law demands. It is a curious type of "neutral" power that disavows responsibility for the system it creates and upholds. Yet this disavowal of responsibility for the law—which is thought to exist prior to and apart from human intervention—is particularly uncanny when placed alongside contemporary Western notions of

The Free Market. Here too we encounter a mechanism for organizing social life that is said to obey its own mystical principles, such that the "spontaneous collaboration of free men" results in far superior outcomes than those planned and directed by any dedicated body.[46] The show doesn't run itself, of course, any more than the law floats through space waiting to be applied in unadulterated fashion. The Free Market was created by people and states to serve certain ends and cannot exist but for continual support and intervention by its partisans. It is the *denial* of this fact, like the disavowal of sovereignty from which it springs, that characterizes this formidable type of modern power.

How is this power made manifest, and what aims does it serve? What type of political action is available to individuals who have disavowed their own sovereign force? And how should we think about the relationship between the goal of contemporary jihad and its chosen means? Chapter 5 will take up these questions in earnest.

5

Means without Ends

The images have been seared into collective consciousness: rubble-strewn streets, smashed cars, policemen, body bags, and of course the journalist reporting from the scene of the latest suicide bombing/car explosion/truck ramming/ mass shooting/et al. Since the turn of the last century we have witnessed a steady stream of violence targeting places of public gathering worldwide: transit hubs, holiday markets, places of worship, school, museums, hotels, and outdoor cafes. Such acts are often referred to as "senseless," and indeed, seem to generate as much confusion as shock. What greater strategic purpose is achieved by detonating a suicide vest at an Ariana Grande concert? Indeed, while Islamic State–planned or inspired attacks against European and American targets serve several purposes in the ongoing war of affect, they have not shifted the overall balance of power in material terms. That is to say, their strategic impact is negligible notwithstanding the genuine human loss. For many observers, this fact is taken to confirm the origin of such violence in religious fanaticism or pathology—either way, "evil" lurks as the dominant explanation for what is otherwise nonsensical.

The sense of befuddlement on display in the wake of such attacks is both meaningful and ultimately misplaced. Meaningful because it highlights the urge to seek out a reasoned relationship between cause and effect, to search for "root causes" and to think of political violence as symbolic of something else—something bigger and more meaningful, something that helps explain and rationalize, if not necessarily justify, the nature of the deed. Misplaced because jihadi attacks against so-called "soft targets"—like those perpetrated by their closest corollary, the American mass shooter—are essentially nihilist. There are no demands to communicate or even goals to achieve; there is only destruction and the pursuit of death, both of the self and of others. Differing from both classic hagiographies (in which death is accepted but typically not sought), or traditional hero narratives (in which death is skirted), this aspect of the new jihad renders the negation of life as the spiritual apex of the individual's time on Earth; the meaning of life is best grasped at the moment of its dissolution. In Olivier Roy's framing, "Violence is not a means. It is an end in itself. It is violence devoid of a future."

Terrorism is not a new phenomenon, of course, nor a singular one. Yet for much of modern history, those accused of being "terrorists" (a fraught word if there ever was one) pursued clear political goals: a ruler's assassination, the end of colonial occupation, or revolution—as indeed, the English term terrorism dates to the French revolution and to the Reign of Terror (*la Terreur*) following the creation of the First French Republic. Terror, Robespierre argued, was an essential foundation of popular government under siege, and the only way to punish enemies of the state with justice that was "speedy, severe and inflexible." As discussed in Chapter One, terrorism is the modern state's preferred term for whatever its enemies pursue, regardless of context, target, or means. Still, it is clear that a new form of stylized, hyper-mediated violence has emerged over the last twenty-five years that differs in fundamental ways from that employed by "freedom fighters" along the lines of the PLO and IRA. As Khaled Abou El Fadl noted in the wake of 9/11:

> While national liberation movements often resort to violence, the recent attacks are set apart from such movements. The perpetrators did not seem to be acting on behalf of an ethnic group or nation. They presented no specific territorial claims or political agenda, and were not keen to claim responsibility for their acts. One can speculate that the perpetrators' list of grievances included persistent Israeli abuses of Palestinians, near-daily bombings of Iraq and the presence of American troops in the Gulf, but the fact remains that the attacks were not followed by a list of demands or even a set of articulated goals. The attacks exhibit a profound sense of frustration and extreme despair, rather than a struggle to achieve clear-cut objectives.[1]

In truth, Americans stunned by the nature of al-Qaeda's attacks had more analytic resources at their disposal than they realized. They just weren't prone to looking for answers at home, which would threaten the integrity of narratives built on the idea of jihad as wholly foreign and exotic. They might have looked at the confused response to the shooting at Columbine High School, just two years prior, where a SWAT team stood assembled outside for over an hour before entering the premises, totally unprepared for the new rules of the game. As AP would note, those officers "had never trained for what they found: No hostages. No demands. Just killing." In an era defined by depoliticization, we find incredible acts of violence devoid of anything that is recognizably political.

It is certainly true that such spectacular acts of violence are tailor-made for a world with instantaneous communication networks, a 24/7 news cycle, and globalized social media. For instance, mass shooters' desire for infamy is often noted, itself facilitated by the abundance of media outlets ready to scour manifestos, diagram the scene of the crime, and enlist psychologists, coworkers, and former neighbors to dissect the trajectory of the assailant's troubled life. The Islamic State thrives in the same media ecosystem, and has even shown "thought leadership" in making use of new channels and formats. Still, there is something more elemental to explore beyond the mutually constitutive nature of terrorism, media, and spectacle. How, for instance, should we understand the randomized nature of both jihadist attacks and mass shootings, whose indiscriminate and almost casual killing is said to differentiate them from the rational and proportional use of violence by the state? Why has jihad under Islamic State auspices assumed *this* form at *this* time, and how does this choice of means correspond with the stated end of ushering in a world under divine sovereignty? If nihilism is in fact the proper frame for approaching this type of violence, why has it reared its head at this particular historical juncture? In short, where does the "no future generation" Olivier Roy implicates in contemporary terrorism come from? Asking what this generation wants may already be beyond the pale. We might rather ask why it no longer wants anything this world can offer.

The Makings of Spectacle

The use of violence as spectacle dates back millennia, encompassing many forms and serving multiple purposes, from amusement and patronage (e.g. the Roman Gladiators games) to punishment and determent (e.g. public executions). In the *Iliad*, Achilles allows his Myrmidons to stab the corpse of his vanquished foe, Hector, before he drags it behind his chariot below the walls of Troy, gesturing at the link between bodily mutilation and humiliation that is often part of violence as spectacle. Stuart Carroll refers to this as vindicatory violence, deployed to "repair an honour or injury."[2] The violation of bodily integrity involved, anthropologists suggest, is a means of denying the humanity of the victim. The use of public torture and execution was a well-known feature of medieval life in Europe, though it had mostly fallen out of favor by the nineteenth century. It was with the simultaneous rise of the disciplinary society, famously described by Michel Foucault, that the site of punishment shifted from the body to the soul of the accused. From this point forward, punishment becomes the most hidden part of the penal system: executions take place behind prison walls instead of in public squares; torture as a form public spectacle (it continued in private) becomes yet another barbaric practice vanquished by Enlightenment progress.

The history of violence as spectacle follows a somewhat different trajectory in Islamic lands. Leaving aside notions of "Oriental despotism," it seems that pre-modern Muslim rulers differed little from contemporary European ones. Yet one interesting point of distinction is that, rather than aiding and abetting in the pursuit of bodily torment, Muslim jurists widely condemned the use of torture and bodily mutilation. In contrast to Roman law, "torture of witnesses was unknown in Muslim jurisprudence" until the late thirteenth century onward, running "roughly parallel to the rise of judicial torture in Europe." Jurists also showed great reluctance to implement the statutory punishments (*ḥudud*) stipulated for serious crimes in the Qur'an and hadith. Surveying this territory, historian Christian Lange has noted:

> Jurists opposed the staging of public spectacles of state violence, such as the statutory punishments (in particular crucifixion, the punishment for brigandage) usually implied. Violent punishment had been from early Islamic times the province of the government and its agents of public order, less so of the developing class of legal scholars and judges. The chronicles from early Islam up to Ottoman times provide many cases in which the authorities made an example of offenders against the public order by publicly shaming, torturing and executing them. Thus the fact that the jurists developed doctrines that painstakingly circumscribed statutory crimes and punishments can be interpreted as an attempt to rein in state violence.[3]

In practice jurists had little control over the conduct of rulers, who relied on a well-developed body of law that largely stood apart from shari'a to justify their actions, but the reluctance to sanction such spectacles must be counted as another instance in which the Islamic State's "return" to the past betrays its own modernity. In practice such spectacles were common under a variety of dynasties and continued under the Ottoman Empire until the mid-nineteenth century, after which reforms in the legal code rendered capital punishment a rare occurrence.

Just as modernizing states, the Ottoman one included, were enacting "civilized" penal codes in the nineteenth century—effectively putting an end to the most common form of violent spectacles at the hands of the state—a different form of violence was emerging in the public sphere. This was, in the words of the Italian revolutionary Carlo Pisacane (d. 1857), the "propaganda of the deed"—the assassinations and bombings embraced by anarchists and other anti-state factions in the late nineteenth and early twentieth centuries. National liberation groups of the last century belonged to this tradition as well, using terrorism as a tactic to generate attention for their cause as well as to inflict harm on the state and its supporters. Debates might have raged whether "the ends justified the means," but there was little doubt what the ends were: liberation and independence, from Northern Ireland to Palestine and Sri Lanka.

In such cases the use of terrorism is often attributed to the deep asymmetries between the military capabilities of insurgents and the states they fight. This structural imbalance meant that publicity assumed an outsized significance, even when compared to traditional war propaganda, leading Brian Michael Jenkins to observe (in 1975) that "terrorists want a lot of people watching, not a lot of people dead." Compare, for instance, the typical airplane hijack scheme of the 1970s or 1980s with the Islamic State's more recent advice regarding hostage taking:

> The objective of hostage-taking in the lands of disbelief—and specifically in relation to just terror operations—is not to hold large numbers of the kuffar (disbelievers) hostage in order to negotiate one's demands. Rather, the objective is to create as much carnage and terror as one possibly can until Allah decrees his appointed time and the enemies of Allah storm his location or succeed in killing him.[4]

As Philip Bobbitt has noted, "market state terrorists [meaning those like al-Qaeda that arose with globalization] want a lot of people dead *and* a lot of people watching."[5] This violence does not have a political endgame save destruction.

What modes of spectacular violence are in circulation today? Adriana Cavarero has given us a useful typology in differentiating between *terrorism*—attacks that sow fear and panic on those directly affected and in close proximity to the event—and *horrorism*, highly mediated acts of violence that are often performed for distant audiences and yet act with extreme cruelty on the bodies of victims, whose helplessness is part and parcel of the spectacle of domination.[6] While terrorism is witnessed, horrorism is meant to be watched. The Islamic State's execution videos—the burning alive of Jordanian pilot Muath al-Kaseasabeh, for instance,

or the beheadings of American and European hostages
—fit squarely in this latter category. Yet they also have the
character of what Stuart Carroll calls vindicatory violence,
"such as revenge killing or the duel, which repair an honour
or injury and which are suggestive of a reciprocal relationship
between the parties." The issue of reciprocity is key, as the
Islamic State's atrocity videos are meant to skillfully mirror
the "legitimate" violence of American Empire: victims about
to be executed appear in the same orange jumpsuits made
notorious by prisoners at Guantanamo Bay, and the act of
killing is always narrated as retaliation in a tit-for-tat style.

Perhaps most importantly, these videos strive to make
death visible to a public that is used to either witnessing it
from afar (e.g. cable news footage of "Shock and Awe") or
ignoring it altogether (e.g. the victims of American drone
strikes in Pakistan, Afghanistan, or Yemen). Often, as with
a 2019 executive order that revoked the requirement for US
intelligence to report on civilian casualties outside of areas
of "Active Hostilities," there is a clear desire to render death
invisible.[7] As critics of America's endless wars have noted,
the issue of body counts raises the question as to whose
bodies count; the careful tallying of "our" losses stands in
stark contrast to the imprecise figures—the very conservative estimate is between 244,124 and 266,427 civilians
killed as a result of the wars in Afghanistan and Iraq[8]—that
characterize "their" deaths. The retail version of Western
humanism remains remarkably untroubled by the suggestion that certain group are less than human.[9] In this sense,
ISIS execution videos that "challenge Western rules of 'taste
and decency' ... simultaneously mirror back and expose

Western practices of death at war that largely remain invisible to its publics."[10]

   It is interesting to note, following Stuart Carroll's argument, that vindicatory violence has historically been central
to the feud—a state of conflict that sits between the purely
private violence of the domestic sphere and the international
wars of states. And indeed, reviewing the characteristics
scholars have identified as defining a feud, one is struck
by how applicable they are to the current state of enmity
between the Caliphate and its foes. As Carroll writes, the
feud is a hostile relationship between two groups that are
nonetheless bound together "by ties of kinship, vicinage,
clientage, service etc." That is to say, the feuding parties
are part of the same world and shaped by its constraints,
indeed intimately bound to one another like two sides of a
single coin. Feuds also tend to invoke a sense of collective
liability. "The target need not be the actual wrongdoer, nor
the vengeance taker must be the person most wronged."
In an age of globalized identity, no longer bound by the
strictures of territory or the conventional rules of warfare,
a cosmic battle between "Islamic terror" and "the West"
generates no shortage of possible targets. One need not kill
the king; any old Frenchman will do. Likewise, it does not
really matter whether those held at Guantanamo Bay have
personally committed any crime; they are brown and were
living in proximity to a named terrorist organization. A logic
of exchange governs the process, "a rhythm of riposte and
parry in which each party takes its turn." And perhaps most
importantly for the workings of spectacle, "people keep
score."[11]

The feud is not a perfect fit for contemporary violence, of course; nor does the overlap I am suggesting here prove that the Islamic State is really a grotesque medieval phenomenon. Much as political theorists have started to view the emerging constellation of security and violence described in Chapter One through the lens of neo-feudalism, we might also think about contemporary jihad, and the responses it generates, as a globalized, hypermodern feud. As we witness the breakdown of the modern state's capacity to monopolize violence, complete with a proliferation of "non-state actors" that disrupt sovereign claims, it is not surprising that the analytic categories from a time prior to nation-states suggest themselves. However, we must use them with caution lest we lapse into thinking that contemporary phenomena are merely a return to the past: no such trips are possible, and it is rather the innovative redeployment of older concepts and practices makes them noteworthy.

The fully globalized scale of this feud also helps make sense of its randomized nature. Creating a perpetual sense of insecurity is in fact constitutive of this type of violence: it can happen to anyone, in any place, at any time. In this sense, it represents a generalized acceleration of modern warfare's assault on experience, famously described by Walter Benjamin. "Never has experience been contradicted more thoroughly than strategic experience by tactical warfare, economic experience by inflation, bodily experience by mechanical warfare, moral experience by those in power."[12] Benjamin described a new world coming into being in the trenches of World War One, one in which personal attributes (merit, intelligence, skill, bravery, courage, etc.) were rendered irrelevant, effectively breaking the commonsense link between individual behavior and survival, cause and effect. Violence, here of the state and the market, becomes arbitrary precisely because *it does not matter* whether the soldier was heroic or the merchant honest. The liberal dream of individual freedom and individual responsibility—not only can you chart your own path, but you are only held liable for your own transgressions—is exploded in the face of such violence. The bombs were never designed to discriminate.

In accounting for its targeting of non-combatants, the Islamic State repeatedly invokes a sense of reciprocity, pointing out that airstrikes do not distinguish between fighters and civilians. In accounting for the beheading of American journalist James Foley, for instance, it was an appeal to the logic of exchange rather than to shari'a that ruled the day. Indeed, the "complete message from James Foley," included in *Dabiq* as a sort of last will and testament, presents someone quite sympathetic to the Islamic State's critiques of American empire. Casting him in such light makes very little sense if one is trying to justify his killing on the basis of guilt. Rather, the presentation assumes a sacrificial tone: Foley had to die because the Obama administration refused to negotiate for his release. The denial of sovereign agency discussed in Chapter Four is on full display: "Foley's blood is on Obama's hands." Yet Foley's death only became meaningful in a larger sense because it served the purpose of spectacle. Absent video technology and global networks of communication, the execution of a hostage in the Syrian desert has very little impact in military or strategic terms. His death was meant to inflict on a psychological level the type of blow that was impossible on a material one—the rare opportunity to humiliate the world's greatest superpower before a global audience. Foley became, in this sense, an instrument of spectacle. His individual behavior, faults, or opinions are simply irrelevant to this mode of violence. Either everyone is potentially guilty—we should note that some form of guilt by association lurks behind most justifications of "collateral damage" by American forces as well—or guilt and innocence are no longer meaningful categories for making sense of violence.

Like a funhouse mirror held up to the National Security state—with its obsessive focus on risk mitigation and threat assessment—the Islamic State promises constant insecurity and danger, directing its followers to make Western cities resemble the war-torn streets of Iraq and Syria. It has proved particularly adept at mobilizing its global fanbase to launch attacks wherever they might be—something that became increasingly important as the group lost most of its core territory. While most high-profile attacks are still centrally planned and coordinated, attacks by "lone wolves" or small groups have become commonplace. Sometimes assailants swear allegiance to the Islamic State during their attacks, as in the 2016 shooting at the Pulse Nightclub in Orlando; sometimes they merely exhibit "jihadi sympathies," like the 2018 attack on a music festival in the Jordanian city of Fuheis. Often, they are found to have acted without explicit direction, using whatever tools of the trade are available: kitchen knives, rental trucks, even scissors.

The third issue of the ISIS magazine *Rumiya* included a feature (part of the series on "Just Terror Tactics" discussed below) specifically designed to serve the needs of would-be lone wolves in the West: "Stationed behind enemy lines, the just terror mujahid has at his disposal a multitude of weapons and techniques that he may employ at any given time." Citing the truck attack in Nice on Bastille Day 2016 as inspiration, the article offers practical advice to those wishing to emulate this example: criteria of the ideal vehicle, suggested targets, and day-of directions.

"An appropriate way should be determined for announcing one's allegiance to the Khalifah of the Muslims and the goal of making Allah's word supreme, so that the motive of the attack is acknowledged. An example of such would be simply writing on dozens of sheets of paper 'The Islamic State will remain!' or 'I am a soldier of the Islamic State!' prior, and launching them from the vehicle's window during the execution of the attack."

Sayfullo Habibullaevich Saipov followed these instructions to a T when he drove a truck onto New York City's Hudson River Greenway in 2017, killing eight and wounding eleven. The note he left read, "The Islamic State will endure forever."

The new age of private violence is thus also one of random violence, wherein the carnage spills over the conventional floodgates meant to distinguish between war and peace, and the battle is waged not merely in material terms, but in symbolic ones as well. The mere existence of the Caliphate, binding together a new type of imagined community, lends unity and coherence to instances of violence that are otherwise disparate and disjoined. Creating a global network of actors outside the rubric of the state means that even the lowliest attack using the most rudimentary of means can be claimed as a victory for the true *umma*—everywhere existent even if nowhere sovereign. It is, of course, modern media and communications technology that facilitates this network of meaning—that brings us news of attacks on different continents by assailants from different backgrounds, speaking different languages, and using different methods, yet all tied together in a web of signification provided by the Caliphate. It is the existence of this organizational network that most distinguishes Islamic State terrorism from its closest living relative, mass shootings by disaffected, predominantly white men. But as we shall see, here too jihad might gesture at the future rather than the past.

The Threat Within

On March 15, 2019, a twenty-eight-year-old Australian man used a helmet camera to begin a livestream on Facebook. Playing the role of performance artist, he had taken care to share the video link and a related manifesto on Twitter and 8kun (formerly 8chan) in advance of the big show. Those who tuned in would see him approach the al-Noor Mosque in Christchurch, New Zealand, his beige station wagon loaded with weapons and ammunition. You can watch as he enters the building and fires indiscriminately at worshippers before returning to the car to reload, entering the mosque a second time, and eventually driving off—leaving forty-two dead and dozens injured. The seventeen-minute video cuts off as the assailant was making his way to the Linwood Islamic Center, where he managed to kill seven more people. The attack was notable for a number of reasons. It was the first of its kind in New Zealand, which has gained an international reputation for being a tolerant and highly functional democracy. It was also among the first instances of livestreamed mass shootings, though others have come in its wake. In October 2019, for instance, a right-wing assailant broadcast his attack on a synagogue in Germany on Twitch, a platform largely used by gamers. In February 2020, a Thai solider took to Facebook to livestream his assault rifle–fueled rampage at a Buddhist temple and shopping mall in the city of Nakhon Ratchasima, in which thirty people were killed and dozens more wounded.

I have argued throughout that jihad is not an unbroken chain that can be accounted for by remaining within the comfortable bounds of Islam, or even the broader category of religious violence. On-screen executions and violent attacks on public places, without warning or demands, do not evolve naturally out of theological treatises on jihad; nor do they merely continue the insurgent tradition of last century's national liberation movements. On the contrary, they have quite a bit in common with the mass shootings that have become an increasingly commonplace experience—not just in the United States with its infamous gun-lust, but the world over. Moreover, there are certain structural features present within both modes of violence: attacks are randomized; the assailant's death is almost always part of the plan; no demands are given, as killing is the aim, rather than some concrete political outcome; and perpetrators seek maximal publicity. Increasingly, the action is itself broadcast in real time, taking advantage of the Internet's various chat rooms and streaming platforms.

All this said, there remains an ardent desire to distinguish between run-of-the-mill mass shootings in the United States —like those perpetrated at Sandy Hook Elementary School or at a bar in Thousand Oaks, California, by "troubled" young men—and similar attacks undertaken by "jihadi terrorists," such as the 2015 shooting at a San Bernardino office building. In the latter instance, a married couple—one of whom worked as a county health inspector—targeted a Department of Health employee Christmas party, killing fourteen and injuring twenty-two more. Two days after the attack—the 355th mass shooting of 2015—the FBI announced that it was investigating the shooting as "an act of terrorism" on account of the fact that the female shooter had given *bay'ah*, an oath of allegiance, to the Islamic State via a Facebook post. A similar logic played out in the aftermath of the Pulse Nightclub attack in Orlando, Florida, whose perpetrator similarly pledged *bay'ah* in a call to 911. Yet when Dylann Roof killed nine black parishioners at a church in South Carolina, or Robert Bowers killed eleven congregants at a Pittsburgh synagogue, there was no such rush to characterize the attacks as terrorism, despite the far-right and white supremacist politics of both.

This was ostensibly on account of the fact that "lone wolves" lack any clear affiliation with designated terrorist groups or terrorist ideologies—which as of this writing does not legally encompass white supremacy.[13] Rather, according to the US Department of State, terrorism is "premeditated, politically motivated violence perpetrated against noncombatant targets by subnational groups or clandestine agents, usually intended to influence an audience."

In laymen's terms, we consider terrorism as something foreign that infects the body politic from without, gesturing at a deep-seeded desire to differentiate "our" violence from "theirs" regardless of its actual form. As Khaled Beydoun has argued, "whiteness generally insulates white culprits of violence, like Paddock [the gunman in the 2017 Las Vegas strip shooting], from the presumption of terror conspiracy and the reciprocal burden of collective guilt"—meaning that they are presumed to be acting on their own, and that their actions are not held to be representative of anything larger. The operative assumptions are very different for "Muslim culprits of violence," who are presumed to be actors in a broader terrorist network "even when the evidence is non-existent or tenuous."[14] Religious affiliation becomes an all-encompassing, almost magical explanation, even when facts point to a more complex reality. Workplace violence is certainly not an unknown phenomenon in the United States, for instance; likewise Omar Mateen's decision to target a gay club may have been related to his own conflicted sexuality. The point is not to choose a single motivation to the exclusion of all others, which is in most cases a fool's errand. The point is rather that the logic of "terrorism" as applied in these examples renders everything outside Islam obsolete.

A central contradiction therefore undergirds America's obsessive pursuit of national security: billions are spent annually to guard against terrorism, while mass shootings by white assailants appear like the natural order of the universe about which little can be done. The logic of difference performs very important political work but cannot quite solidify the boundary between "jihadi" terror (of the sort undertaken by Mateen and Saipov) and functionally equivalent attacks by "homegrown" killers (like Roof and Bowers). Making matters worse, the Islamic State has repeatedly entreated supporters to take advantage of America's lax gun laws in order to undertake attacks, and even dedicated an article in a 2017 issue of *Rumiya* to this end:

> In most U.S. states, anything from a single-shot shotgun all the way up to a semi-automatic AR-15 rifle can be purchased at showrooms or through online sales—by way of private dealers—with no background checks, and without requiring either an ID or a gun license.

Indeed, the plausible ambiguity involved in determining the nature of mass shootings led the Islamic State to claim responsibility for the Las Vegas attack, alleging that Stephen Paddock had begun a conversion to Islam six months prior. No evidence has substantiated this claim, but it offered a telling example of just how blurry the boundaries between "our" violence and "theirs" has become.

The abovementioned article in *Rumiya* was part of a four-part series entitled "Just Terror Tactics," which offered practical advice on planning and executing attacks with trucks, knives, arson, and firearms. Importantly, articles in the series cite as inspiration prior attacks that had occurred in the West without any direction from ISIS Central: the Nice truck attack and shootings in several locales (including San Bernardino and Orlando). Rather than an all-powerful Caliphate issuing commands to its followers, this fact points to a more cyclical exchange that in many instances originates on the edges and is retroactively absorbed into the Islamic

State's theological reasoning and operational logic. The ambiguity occurs on a broader scale as well, particularly if we consider that Islamic militant groups may have *borrowed* the mass shooting tactic from America. Attacks in the 1980s and 1990s tended to be bombings—for instance, the 1998 US embassy bombings in Dar es Salaam and Nairobi, planned by al-Qaeda. The tools of the trade have shifted in the last several years, roughly running parallel to the global surge in mass shootings. A short list includes: the 2008 attacks in Mumbai undertaken by Lashkar-e-Taiba; a 2014 attack by gunmen in al-Dalwah, Saudi Arabia, targeting the Kingdom's Shi'a population; a 2016 shooting at a resort in Grand-Bassam attributed to al-Qaeda in the Islamic Maghreb; and several high-profile Islamic State attacks, including those in Paris (2015) and Ataturk Airport in Istanbul (2016).

Yet, in a way that mirrors the American debate regarding mass shootings, the Islamic State too is fixated on differentiating its campaigns from others.

"Lest the operation be mistaken for one of the many random acts of violence that plague the West, it is essential to leave some kind of evidence or insignia identifying the motive and allegiance to the Khalifah, even if it is something as simple as a note pinned or attached to the victim's body, or a final testament if the operation will be of a nature where the expected outcome is one's shahadah [martyrdom]."[15]

Likewise, the article clarified (in a footnote no less), "Instead of using the term 'lone wolf,' we will refer to operations in Dar al-Kufr [the Abode of Disbelief] executed by mujahidin with bay'ah [allegiance] to the Khalifah as 'just terror operations'." Lest the obvious continuities unsettle the narrative of difference, potential points of overlap must be preemptively undermined.

Detractors will claim that the most important differentiating factor between Islamic terrorism and pedestrian mass shootings is that perpetrators in the latter case lack a clear ideological agenda, and do not tend to belong to any defined organization. This has been the case in some instances, though this characterization is increasingly at odds with the nature of such attacks. As was noted in the wake of the Christchurch attack, "Rather than focusing on only domestic grievances, white-supremacist nationalists are increasingly taking their cues from incidents around the world, championing international supporters of their cause and condemning what they see as injustices around the world."[16] Indeed, the Christchurch shooter pointed to the attacks by Dylann Roof and Anders Behring Breivik— the far-right assailant who killed 77 people in Norway in 2011—as inspiration, and correctly identified Donald Trump as the most influential leader of this resurgent white identity (though even he doubted Trump's skills as a policy maker). Likewise, appeals to forestall the great replacement through attacks on "outsiders"—a capacious category that can include blacks, Muslims, Jews, leftists, and people of color more generally—can and should be situated alongside the Caliphate's purported campaigns to protect and avenge the *umma*.

In both instances we find global networks of true believers making use of media platforms to share ideas, encourage attacks, and indeed, create a sense of community for those within. It is not among their immediate social and familial settings that they are their fully realized selves, but often online, in chat rooms and down conspiratorial rabbit holes. In this sense they are characterized by simultaneous engagement and withdrawal, and indeed by the displacement of the local and even national community for a self-selecting, globalized one. Yet, according to the conceptual limitations inherent in the legal definition of terrorism, expressing "jihadi sympathies" makes one eligible for membership in the Islamic Terrorism Club while professing white supremacy, neo-fascism, or rabid nationalism is not viewed as "ideological," nor do adherents to such views seem to represent part of a larger community. This in no doubt stems from the fact that elements of all three are so deeply embedded in our politics so as to appear the default position. Unsettling this logic entails thinking across different forms of reactionary and nihilist violence to consider their points of commonality, and likewise resisting the urge to regard them as unrelated phenomena. Rather, we should be asking what the proliferation of such violence indicates about political and social life more broadly. To do so, it is helpful to once again return to the Islamic State.

Value for our Shareholders

There have been hundreds of articles and books written about the Islamic State's media practices, augmenting an already formidable mass of work regarding the role of media in shaping contemporary acts of violence. Importantly, many of them have attended to the mutually constitutive relationship between spectacular violence and the media ecosystem it thrives within. "Rather than marveling at the barbarians at the gate," scholars have argued, the task is to "understand just how global media infrastructures facilitate ISIS's style and, just as important, how ISIS's media practice reveals much about 'our' cultures of mediation and contemporary spheres of conflict."[17] This is not the place to re-hash these arguments in detail, but to place them in conversation with our central question: What type of politics are implicit in violence as spectacle? Why these means, and for which ends?

Islamic State media is most infamous for its gore, but there's no shortage of kitsch either, particularly in productions from the early years of the Caliphate. Upon viewing the introductory sequence of "The Structure of the Caliphate," for instance, my husband quipped that its creators may have watched *Braveheart* too many times. Indeed, kitsch and gore are the bookends of the video's otherwise quite corporate overview of its organizational structure, with the final minutes cutting without warning to graphic execution footage. There is a clearly performative aspect to much of this media, whereby Islamic State fighters appear eager to play the role of fanatic assigned to them by the West. As Amanda Rogers has argued, "Evil™" is the Islamic State's chief commodity export—and media is crafted to reflect an Orientalist mix of fear and fantasy.[18] If there is something familiar looking about the sword-wielding executioner, that is because you've seen this movie before.

The cinematic quality of certain Islamic State productions —including those execution videos, which were known to include several takes—brings to mind the sense of hyperreality some reported in watching the Twin Towers collapse: Is this a movie, or actually happening? With the ascendance of VR and social media, and the attendant ways to increasingly live life online, this sensory confusion has become part of our everyday experience. Mass shooters who livestream their "performances" as if they were part of a video game exist within this same realm of spectacular violence, as do the drone pilots who unleash death from the skies over Yemen or Pakistan from the safety of their desert bunkers. Within this highly mediated context, violence as spectacle risks becoming yet another thing you watch or share, losing sight of the material violation of human dignity involved. Rather, human bodies are largely disposable within a political order built on spectacle, serving as a mere instrument to produce the latter. In Donald Trump's America, this surely cannot seem foreign, whether we look at the tear gassing of peaceful protestors for the sake of a photo op in front of St. John's Church in Washington, DC; his decision to hold an indoor campaign rally in Tulsa, Oklahoma, in the midst of the coronavirus spread; or the cosplaying mob that stormed the US Capitol in January 2021, which had no plan to seize power but was willing to assault police officers and endanger life while mugging for the camera.

"Fascism sees its salvation in giving these masses not their right, but instead a chance to express themselves," Walter Benjamin observed in 1936.[19] That is to say, spectacle is part and parcel of the aestheticization of politics whose chief "virtue" is offering the masses a sense of excitement and purpose while preserving the underlying power structures that oppress them.

This order is built upon the almost casual degradation of human dignity, but that is not to say that it is an irrational one. Look for instance at *al-Naba'*, the Islamic State's Arabic-language newsletter: Part news bulletin, part corporate report, *al-Naba'* recounts the military operations IS operatives undertook during the prior week, details how many enemies of varying stripes were killed or injured, and celebrates the spoils of war. The reader can quickly absorb much of this information by consulting charts and graphs that present different data points on a single page—an executive summary, if you will. What kind of religious fanatics feel compelled to issue progress reports? And what are the material markers of its success?

Lacking many of the design features that the group's English-language glossies (*Dabiq* and *Rumiyah*) were known for, *al-Naba'* is more school newspaper than *Vanity Fair*. Yet the newsletter has also proved the most enduring title within the Islamic State media empire, publishing more or less continually since October 2015. Headlines are formulaic and create a blissfully context-free sense of accomplishment: "Caliphate soldiers kill 6 American soldiers in Khurasan" (No. 50). Or: "43 members of Shi'a crowd killed in a failed raid on the village of Bashir [in northern Iraq]" (No. 26). Against the background of the Islamic State's defeat in Iraq and Syria, *al-Naba'* still managed to find something uplifting to feature, often from its regional affiliates elsewhere, such as "30 apostates hit and killed from army of Niger" (No. 173). Not even the death of Abu Bakr al-Baghdadi caused a departure from this general formula. At the level of affect, this format conveys the same sense of perpetual motion evident in many IS videos: here, finally, Muslims are *doing* something—taking action instead of merely lamenting their woes. This robust vision of personal agency sits diametrically opposed to the feeling of helplessness that is the more common experience of the modern political subject.

Roughly translated into English as "the announcement," *al-Naba'* is also the name of several TV stations in Arabic-speaking countries, gesturing at a sort of mainstream mimicry. And indeed, it is worth noting just how closely *al-Naba'* hews to the formal conventions of contemporary journalism. The form of its stories suggests nothing less than the front page of a major newspaper, looking to cover the story from all of the standard Five W angles: What type of assault was it? Where did the attack happen? Who carried it out, and how was it all coordinated? As we have seen from alt-right publications in the West, the point is not to explode the genre but to master it. Recounting tales of the vanquished foe is of course a very old literary trope, but it would be an error to attribute the Islamic State's approach to this ancient convention. The latter serves as a stylistic tool, not an attempt to convey facts. And therein lies the difference: the Islamic State aims to inform, to communicate data with accuracy and precision, attending to details in a way which would have been completely foreign to their ancient counterparts. While the writers of *al-Naba'* deploy a number of stock phrases and lean on linguistic ambiguity to amplify success—adversaries often are "killed and wounded" without specifying how many fall into which category—their accounts are by no means fictitious. Even the body counts are mostly accurate. Thus, rather than reflecting some sort of fantastical universe, *al-Naba'* peddles sober reporting for the jihadi set.

The adoption of this communication style is arguably reflective of a broader set of concerns, ones so pervasive in a world organized around market-based thinking that we must stop ourselves from taking them for granted. The Islamic State feels compelled to analyze its missions, report on its activities, and implicitly, to justify itself through its results. This also generates an alternative explanation for its abundant gore: mangled bodies and severed heads serve as evidence, offering supporters confirmation that no gap exists between the Caliphate's words and deeds. But gore is not the preferred method for communicating this data, which is rather presented in more sober formats. Take, for example, the charts below. The graph on the left represents the number of people killed and wounded in different Islamic State provinces, while the pie chart on the right indicates the number of operations undertaken in each as a percentage of the Caliphate's total activities. The figures at the bottom provide further detail about attacks carried out in Iraq and Syria.

It seems safe to say that pie charts and bar graphs are not what comes to mind when you think about the Islamic State, but infographics of this sort are a regular part of the media mix. One of the few scholars to turn their attention to this fact is Rebecca Adelman, who has argued that the adoption of such graphics both mirrors its adversaries' own instrumental logic and undermines the characterization of the Caliphate as backward and irrational.[20] In a similar vein, later issues of *al-Naba'* introduced a regular feature called "Harvest of the Soldiers" which details the number and type

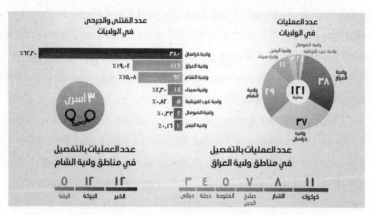

Infographic from al-Naba' No. 153 documenting the number of operations and combatants killed and wounded by province

of adversaries killed or wounded and the military equipment either captured or destroyed. No. 206, the first issue published after the death of Abu Bakr al-Baghdadi, noted that more than 179 opponents were killed or wounded in 71 campaigns that week, including "116 infidels and apostates" and "15 crusaders," among whose ranks were five officers and commanders. The focus on precision is noteworthy. Even in the face of minimal material progress, the Islamic State will have you know it is not slacking on its record-keeping.

We would search the records of pre-modern Muslim conquerors in vain for anything that resembles this reporting style. On the other hand, *al-Naba'* seems right at home alongside the periodic updates issued by many NGOs, corporations, or even government agencies: "This year we held X events, produced Y publications, served Z participants, in Q cities." It is the boring familiarity of surveying data in this fashion that accounts for the uncanny experience of confronting death via pie chart. For comparison's sake, take the following summary page from Glencore's 2019 annual report. One of the world's largest natural resources extraction firms, Glencore too boasts of the global scope of its operations and reports its earnings in graphical formats that are easy-to-access.

This is not an argument for equivalence between radically different organizations, but an observation about how the tendency to rationalize oneself through recourse to "the results" is pervasive, even in the most reactionary quarters. In a world obsessed with statistics and outcomes, such reports serve as a key communications strategy for organizations seeking to justify their existence by recourse to market thinking. We all must account for ourselves and our activities, and in this the Islamic State is keeping fully with the times.

The reduction of human lives to data points brings to mind some of the darkest moments of the last century, and in particular, the meticulous accounting of totalitarian states. But even they could argue to be advancing some greater aim in this world: cue Stalin's infamous quip that one death is a tragedy while a million deaths is a statistic. But the Islamic State is not, nor will it ever be, the Soviet Union. It is here the essential nihilism of a political order built around spectacle comes into focus. Death is synonymous with victory, regardless of context or strategy. "You [Americans] fight a people who can never be defeated," Abu Muhammad al-Adnani argued in a well-known speech from 2014. "Being killed, according to their [the Islamic State's] account, is a victory. This is where the secret lies."[21] The reality is that a functioning Caliphate, one that replaces secular political

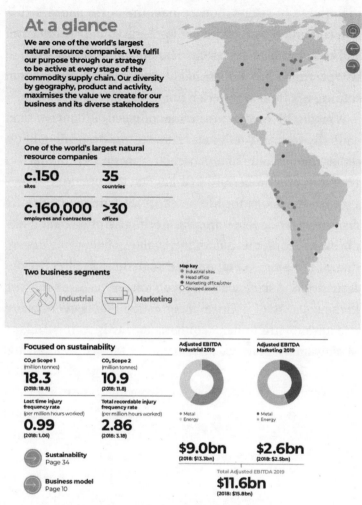

An overview of Glencore's global operations

models with divine sovereignty, remains an elusive, if not impossible, goal. Still *al-Naba'* conveys a sense of action and purpose, pointing toward a fixation on means that is shaded by the absence of ends. It is frenetic activity for its own sake, because death—of others as well as oneself—has become

the marker of success. Of course, the death and destruction recounted therein are not figments of the imagination,
and each headline represents real human suffering. But, to
borrow from Patrick Blanchfield speaking of American gun
culture, it is human suffering not as sacrifice but as waste.[22]

A nihilist pivot toward a politics of spectacle does not stem
naturally from any religious text or cultural tradition, but is
rather the outcome of a particular historical encounter—a
symptom of a modernity that has run out of steam, where
alternative visions for life on earth are harder to come by
than apocalyptic fever dreams. At the risk of sounding like
a broken record, this is not the way things have always been.
Radicals of past generations had something to offer besides
destruction. Asking why that is no longer the case brings us
to the collapse of political imagination that is everywhere
a feature of life under neoliberalism. It is to this lack of
worldly alternatives we now turn.

6

At History's End

I do not believe that things will turn out well, but the idea that they might is of decisive importance.

—Max Horkheimer, in Theodore Adorno and Max Horkheimer,
Toward a New Manifesto

Events were not looking promising for the Islamic State in April 2019, when Abu Bakr al-Baghdadi made his first video appearance since the announcement of the Caliphate in 2014. Donning a military-style vest over his black robes and seated beside an AK-47, al-Baghdadi's appearance mirrored the strategic shift toward guerrilla warfare necessitated by the group's territorial losses. The Islamic State had seen challenges before (particularly the post-Sahwa period from 2007 to 2010), allowing its leadership to retool the current nadir into a narrative of triumph over tribulation, urging patience and sacrifice in the face of hardship and faith in the eventual turn of events. Addressing his supporters, al-Baghdadi related that "our battle today is one of attrition and struggle for the enemy. They need to know that jihad is continuing until the Day of Resurrection, and that Allah ordered us to wage jihad and not to achieve victory."[1] Offering a succinct summation of the tendency to elide ends and means—and the corresponding move of endowing jihad with an intrinsic spiritual worth akin to prayer or fasting—al-Baghdadi promoted jihad *for its own sake*, absent any strategic advances it might generate. The only barrier before it, he argued, was the apocalyptic one: jihad must continue until the Hour (*al-sa'a*) draws near, the final battle commences between the forces of the faithful and those of the Antichrist, and God's subsequent judgment and resurrection completes the eschatological cycle.

This was hardly the Islamic State's first invocation of the apocalypse, whose images and narratives figured prominently in the group's propaganda even during the height of its power. It chose to name its English-language magazine after Dabiq, the town in northern Syria in which, according to a hadith narrated by Abu Hurayra, the final showdown will occur between the forces of Rome (the West) and Islam. In the ensuing battle, a third of the Muslim forces will retreat, a third will be killed, and a third will emerge victorious, leading them to conquer Constantinople before withdrawing to Syria to face the Antichrist. After the call to prayer, the Muslim forces will receive an assist in the form of 'Isa Ibn Maryam (aka Jesus), who will defeat the Antichrist and usher in the Day of Judgment. The symbolic importance of Dabiq was such that the Islamic State expended significant resources to conquer it in August 2014, despite its unimportance from a military–strategic perspective.

Graeme Wood tackled this apocalyptic turn in an influential article published in *The Atlantic* in 2015, attacking the view that the Islamic State was a product of modern political crises rather than the expression of genuine religious fervor. Pushing their professed ideology to the forefront, Wood argued that "much of what the group does looks nonsensical except in light of a sincere, carefully considered commitment to returning civilization to a seventh-century legal environment, and ultimately to bringing about the apocalypse." Wood asserted that the Islamic State was motivated by a well-defined tradition of medieval thought about jihad, and there was no sense in pretending that its more unsavory bits were somehow not part of "real" Islam.[2] Though technically correct—to recognize religions as historically evolving, socially embedded, and highly contested phenomena means rejecting the idea that there is a true form of Islam that excludes radical interpretations—this explanation suffers from the same deficiencies that I outlined in the Introduction. If these medieval texts have been in circulation for 700+ years, why have they proven so compelling at the turn of the twenty-first century? What is it about the present that makes apocalyptic thinking so attractive? Once again, the reassuring recourse to theology serves to obviate the work of historical and political analysis. It obscures the material shifts that make eschatology appealing and blocks our view of the underlying commonalities between "Islam" and "the West"—not just in terms of political destabilization and turns toward right populism, as I have outlined, but in ideas about the nature of history and time.

Yet any serious analysis of the apocalyptic turn in contemporary Islam turns up some surprising facts, the most relevant of which is that invocations of the End Times were infrequent prior to the 1980s and that it was not until after the US invasion of Iraq in 2003 that this fringe position began to move to the mainstream. In a report from 2012, the Pew Research Center found that "in most countries surveyed in the Middle East and North Africa, South Asia and Southeast Asia, half or more Muslims believe they will live to see the return of the Mahdi."* The Pew survey noted a great deal of variation in Muslims' messianic expectations. Only 14 percent of respondents in Bosnia-Herzegovina expected the Mahdi to appear in their lifetimes, versus 29 percent in Bangladesh, 40 percent in Egypt, and 57 percent in Thailand. The greatest anticipation seemed to be found in conflict zones, including Iraq (72 percent) and Afghanistan (83 percent).[3] Much as medieval Islamic apocalyptic literature flourished in the shadow of the Crusades and of the Mongol invasion, the prevalence of contemporary eschatological thinking clearly parallels the deterioration of material conditions. The ebb and flow of apocalyptic thinking uncovered by historical analysis brings our attention back to the way in which the end of the world is indubitably tied to the experience of living within it.

Moreover, the attempt to account for the Islamic State's apocalyptic thinking in vertical terms—that is, through recourse to the classical or medieval Islamic tradition—rather than in relation to the robust output of contemporary

---

* Sunni Islamic theology contains numerous different traditions regarding the Mahdi, but the general idea is that he is a quasi-messianic figure who will usher in the End Times, restoring righteousness to Muslim communities and battling the forces of the anti-Christ in an epic showdown.

apocalyptic, dystopian, and postapocalyptic cultural products is both misguided and illustrative. As numerous cultural critics have noted, we are living in a golden age for apocalyptic fiction and film, spanning genres and languages worldwide. From the pulp and conspiratorial to the highbrow and award-winning, there is no shortage of contemporary film and writing about the end of the world. The impulse to consider the Islamic State's apocalyptic musings in relation to medieval times rather than our current cultural moment offers yet another example of the ardent desire to separate "us" from "them" and to return to the comforting myth that the Islamic State is part of another world entirely. Yet it is a reading that breaks down almost entirely once you consider *Dabiq* alongside literary gems like *The Turner Diaries*, or more recently, the American Christian author Mark Goodwin's *The Beginning of Sorrows* series, which chronicles how a cabal bent on undermining national sovereignty brings about the apocalypse through gun control and the socialist revolution.

In short, we should not shy away from the centrality of ideology in explaining the Islamic State phenomenon, but neither should we be content to take its spokesmen at their word when they profess disdain for the modern world. One need not dismiss theology as a smokescreen for "real" political and economic goals in order to historicize the former, after all. While the Islamic State has often drawn on the apocalyptic canon, this does not mean what observers like Wood think it does—certainly no more than one can square the group's appeals to seventh-century values with its embrace of corporate market thinking. Despite all its invocations of the past, the Islamic State's apocalyptic thinking is profoundly future oriented—or rather, it is what is offered in place of a better future *in this world*. The full embrace of violence as spectacle charted in Chapter 5 is a symptom of this impoverished imagination. That is, unlike the revolutionaries of the 1960s or 1970s—for whom terror was a tactic linked to particular political aims—the current fixation with death and afterlife reflects a diminished sense of what is possible here on Earth. In this sense, the Islamic State's "medieval" sensibilities start to look less like throwbacks from the past and more like a nihilist response to a world that supposedly has no alternative.

The Return of the End

As is the case with Christianity, Islamic apocalyptic literature comes in many hues. The Qur'an itself says relatively little about the End of Days, so much of what is purported to be known about the Hour comes from hadith collections.[4] In the Sunni tradition, the general story includes some sort of final showdown between the faithful and the forces of Rome (that is, the Byzantine empire, as many early texts reflect its arch-rivalry with the early Islamic states). Led by the Mahdi, the Muslim forces will triumph in Constantinople and return to face the Antichrist (*dajjal*) in Syria, a figure who is ultimately defeated by Jesus. The details are fuzzy: some say the Mahdi will arise in Khurasan (the name for the central Asian region encompassing northeast Iran and parts of Afghanistan), others claim he will come from Morocco. Jews figure prominently in some hadiths: one tradition reports that 70,000 Jews from Khurasan will accompany the Antichrist.

But as I demonstrate below, contemporary apocalyptic literature far outstrips its medieval predecessors in terms of assigning a maniacal role to world Jewry, a development that has far less to do with the content of hadiths than with the modern importation of anti-Semitic literature into the Middle East. It does not often happen that I quote the late Bernard Lewis as an ally, but here his pioneering work on Muslim anti-Semitism deserves mention:

> From the late nineteenth century, as a direct result of European influence, movements appear among Muslims of which for the first time one can legitimately use the term anti-Semitic. Hostility to Jews had, of course, roots in the past, but in this era it assumed a new and radically different character.[5]

Importantly Lewis argues, "the unmistakable language of European Christian anti-Semitism" first appeared among Christian communities in the Middle East, and the first anti-Semitic tracts in Arabic were translations from French of literature produced during the Dreyfus affair.[6]

There are many variations in the eschatological drama to contend with, and Shi'a Muslims possess a different version altogether. Sorting through the intricacies of these varied traditions—which, while often fantastical, are not inherently stranger than Christian apocalyptic writing—is beyond our immediate concern.[7] The question here is historical rather than theological: Given its existence within the Islamic canon for centuries, what explains the ebbs and flows of apocalyptic thinking? Why do narratives about the end of the world have purchase at some times and not others?

In his work on the subject, Jean-Pierre Filiu notes that apocalyptic thinking did not exercise much pull in the orthodox Sunni world prior to the end of the twentieth century. Looked upon with suspicion by the ulema and the political classes alike, apocalyptic speculation was associated with the sort of disreputable superstitions espoused by the masses—not the stuff of serious scholarly inquiry. The tide began to turn in 1979, after militants led by a self-proclaimed Mahdi occupied the Grand Mosque in Mecca and held hundreds of worshippers hostage. Revolution in Iran and the Soviet invasion of Afghanistan—which famously drew thousands of mujahideen to Khurasan, with all its messianic associations—further propelled apocalyptic expectations. Yet these elements remain rather fringe, and Filiu cautions against assigning them too much importance. As he notes, the popularity of Muslim apocalyptic writers spewing eschatological musings and conspiratorial thinking in equal parts still paled in comparison to best-selling authors like John Walvoord, whose *Armageddon, Oil, and the Middle East Crisis* tried to map biblical prophecy onto contemporary geostrategic struggles in the region. Indeed, judging by literary output, it was not until relatively recently that the Islamic world started to "catch up" with the robust apocalyptic tradition of the United States.

The Islamic State's fulsome embrace of apocalyptic speculation is one factor that differentiates the group from its immediate predecessor, al-Qaeda. As the scholar William McCants has argued:

For Bin Laden's generation, the apocalypse wasn't a great recruiting pitch. Governments in the Middle East two decades ago were more stable, and sectarianism was more subdued. It was better to recruit by calling to arms against corruption and tyranny than against the Antichrist.[8]

Filiu too notes that judging by their internal correspondence, al-Qaeda "was for many years impervious to apocalyptic temptation"[9] and would even mock attempts to predict the onset of the Hour. Perhaps reflecting the class status of its key leaders, Bin Laden and al-Zawahiri, al-Qaeda regarded itself as an elite vanguard rather than a vehicle for indulging popular superstitions. There was an afterlife to look forward to, of course, and martyrdom was said to secure one's place in paradise. But belief in life after death does not necessarily come with an imminent expectation that the end is near.

Postwar Iraq provided an extremely fertile breeding ground for thinking about the Hour and served as the immediate context in which the eschatological strain became more prominent among ideologues of the new jihad. It was the figure of Abu Mus'ab al-Suri (the *nom de guerre* of Mustafa bin 'Abd al-Qadir Setmariam Nasar) who most influentially merged millenarian expectations with jihadi practice. His 2004 magnum opus, *The Call to Global Islamic Resistance*, weighed in at 1,600 pages, the last hundred of which he dedicated to the coming apocalyptic showdown. Highly critical of al-Qaeda's shepherding of the global jihad movement, and seeking to create a more popular and widely distributed basis for its support, al-Suri's treatise is chiefly devoted to articulating a new strategy for jihad to accommodate the operational constraints stemming from the global war on terror.[10] As discussed in Chapter 2, al-Suri advocated the "jihad of individual terrorism" in lieu of a jihad centered around revolutionary organizations like al-Qaeda—a shift borne out of strategic necessity that has helped inspire attacks by "lone wolves" wherever they might be. In Filiu's interpretation, al-Suri's full embrace of the eschatological tradition stemmed at least in part from his attempt to embed jihad in a more populist sensibility.

While less fantastical than other contemporary visions of End Times (see below), al-Suri's treatise is no less a creature of the modern world. At the most basic level, his text is a prime example of the drive to detach jihad from the state, to moralize its practice, and to offer it to individuals apart from any organizational structure. The idea that jihad possesses its own intrinsic worth—apart from any strategic or military calculations, or indeed, earthly goals at all—is the animating force behind this individualizing gesture. Because enmity between the forces of Islam and those of Rome will remain until the end of time, it is only the entrance of God into history that obviates this duty.[11] Drawing on a well-known hadith, he writes "the obligation of jihad remains until the establishment of the Hour." Despite setbacks, a faction knowledgeable about the truth of religion will continue in this task undeterred until it faces the Antichrist at last.[12] As was the case with al-Baghdadi's address, victory in any material sense is beside the point if jihad is no longer a means to either defend the abode of faith or even aggressively spread it, but rather the end itself. A video message released amid enormous losses in September 2018, titled

"Jihad continues until the establishment of the Hour," similarly conveyed the sense of jihad as an unending obligation
regardless of its effects.[13]

Despite drawing on the hadith, this notion of continual
and perpetual war is at odds with many foundational sources
as well as classical interpretations. For instance, militants
often invoke a Qur'anic verse (Sura al-Baqarah, 191) that
says, "And kill them whenever you find them and turn
them out from where they have turned you out ... such is
the recompense for disbelievers." But the very next verse
states, "But if they cease, then God is oft-forgiving and most
merciful," effectively tempering the command. The world
according to the jurists was not divided—as the Islamic State
repeatedly claims—into the abode of Islam and that of war,
but rather includes a number of intermediary categories (*dar
al-sulh* or *dar al-'ahd*) wherein Muslims have a contract with
non-believers, and no aggression toward them is thus permitted for a certain period of time. Even Ibn Taymiyya, the
perennial favorite of contemporary militants, advised that
one should not wage war on those who do not harm Muslims
or forbid them from practicing their faith.

So too, jihad does not appear in classical discussions as a
practice detached from pragmatic considerations, including
the maximum number of enemies one should face in lieu of
retreating, and the care that should be given to armaments.
The notion of jihad as perpetual and even bereft of strategic
considerations is not, in short, the natural reading of these
classical debates and legal restrictions. Yet it would be easy
to miss this fact by listening to jihad's contemporary champions, who often celebrate it as an end in itself. One might

quibble as to whether today's jihad is really, as I suggest, lacking in strategy given that a whole subgenre of manuals can be found online. Yet the strategies in question—for instance, in advising uncoordinated attacks by individuals against whomever is nearby—are not the stuff of military or political victory. They rather advance a sort of irrational rationality that reflects the confusion between ends and means that is so characteristic of modernity.[14]

The notion of a small, dogged, and fiercely dedicated band of warriors (the mujahideen, but more specifically the victorious faction, *al-ṭa'ifa al-mansūra*) facing off against an adversary who is far superior in material terms is a regular feature of the apocalyptic confrontation. On the one hand, this narrative recognizes the numerical strength and superior military capabilities of the Islamic State's adversaries, conjuring up the triumph of a seeming underdog. The Prophet too faced incredible odds, they are quick to point out, but divine favor ultimately triumphed in the large-scale conquest of the Middle East and North Africa. In itself there is nothing unique about this notion of the divine will expressing itself through military victory, of which one can find innumerable examples among Christians and Jews, for instance. But there is something both fanciful and farce-filled about such delusions of grandeur, which cannot be sustained by any material reality. This does not mean the Islamic State is without power—on the contrary, it manages to compel action from numerous states and dominate media and policy discussions in a way that is wholly disproportionate to its actual capabilities. Moreover, fantasies about conquering Europe and enslaving its inhabitants help fuel Islamophobic narratives

about the incompatibility of Muslims with democracy—
making it easier to ban or bomb them.

The fact that the Islamic State says things that are patently
not true *does not matter* in this mode of politics. Until recently,
the United States was run by a president whose delusions
and lies are the stuff of legend, yet they had no appreciable
impact on his popularity. The delusional is quickly becoming the twenty-first century's dominant political mode. The
material world is no longer determinative or even mallea-
ble, as was the case with twentieth-century fascists who
believed they could bend reality in accordance to their will.
It is irrelevant. This context also helps explain the significant time and resources the Islamic State has devoted to its
media operations, which it correctly identified as a critical
part of its arsenal. As the group wrote in a document posted
on its official Telegram channel in 2016, "This is a time in
which most—if not all—of the mainstream media is driven
by daily lies and professionalized falsification." Fake news!
Thus the mujahid who mans the news desk is no less important to the fight than he who engages in direct combat. "The
media operative is an *istishhadi* [suicide bomber] without a
belt!"[15] The urgent task, in short, is to situate the Islamic
State's apocalyptic turn within a far broader contemporary
context than is often done, one that requires looking across
cultures and geographies. Doing so helps clarify that there
are also far more interesting avenues to explore regarding
this development than the question of false consciousness—
the ever-present impulse to ask if ideologues "really believe
this stuff."

It does this story no justice to pretend its major players

and plot twists are unrelated to the world outside Islam. On the contrary, apocalyptic themes play a starring role in a robust subgenre of films, novels, comic books, and video games in the West. What relationship, if any, can be found between these cross-cultural instances of apocalyptic thinking? Should the belief that we are on the cusp of a cosmic confrontation sound strange to Western ears supposedly unaccustomed to "arcane theological debates"? If we peel back the curtains a bit, we begin to see that signs of the Hour are everywhere.

Strange Beasts and Puppet Masters

The novel opens innocently enough, with a rugged man teaching his wife how to shoot an AR-15 on the family compound. Society has collapsed and most people are stuck in long lines petitioning the new world government for basic food staples. A car appears, carrying none other than our protagonist's sidekick, an Immigration and Customs Enforcement agent who has brought the gift of a gagged Saudi national to be interrogated. But this action is merely a sideshow compared to the real drama. The second horseman of the apocalypse, the Red Virus, has already killed 500 million people worldwide. (This book was written and quickly published during the initial wave of Covid-19 in the United States.) A small band of well-armed Patriots is trying to ride things out before the Rapture, mapping ongoing upheavals onto biblical prophecy: here too heroic notions of "the few against the many" prove a tried and true narrative hook. Taking its literary cues from conspiratorial predecessors like *The Turner*

Diaries, the novel packs more reactionary tropes per page than you thought might be possible.

Taken from book two (*World Order*) of Mark Goodwin's three-part series *The Beginning of Sorrows*, these mostly unoriginal plotlines narrate the world's descent into chaos and march toward the final judgment. The series abounds with conspiratorial themes: a global currency meltdown and the return to gold and silver; a technocratic cabal that confiscates Americans' guns; and a new global government that tramples on national sovereignty, all against the backdrop of shady wars involving Israel, Iran, Saudi Arabia, the global oil market, and people with names that "sound Middle Eastern." As such, it reads like a parodical mash-up of patriarchal, anti-government, anti-Semitic, anti-leftist, and Islamophobic tropes. The plot follows Joshua Stone, a Department of Homeland Security officer who gets wind of the coming storm and retreats to a Kentucky farmhouse with a group of allies to ride out the reign of the Antichrist, who is actually the tech guru appointed to save the world from catastrophe through elite management and global governance. Josh is wise enough to know you can't trust the news, the government, or the experts, but you can trust the book of Revelations. As he counsels his befuddled yet still trusting wife, "whether it comes at the hands of the Saudis or by some other means, times are about to get a whole lot rougher. The Bible hasn't missed a prophecy yet, I wouldn't expect it to start now."[16]

According to the preface, Goodwin wrote the book both to entertain and "to enlighten some to the rapid cultural shift which is pushing America and the globe closer to the dark, one-world government of the anti-Christ."[17] Not surprisingly, Goodwin is an avid prepper in addition to author, and he runs a website called Prepper Recon, which readers are directed to visit in order to download a free PDF of *The Seven Step Survival Plan*. (He is nothing if not a savvy cross-marketer.) Goodwin's books are only a tiny part of a new far-right cultural universe devoted to preparing the masses for race wars and other tribulations, as indeed, the secular and the divine apocalypse are intertwined phenomena.

But it is not only on the right fringes that apocalyptic themes have gained currency, as a surge of such films over the last twenty years—from *The Day after Tomorrow* and *World War Z* to *Snowpiercer*—attest. Indeed, the genre has become popular enough to beget its own parodies, such as the 2013 film *This Is the End*. These films often center on the remnant of humanity that has survived a world-ending event—which in past decades tended to be nuclear Armageddon but is now more often related to climate change, runaway viruses, zombies/robots, or some combination thereof. These secularized versions of the apocalypse are heirs to those centered around nuclear war or alien invasions, both of which were mainstays of post–World War II culture. While apocalyptic writing is plentiful within the Christian and, to a lesser extent, Jewish religious corpus, it only became a mass popular genre in the West after World War II. "A good apocalypse," one young critic has noted, merely "takes advantage of the predominant cultural fear of the time—nuclear destruction during the Cold War, alien invasion during the space race, a contagious lethal virus in the age of Purell, God's judgment at a time of declining morality."[18]

Spanning multiple genres and encompassing varied ideo-logical commitments, the culture of apocalypse is too vast to be singularly characterized. On the one hand, it includes books like *The Beginning of Sorrows* that are heavy-handed, reactionary, and laced with the sort of conspiratorial think-ing that is the handmaiden of fascism. On the other hand, it also includes works like Octavia Butler's *Parable of the Sower*, which explores a world on the brink of collapse due to climate change and corporate greed. Contemporary Arabic fiction writers have also been turning toward apocalyptic or dystopian themes in their work, such as Mohammad Rabie's *Otared* and Ibrahim Nasrallah's *The Second War of the Dog*. There are (at least) two ways of approaching this surge of dystopian and postapocalyptic fiction: either as testaments to the disillusionment and dismay of the present, where the future can only be sketched in dark terms, or as Lina Mounzer has suggested, as an attempt "to imagine alternate worlds or futures that, for all their nightmarish qualities, represent the bold impulse to let one's imagination run onwards as wildly, manically and savagely as possible."[19] That is, invocations of the end of the world are not necessarily reactionary, as the possibility of constructing a new world in its place is often present within such treatments.

The reactionary use of the apocalyptic genre is different in this regard, as the drama often centers not on the remnant struggling to survive in the wake of some world-ending event, but the descent into chaos and the great moment of divine intervention. In contemporary works by Muslim writers, this means detailed accounts of sink holes and fires, Gog and Magog breaching the wall meant to contain them, and of course the great confrontation between the Muslim forces led by Jesus and those of the Antichrist. This fixation on events leading up to the Hour and the great battles it will entail is in part explained by what comes after—heaven and hell, rather than some different version of life on earth. Here too we find a degree of commonality between Islamic apocalyptic literature and that written by Christians like Mark Goodwin, for whom a different—maybe even better— version of life on earth is not within the narrative arc.

However ancient the apocalyptic impulse, such contemporary treatments remain marked by very modern concerns and modes of thinking. Some books use the pretense of scientific inquiry to identify greater and lesser signs of the impending Hour; they are remarkable for their tacit acknowledgment that even apocalyptic speculations should be subject to a quasi-rationalist methodology. But it is the conspiratorial element that most marks current apocalyptic writing as a product of our time and that illustrates certain points of cross-cultural commonality. Both Filiu and David Cook have noted the centrality of conspiracy theories within contemporary Islamic apocalyptic literature, which Filiu divides into two major groups. On the one hand, there are the "pulp" treatments, imaginative and less doctrinally coherent, that find "signs of the Hour in numerological divination and reports of unidentified flying objects." The more "respectable" versions, though "more punctilious in matters of dogma," are still laden with conspiracy theories, often citing *The Protocols of the Elders of Zion* as an authority.[20]

Indeed, allusions to the Jewish puppet-master abound within these texts, whether penned by Muslim reactionaries or members of the American Christian (and even Jewish) right. In Said Ayyub's *Al-Masih al-Dajjal* (The Antichrist), for instance, Jews have "infiltrated political and diplomatic activity in many places in the world, and they have penetrated societies through the channels of communication they control."[21] The notion of a conniving Jewish force secretly controlling the levers of power is not a new idea, but neither is it native to Islam. Adorno and Horkheimer identified it as a central element of Western anti-Semitism eighty years ago: "The fantasy of the conspiracy of lascivious Jewish bankers who finance Bolshevism is a sign of innate powerlessness," they wrote, "the wishful image of those mutilated by power, an image which power uses to perpetuate itself."[22] The image of the puppet-master is evergreen in this context and also noteworthy for its cross-cultural circulation. Compare, for instance, the cover of Muhammad Isa Dawud's *The Hidden Links Between the Antichrist, the Secrets of the Bermuda Triangle, and Flying Saucers*, with that of *From Shadow Party to Shadow Government: George Soros and the Effort to Radically Change America*, by David Horowitz and John Perazzo (see below).

Faced with forces beyond one's control—or even comprehension—conspiracy theories offer a (false) sense of reassurance that *someone* is in charge of this mess. That they flourish under capitalism—with its inherently uneven and often absurd inequalities—and the impersonal, modern bureaucratic state is no coincidence. In the words of political scientists J. Eric Oliver and Thomas J. Wood, conspiracy theories serve "to locate the source of unusual social and political phenomena in unseen, intentional and malevolent

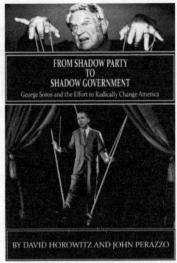

forces" and to "interpret political events in terms of a Manichean struggle between good and evil."[23] While the Islamic State's own apocalyptic invocations are more sober than those favored by mass market authors, they address a populace already primed to think in such terms not just by fiction—but indeed by reality itself. As Lina Mounzer notes, dystopian Arabic novels like *Frankenstein in Baghdad* are not set in some near or far-off future, but the present—in this case, Iraq of 2005, where a junk dealer inadvertently creates a monster by stitching together pieces of various corpses ripped apart by car bombs.[24] "Collective nightmares cannot be banished by demonstrating that they are, intellectually and morally, fallacious," Susan Sontag wrote in a 1965 essay. "This nightmare—the one reflected, in various registers, in the science fiction films—is too close to our reality."[25]

More recently, the Covid-19 pandemic has assumed a starring role in the apocalyptic drama. Given its heavy toll on the United States and European countries, the virus has broadly been greeted as a form of divine retribution against the Islamic State's enemies. At times, the group has responded to Covid-19 pragmatically, regarding it as a distraction that limits the capabilities of Iraqi government forces, for instance. But a "lockdown special" edition of an Islamic State magazine in South Asia turned to more cosmic terms, advising supporters to contract and spread the virus as widely as possible, noting that "no disease can harm even a hair of a believer."[26] None of this should sound terribly outlandish given that conservative Christian preachers in the United States have claimed that Covid-19 was spreading in synagogues to punish Jews for rejecting Jesus Christ (Rick Wiles); argued that the virus is God's punishment for the advance of homosexuality and environmentalism (Ralph Drollinger, who runs a Bible Study frequented by Betsy DeVos, Mike Pompeo, and Ben Carson); and been at the forefront of the anti-mask movement. (One Wisconsin pastor, Matthew Trewhella, compared mandatory mask mandates to Nazi Germany's discriminatory laws against Jews.) The usual retorts are that "there are crazy people everywhere" or "this is why religion is so dangerous." But neither response gets at the question as to why particular types of irrational thinking are embraced at certain times; nor is this a broadly shared trait of religious people and communities as a whole. That is, the salience of conspiratorial, authoritarian, and nihilist readings of religious traditions cannot be explained solely by recourse to a set of texts from which other believers advance diametrically opposed platforms.

The growing tide of conservative Christian thinking about

the apocalypse shares the morally dubious quality present within the Islamic State vision as well: plagues, disasters, deadly conflicts, and human suffering are merely signs of the times. In the best-selling *Left Behind* series, for instance, the virtuous have been raptured and the remaining world descends into chaos. Playing off a familiar theme, the Antichrist is the new Secretary-General of the United Nations, and a remnant must prepare themselves for the coming tribulations before Jesus Christ's triumphant return. True believers are told they will ultimately achieve salvation, and in the Rapture version of history's end, they even miss out on the worst of things. As such, crises—whether man-made or naturally concocted—are not so much to be resisted as embraced. This is a sort of strong messianism, defined by the negation of time and human life here on Earth, which ceases to exist after the apocalyptic showdown. It is a true end of history. To foreclose any possibility of a different, and better, life here on earth is to abandon oneself to nihilism, of which the current apocalyptic fever is merely one symptom.

It is telling that most researchers writing and speaking about the Islamic State's apocalyptic references almost never situate them within this broader comparative context. It is as if we have been conditioned—once something has been labeled "religious"—to plumb the depths of history and tradition to make sense of what might be more fruitfully considered alongside contemporary political and cultural phenomena. The point is not that the Islamic State is made up of budding science fiction writers, but that it is hardly the only group mobilizing apocalyptic themes, preparing for the final confrontation, or propagating a Manichean worldview.

Perhaps most importantly, there is no need to return to medieval Europe or the so-called Wars of Religion to locate a corollary to the Islamic State's vision of the future: it's all around us.[27] That is because the West too is teetering on the End of History. It should come as no surprise that the apocalypse appears as an increasingly viable choice in a world with no alternative.

In the Shadow of the End

In 1989 Francis Fukuyama authored an influential essay in *The National Interest* entitled "The End of History?" Fukuyama made the case that liberalism—that ideological stew composed of free markets, representative democracy, and respect for individual liberty—had won the ideological game. "The triumph of the West, of the Western idea, is evident first of all in the total exhaustion of viable systematic alternatives to Western liberalism," he wrote, as the fall of the Berlin Wall signaled the collapse of communism. The result was that those of us lucky enough to live in the West had exited from "history" itself:

> What we may be witnessing is not just the end of the Cold War, or the passing of a particular period of postwar history, but the end of history as such: that is, the end point of mankind's ideological evolution and the universalization of Western liberal democracy as the final form of human government. This is not to say that there will no longer be events to fill the pages of Foreign Affair's yearly summaries of international relations, for the victory of liberalism has occurred primarily in the realm of ideas or consciousness and is as

yet incomplete in the real or material world. But there are powerful
reasons for believing that it is the ideal that will govern the material
world in the long run.[28]

Offering a neo-Hegelian read of history—wherein it is
chiefly ideas that propel political and social change rather
than material conditions—Fukuyama argued that the ideals
advanced by the American and French Revolutions are
not subject to revision. Rather, "their theoretical truth is
absolute" and cannot be improved upon. While these revolutionary projects had their attendant blind spots—he
admits that considerable work remained in their wakes, little
things like "abolishing slavery and the slave trade, extending the franchise to workers, women, blacks, and other
racial minorities, etc."—that was the result of the imperfect application of liberalism rather than any structural flaw
within it. He claimed that the class conflict had been effectively resolved and that the end of history left no struggles
over "larger" issues: "What remains is primarily economic
activity."[29]

From today's vantage point, Fukuyama's oft-cited essay
seems smugly myopic. Liberalism's definitive triumph
looks much more precarious as we witness the slide toward
authoritarianism in Poland, Hungary, Russia, Brazil, the
Philippines, Turkey, Israel, and (of course) the United
States. This fact arguably has much to do with the inner
workings of (neo)liberalism itself. The quest to make the
world safe for capital—if not necessarily for people—has
born bitter fruit in the form of staggering inequality, environmental degradation, and falling developmental indexes.

That these factors are destabilizing even within the world's oldest democracies has become almost axiomatic.

For our purposes, Fukuyama's thesis is most noteworthy for its inability to account for the fact that only some places had reached history's end. It was chiefly in "the West" (which, as it includes much of East Asia, is more an imaginative category than a geographic one) that this goal had been reached. The fact that many parts of the globe were still mired in the stuff of history could do nothing to upset this narrative:

> Our task is not to answer exhaustively the challenges to liberalism promoted by every crackpot messiah around the world, but only those that are embodied in important social or political forces and movements, and which are therefore part of world history. For our purposes, it matters very little what strange thoughts occur to people in Albania or Burkina Faso, for we are interested in what one could in some sense call the common ideological heritage of mankind.[30]

Because it is only in the West that the "common ideological heritage of mankind" seems to reside (offering an excellent example of the particular dressed up as universal), the Global South is an afterthought within this construction, discussed only to highlight its deficiencies in relation to developmental models and matrices. So too imperialism is viewed as the imperfect application of liberalism rather than a foundational component of actually existing capitalism, with its never-ending quest for materials and markets. Rather than regarding the victory of liberalism in the West as somehow related to the ongoing struggles with "history" elsewhere, Fukuyama exemplifies the tendency to separate these two experiences entirely.

Yet there are good reasons to consider the rise and prolif- eration of contemporary jihadist movements as products of the precise triumph of liberalism that Fukuyama celebrates. We might remember, for instance, that Anwar Sadat sup- ported Islamist politics and parties throughout the 1970s as a counterweight to leftist groups that opposed his attempts to liberalize and "open" Egypt's economy to foreign invest- ment. Similarly, the United States notoriously aided the "freedom fighters" combating the Soviet Union in Afghan- istan, whose most famous alumna would later lead al-Qaeda. And perhaps most importantly when accounting for the rise of the Islamic State, the US invasion of Iraq was a hubristic expression of liberal triumphalism par excellence. Informed precisely by the flawed assumptions found in Fukuyama's argument—that Western liberalism was the highest form of political development; that its spread was inevitable; and that there existed some necessary link between economic and political liberalization—the quest to bring freedom to the Iraqi people remains this century's greatest foreign policy blunder. Beyond securing access to fossil fuels, however, we should recall that Iraq was reconstructed as a sort of neoliberal Candyland, complete with rapid deregulation, privatization, and laws catering to foreign investment. It is indeed noteworthy that Iraq offered US leaders a chance to realize policy dreams that were still elusive at home, such as the introduction of a regressive flat tax. Rather than viewing liberalism's triumph as something apart from this history, we might do better to recall Walter Benjamin's memorable claim that "there is no document of civilization which is not at the same time a document of barbarism."[31]

Notably for our purposes, Fukuyama argued that the end of history does not require that all countries settle into the comforting arms of liberal democracy—only that they abandon "their ideological pretensions of representing different and higher forms of human society."[32] This element of his argument is of particular significance because it is an artifact of a particular moment in history when it was possible to believe that the work of political thought was over. Envisioning alternatives to the current model of Western capitalism, warts and all, was simply beyond the imaginative capacity of Fukuyama—as it remains, we should add, to his contemporary acolytes. Here we can clearly discern the collapse of political and social imagination that is so typical of neoliberalism. Following political theorist Wendy Brown, it is clear that this narrowing of possibilities is constitutive of the attack on "the social" and "the political" as sites of democratic action.[33] It might seem paradoxical, but it is this inability to articulate any alternative to the status quo—the bitter fruit of hegemony—that makes neoliberalism quite compatible with the end-of-the-world thinking adopted by the Islamic State. The apocalypse and the end of history are not diametrically opposed political projects, but two distinct symptoms of the collective inability to envision and strive for something better here on earth.

The fall of Soviet communism has often been credited with sucking the lifeblood out of leftist opposition to autocratic regimes in the Global South. In the Middle East the loss of Soviet patronage was the final nail in the coffin for postindependence socialist movements, which almost without exception devolved into dictatorships—as was the case in Iraq, Syria, Libya, Tunisia, and Egypt, all of which, we might note, have become staging grounds for jihadi militancy. As the Algerian writer Kamel Daoud noted in 2016:

> Paradise as a goal for the individual or the group has gradually replaced the dreams of development, stability and wealth promised by postwar decolonization in the so-called Arab world. These days, one imagines happy tomorrows only after death, not before.[34]

The socialist vision of paradise here on earth has aged poorly in the face of entrenched dictatorships and the failures of the Arab left, Daoud argues. We need not romanticize Soviet communism in noting that its collapse made plausible the sort of nihilist impulse into which all talk of history's end must devolve.

In positing that there is nothing else to hope for—no better, more just, or ethical order to bring about—liberalism's triumph also marks its exhaustion. The symptoms of this exhaustion and inability to imagine a different sort of future are all around us, finding expression not merely in the nihilist violence discussed in Chapter 5 but in the widespread apathy toward politics as a means of effecting meaningful change. The oft-heard dismissal of politicians as "all the same" is another symptom of this sense of fatigue, and it is worth noting just how advantageous this demobilizing and depoliticizing trend is for those promoting an antidemocratic, authoritarian liberalism.

In *Jihad and Death*, Olivier Roy circles around this convergence of nihilist currents on the European continent, offering one of the few accounts that explicitly situates jihad alongside other forms of contemporary, secular violence. Rather than thinking in terms of the "radicalization of Islam," Roy argues that the disappearance of viable leftist challengers to the status quo has led to the "Islamicization of radicalism." In this regard, Roy suggests that those who take part in European jihad today are the heirs to an earlier radical tradition:

> The two forms of protest (extreme leftism and radical Islamism) have a similar structure ... From the Cultural Revolution to the Baadar-Meinhof Gang and up to ISIS, elders are accused of having "betrayed" the revolution, democracy, or Islam and of not handing down the truth. It then becomes a matter of wholesale revolt against the world order, and not a national liberation movement. This global ideal was first THE revolution (permanent and worldwide, by creating "three or four Vietnams" and multiplying hotbeds of insurgency according to Che Guevara's foco concept). Now it is THE jihad, with the multiplication of local emirates, new foco, and the same determination to draw Western troops into a quagmire.[35]

As evidenced by the Islamic State's embrace of insurgency tactics associated with communist leaders, interesting points of overlap do exist between an earlier generation of revolutionaries and today's religious militants. Yet the assertion that contemporary jihad is the heir to leftist politics runs afoul of Roy's own assertion that today's militants are not interested in the construction of an alternative political and social order, only the nihilistic destruction of our current one. Whatever one might think of the leftists of old, the fact that they were deeply committed to imagining and creating alternatives to capitalism can hardly be disputed. The more compelling explanation is not that contemporary jihad is the heir to the radical leftist tradition, but a symptom of its decline. If we are truly living—in Dame Thatcher's immortal words—in a world to which there is no alternative, nihilism is exactly the form of anti-politics one would expect to find in this age of civic exhaustion. Here the apocalypse and the end of history stand shoulder to shoulder, not as identical formations, but rather as different manifestations of a shared sense of futility.

In closing, it is worth reiterating that the social and political order the Islamic State invokes does not represent a real alternative to decades of corruption, poverty, or war, despite the group's delusions of grandeur. The Islamic State will no sooner solve the genuine problems of the world's Muslims than corporate tax cuts will help working-class Americans. In lieu of respite, or of a different type of political and social life, the Islamic State offers a highly punitive police state enforcing piety from above, authoritarianism filtered through a "populist" sieve, a depoliticized form of governance that serves to shield those who actually wield power, and a vague promise that capitalism's failings will be remediated by charitable giving and removing women from the workforce, all bundled up with a view of violence as an end in itself. If the apocalyptic dream seems to lurk around every corner, that is because the freedoms sought—peace, prosperity, comfort, and a far more expansive version of "security" than is often invoked—can only be realized in another world. Any response from those of us still interested in earthly delights must begin by asserting that, in the words of Ajay Singh Chaudhary, there can only be alternatives.[36]

Conclusion: Two Futures

By most conventional accounts, the story of the Islamic State ended in 2019. Merely five years after the proclamation of the Caliphate, most of its core territories had been lost and its leader, Abu Bakr al-Baghdadi, was dead. President Trump declared that the Islamic State had been defeated, though another US claim of "mission accomplished" in the region inevitably raised some eyebrows. Maybe they will return, experts said, or continue to launch attacks regardless of their setbacks. Both of these statements are highly probable, and indeed I have argued that one of the Islamic State's chief innovations is decoupling identity and political violence from territory. But this view, focused as it is on Islamic militancy as a security threat, misses much of what is important about contemporary jihad. It remains firmly within a comforting framework that would assert that jihad is some strange phenomenon that is ravaging the Islamic world, but that—other than demanding continued military vigilance—has very little to do with the problems facing advanced Western democracies.

I have told a different story here, one that regards contemporary jihad as a useful site for theorizing about agency, identity, governance, and violence on a global scale. I have argued that the Islamic State is in no way alien to the modern world but rather exemplifies its rationale. I have further argued that the transformation of jihad over the last century parallels a broader shift away from states as the chief wielders of violence, and that the empowerment of individuals and a wide variety of non-state actors is perfectly compatible with the logic (if not intent) of neoliberalism. So too, this analysis underscores that "our" crises—a distrust of elites and expertise, a drive toward homogeneity as a prerequisite to political life, a constricted view of freedom, served with a side of conspiratorial and apocalyptic thinking—are not uniquely Western phenomena. As I have suggested throughout, the nihilist element of contemporary jihadi violence finds its corollaries not in medieval attempts to dislodge the Crusaders, but in mass shootings in shopping malls. The continued recourse to the "medieval" nature of such violence illustrates just how uncomfortable we are with the modernity it lays bare.

One way out of this trap is to historicize religious ideas and the actions they inspire against a broader material backdrop. The abiding insight of studying religions over time is that there is nothing stable about them, regardless of what their adherents might claim. For instance, the authoritarian dimension within radical Sunni thinking today is diametrically opposed to liberal arguments that linked "true Islam" with democracy a century ago. Which one is supposed to represent Islam's stance toward democracy? Abandoning an essentialist frame allows us to survey the recent past from different territory. The fact that the Islamic State— not to mention state clerics in Saudi Arabia—has repeatedly emphasized the virtues of obedience does not represent a return to the premodern practice of political quietism. Rather, current calls for obedience occur in democracy's waning shadow, coupled with an aggressive attack on the very idea of popular sovereignty and a continual appeal to law (either divine or natural) as something beyond human control. Here too Islamic reactionary elements find their mirror image in formations closer to home, including a Christian nationalist movement that is "authoritarian, paranoid and patriarchal at its core," as journalist Katherine Stewart has aptly character- ized it. "They aren't fighting a culture war. They're making a direct attack on democracy itself."[1]

The points of correspondence that I have traced in this book raise a conundrum. How is it that we are to account for overlapping formations that are part of radically differ- ent social, economic, and political processes? After all, the modern history of the United States or the United Kingdom has little in common with that of Iraq, Syria, or Egypt. Cer- tainly, the most common mode of dealing with this issue is to avoid it by treating developments in the West as something apart from those in the Middle East, North Africa, or South Asia. In the usual version of the story, colonialism and its legacy in varied forms of neo-imperialism have shaped the modern history of these regions, whereas neoliberalism is the preferred frame for accounting for developments within

Western democracies. It is not that these two systems are regarded as wholly separate; indeed, scholars like David Harvey have long recognized the interrelations of the two. But even with such examples like the Iraq War, there is a tendency to think that neoliberalism at home leads to neo-colonial exploits abroad, such that developments in the West remain the moving force of history. But I believe there is another way of framing the relationship, one that is more attentive to the bi-directional circulation of ideas and practices: neoliberalism as a form of colonial blowback, in which populations in the global West and North are subjected to the same types of degradation that long typified colonial rule in Asia, Africa, and South America.

This would help explain why so many of the social and political crises evident in the West today look familiar to those of us trained as scholars of colonialism—for instance, the private security forces that have long been mainstays of elite life in the Global South, now guarding the gated compounds of tech entrepreneurs in Silicon Valley. More broadly speaking, British colonies—which a century ago encompassed the modern-state states of Nigeria, India, Pakistan, Egypt, Sudan, Israel/Palestine, Iraq, Kuwait, Jordan, Yemen, and Oman, among many others—were generally governed so as to facilitate private enterprise and investment, with the government striving to keep out of the way of commercial initiatives. In the words of one nineteenth-century colonial administrator:

> It is the duty of every African government, not to provide work for the workless, but so to govern that private enterprise is encouraged

to do so; that trade is allowed to grow without hindrance; that business houses are given every facility and encouraged to start new
productive works.[2]

The primary purpose of colonial governments was to sup-
press popular discontent in the face of such developments
and to ensure that the march of capitalist progress would not
be subject to any sort of democratic control.

Whereas the process of building stable democracies
in Europe and the Americas necessitated the checking of
private power, and indeed, some compromise with labor and
redistributive policies, the story across much of the Global
South was quite different. The colonial economic order was
a shining example of Actually Existing Laissez-Faire, one
that is particularly useful because it reveals just how much
state violence goes into the construction and maintenance
of the "free market." (More recently, we might recall Milton
Friedman in 1982 hailing Chile's economic miracle under
the dictatorship of General Pinochet.) As a rule, colonies
were denied the tools used by Western countries to guard
against the vicissitudes of unfettered markets: tariffs, coun-
tercyclic spending, labor protections, and no less important,
franchise. On offer instead were high rates of taxation,
concessions to foreign capital, and the denial of rights (for
example, of the press, of assembly, of unionization, and of
representative government) that might be useful in organizing on behalf of the public good. The need to maintain "law
and order" also led to outsized budgets for police, prisons,
and the military and scant allowance for social services. In
1946, for example, and after twenty-five years of British rule,

60 percent of Palestinian Arab children still had no access to public primary school, and a single government secondary school existed for the entire country.

This might start to sound eerily familiar at a time when US military spending exceeds 15 percent of the federal budget while over 30 million Americans live without access to health care. Likewise, US cities continue to devote a substantial portion of their annual budgets—and sometimes up to half of their discretionary budgets—to police departments, all the while lamenting racialized poverty, rising homelessness, and crime. It is, activists claim, a vicious cycle that diverts resources from where they are most needed—education, housing, health care, job training—generating the very social problems policing is called upon to solve through punitive means. Adjusted for inflation, state and local spending on policing grew from $42 billion in 1977 to $115 billion in 2017, reflecting a broader punitive turn that has continued apace even as actual rates of violent crime have dramatically fallen.[3] Alex Vitale put this trend in stark terms by noting that "New York City spends more on policing than it does on the Departments of Health, Homeless Services, Housing Preservation and Development, and Youth and Community Development combined."[4]

As familiar as this story has become in the push to defund police departments in the wake of George Floyd's murder, it is important to note that this domestic distribution of resources finds its parallels in US conduct abroad. Both in Iraq and Afghanistan, but also by means of regional alliances in the Middle East and Latin America, the United States has fallen into a security trap—one whose extensive focus on maintaining public order through force undermines the legitimacy of states and fuels even more violence.[5] In his work on Mexico, John Bailey has charted the cyclical and co-constitutive effects of violent crime and state violence, paying particular attention to how the militarization of the police has actually increased violent crime dramatically. A security trap occurs when "crime, violence, and corruption become mutually reinforcing and contribute to low-quality democracy," effectively eroding civic trust in the state.[6] Bailey attributes the phenomenon to the blurring of public and private sector functions, which undermines the ability of governments and their security forces to pursue the public good. As Kristen Martinez-Gugerli characterizes the dynamic, "Criminal organizations infiltrate political bodies and security forces, and citizens begin to trust criminal groups and cartels more than they do their own government. And instead of working to fight crime, the public sector perpetuates it."[7] The resulting cycles of violence and repression do little to make societies safer, but they do a great deal to erode trust in the state. As Wendy Brown maintains, the present—and widespread—legitimation crisis is not what neoliberal ideologues intended when advancing their critiques of rational planning, social justice, or democratic sovereignty, but it remains wholly consistent with their broader project of depoliticization.

In the prior chapters, I have traced how the legitimation crisis lurks in every corner when we try to account for the emergence and continued appeal of Islamic militancy over the last several decades, and in particular, informs the Islamic State's self-narrative as a political alternative to the corrupt and arbitrary dictates of an elite class. I have called attention to the antiestablishment impulse that animates much of the group's rhetoric and which takes aim at traditional religious authorities and institutions as well as despots. Yet the salve on offer, as evident from authoritarian populists elsewhere, is decidedly not a democratic one. It is rather a call to replace entrenched power with new forms of domination, every bit as repressive as the last, but in some ways more formidable on account of the disavowal of sovereign power discussed in Chapter 4. The idea of a law given and made not by human hands but divine imperative aims at the creation of a political and social order with no legitimate alternatives. It is not the antithesis, but rather the mirror image, of a recourse to the "spontaneous" arrangement of market forces that neoliberals hope will dislodge most of human affairs from the realm of politics. Both positions deny the fundamental fact that, as Franz Neumann argued, "the law cannot rule, only men can exercise political power over other men."[8]

I want to clarify that I do not mean to take neoliberalism, a framework that has emerged to account for a broad realignment of political, economic, and social forces in the West, and imply that we can plop it down in the Middle East as a means to explain contemporary jihad. I am all too wary of such "universal" political models. I am proposing something quite different, though no less global in scope: that neoliberalism itself was prefigured—if not actively constructed—in the colonial world. As a mode of utilizing the state to enforce a set of essentially antidemocratic policies that shield private enterprise from the redistributionist demands of popular sovereignty, neoliberalism echoes the

structure of relations between capital and the state that
are familiar from the colonial era. While in the 1980s and
1990s global financial institutions worked alongside the
United States to pressure newly independent nations in the
Global South to accept neoliberalism's prevailing economic
orthodoxies—"my factories for your reform"—in recent
years "reform" has come home to roost.[9] This is one way
to understand the race-to-the-bottom currently being run
by multiple contenders—from US cities offering billions
of dollars in tax breaks in exchange for Amazon's second
headquarters to tax havens like Ireland, which have helped
tech giants including Apple, Google, and Facebook guard
their new Gilded Age profits from public coffers. Lest we
believe that the current era of corporate power operating at
and above the level of state sovereignty is unique, we might
recall that the East India Company ruled South Asia long
before India was formally absorbed into the British Empire.

Within this framework, the Global South is not the secondary market for Western politics *but a key site of their
emergence*, which is why—however counterintuitive it
might seem—the recent history of Islamic militancy speaks
also to social and political trends in the West. The colony
precedes the metropole, and grappling with the crises of
neoliberal governance is consequently enriched by linking
it to the "peripheral" histories that have helped pave the way.
Placing these disparate experiences in dialogue also helps
us attend to that which links domestic and foreign policy,
to note, for instance, the ways in which the global war on
terror has transformed both US policing and civilian gun
culture. Or to return to the broader horizons of this book:

the inadequacy of moralizing frames that make the individual the central unit of political and social change; the ways in which the search for agency amid an overarching sense of futility undergirds a particular type of nihilist violence; or how the effective undermining of democratic governance fuels authoritarian alternatives. Building on the ruins of neoliberalism, a new crop of strongmen has decreed that the old battle between equality and freedom shall be settled by doing away with both.

Security and Sovereignty for the Twenty-First Century

It is notoriously difficult to translate historical and theoretical observations into a plan for action, and I will leave political strategy to those who do it better. But it is clear to me that developing an adequate response to the interlocking modes of domination I have traced here will require a fundamental change in mainstream thinking about two concepts in particular: security and sovereignty. From Hobbes onward, liberal political theory has viewed the two as mutually co-constitutive. The basic premise is that every individual has a natural right to self-defense. The social contract is the mechanism through which people join together to create civil society, and it requires giving up this natural recourse to violence for the sake of creating a system of law to which all are subject. Protection against violence constitutes the state's basic function and, per Hobbes, the basis of its legitimacy. The sovereign who cannot ensure the security of his subjects likewise has no claims to their obedience.

Fast forwarding to the present, this premise still exercises tremendous influence in material terms and has come to shape US foreign policy in a way that favors "law and order" either before—and indeed, often in the place of—ostensibly liberal ideals like freedom, democracy, or respect for human rights. Enormous resources are directed at those institutions that are regarded as the bedrock of law and order: police, military, prisons, and the judiciary—a fact represented not only in terms of budgetary priorities during the US reconstruction of both Afghanistan and Iraq, but in military aid packages, police force development, and counterterrorism training programs for more than 100 foreign countries. In real terms, the idea that other forms of public social provision are possible only after a certain security baseline has been achieved has become near hegemonic. Supporters of this prioritization will argue that it is impossible to have schools, hospitals, or community organizations function effectively if car bombs are exploding outside. But the reality is a sort of catch-22 in that the effective functioning of schools, hospitals, and community organizations are precisely the sort of civic social web required to make car bombings a less desirable proposition.

The notion that stability is best achieved by increasing the coercive apparatuses of weak states has been the dominant position toward military and police aid for decades and one that has garnered a wide degree of bipartisan support. Yet the cracks, and indeed, material shortcomings, of this approach are by now impossible to ignore. Arguments that have long circulated among the left—and have often been reproached as the naïve idealism of those who do not grasp the amoral nature of realpolitik—have likewise moved into more mainstream policy circles not because of any great ethical realignment, but because the attempt to realize security through state violence has proved an abject failure. Surely the $25 billion spent to equip and train the Iraqi Army between 2003 and 2014 did not aid the latter in its fight against the Islamic State. Writing in *Foreign Affairs* in 2017, Mara Karlin argued that "history shows that building militaries in weak states is not the panacea the U.S. national security community imagines it to be." Though she fell far short of questioning the underlying rationale behind such spending—particularly with regard to the sordid history of using American aid dollars and in some cases personnel to undermine leftist opposition groups—she was forced to concede that the nearly $20 billion poured annually into foreign security forces has failed to achieve the long-sought stability. For instance, military aid to El Salvador under the Carter and Reagan administrations, which was intended to crush left-wing guerillas but led to numerous massacres and other atrocities, did not solve that country's political crises but did leave it with one of the world's highest homicide rates.[10]

In a related vein, and surveying the astronomical sums the United States has spent on security assistance to the Middle East, Richard Sokosky and Andrew Miller took to the pages of *American Conservative* to argue:

> Despite $47 billion in U.S. military assistance over 40 years, the Egyptian military has struggled mightily to contain an ISIS-affiliate numbering no more than 1,200 militants. The Saudis barely used their American-made advanced combat aircraft in the U.S.-led

anti-ISIS operation in Syria, and $89 billion in arms sales to the kingdom over the last 10 years has not prevented Riyadh from getting bogged down in an increasingly costly quagmire in Yemen with U.S.-supplied weapons. The U.S. has sold hundreds of billions of dollars in military hardware to Persian Gulf countries and yet collectively they are not capable of defending the free flow of oil from the Gulf against a militarily weaker Iran without U.S. assistance.[11]

Noting that flooding the Middle East with arms has not produced much in the way of regional stability—and has rather tended to encourage belligerence—the Quincy Institute for Responsible Statecraft has called to redefine American interests along more narrow lines, a shift that would reduce the US military footprint in the region as well as military aid to its governments.[12] It is striking that even as these different policy voices clash on the appropriate course of action, they largely agree that after decades of US stewardship, the Middle East is more chaotic in 2020 than at any point since World War I.

The rise and proliferation of Islamic militant groups since the 1980s runs parallel to this diplomatic track, which is not to claim the latter is the source of the former alone. What is clear is that the militant response to Pax Americana, most recently culminating in the Islamic State, feeds off a widespread sense of illegitimacy—of states, leaders, elite functionaries, and clerical bureaucracies. Strengthening the coercive capabilities of governments that lack popular support does not make the region more stable in the long run. This basic fact gestures at the limit of state violence as a means of creating security. Yet this remains the dominant approach, not just in the Middle East, but toward many countries across the Global South—one that has, importantly, been built and defended by a bipartisan group of leaders and policy makers despite its dismal record. Having rightly given up on spreading democracy at gunpoint, there is no reason to double down on US support for autocratic and repressive regimes instead. Even modest shifts—toward conditional aid, for instance, that would tie support to certain governance benchmarks—would represent a positive step. Broadly speaking, a commitment to do no harm is far preferable to the modes of "help" the United States is accustomed to offering.

More ambitiously, we need nothing short of a complete and total overhaul in how security is defined. Taken in its narrow sense as protection against bodily harm, security might seem best achieved through more and better soldiers, policemen, and weapons. But surveying the results of this strategy—not just abroad, but notably right at home—underscores that living without fear cannot be achieved while so many continue to live without dignity. At the very least, security, like freedom, needs to be understood in far more capacious terms than those usually on offer. One promising turn among policy makers is to note the interrelation between government corruption and security and to argue that any meaningful sense of the latter is impossible absent a state that is responsive and accountable to its citizens. As Sarah Chayes, a former Pentagon adviser, stated in a recent interview, "Corruption is not just a fundamental political problem but the most significant driver of most of the security problems we are supposed to be trying to address."[13]

Chayes was speaking about Afghanistan and Iraq, but her observations apply elsewhere as well. Adequate health care, education, housing, and employment opportunities are the building blocks of genuine, broad-based security. Absent these, security is only achieved—and not for everyone— through massive criminalization, repression, and violence. The private police forces who stand guard outside gated compounds reflect both this heightened desire for security *inside* and the deterioration of conditions *outside*. These are, furthermore, related phenomena. While one set of policy choices leads directly into the snare of this security trap, there are alternatives that would redirect attention and resources toward building a more just society. The recent history of jihad does not reside outside of these dual states of security and precarity but is rather symptomatic of their advanced stage of development. It is in this sense that today's jihad can be said to belong not to the past, but to one possible future.

I say one possible future because the course of history is neither predestined nor predictable. There are always alternatives, and it is our job to articulate what they might be. At the risk of restating the obvious, there is no simple lever to pull to eliminate the Islamic State, any more so than one exists to rid ourselves of the Proud Boys. Analysts often acknowledge this fact by insisting that states must rather tackle the ideology that radicalizes young people—likewise throwing their support behind re-education programs and "moderate Islam." But this is both a shallow way to think about ideology and, in the immediate instance, a misstatement of the facts. Convincing militants that the Qur'an "really" says something other than what they have heard in Islamic State recruiting videos is largely irrelevant if, as the evidence suggests, they are not all that interested in Qur'anic exegesis. In the words of Usman Raja, who runs a mixed martial arts gym geared toward reintegrating former militants, "The biggest thing these extremists get from it is community."[14] It is important to note that Raja's approach has been statistically more successful than typical programs focused around religious reeducation.

This suggests that the vast resources currently being devoted toward the religious reprogramming of militants might prove ineffective or simply inconsequential. If instead of treating mujahideen as evil incarnate, we regard them as individuals seeking agency, community, and meaning in a world that is short on all three, it becomes clear that tackling the conditions that produce them requires changes that are both sweeping and rather basic: How do we build and sustain robust communities without abandoning a commitment to individual freedom? How do we create governments that are strong because they are truly responsive to the needs of their people? How do we revitalize some sense of the common good, against which private gains must be weighed? How do we extend our powers of imagination such that a better world is possible, not just at history's end, but in its still-unfolding present and future?

These are not utopian or even particularly radical questions, but the bare minimal framing needed to address "root causes." Nor are these questions only of relevance abroad. It has become painfully ironic that Western democracies, with

236 THE APOCALYPSE AND THE END OF HISTORY

the United States at the helm, have long counseled countries in the Global South regarding responsible and accountable governance. Yet the signs of trouble at home are everywhere, with legislative gridlock, voter suppression, and unchecked corporate power effectively undermining faith in democratic government. The dismantling of the social good that was so desired by neoliberal leaders like Margaret Thatcher is not without cost. Far from belonging to a different history, Iraq has been rebuilt as a neoliberal laboratory in which everything is for sale, producing its own gilded class—not of tech entrepreneurs, but of militia leaders and contractors to the US government. The results have been predictable: numerous armed separatist groups vying for power, a government that few trust (a fact that facilitated the Islamic State's rapid spread across Sunni regions), and protestors taking aim at the staggering levels of inequality and ineptitude of the government response.

This brings us to back to the question of sovereignty and in particular to the state as a vehicle for expressing democratic sovereignty and exerting democratic control over violence. It might seem quaint to talk about sovereignty—a concept with decidedly medieval roots—in an age shaped by power that is nonsovereign or even suprasovereign, as in the case of the multinational corporate behemoths that have come to hold incredible sway over everyday life. We need a theory of democratic power that is able to contend with such actors, and any attempt to construct one must begin with the state even as it looks outward to international coordination. From my vantage point, any disavowal of sovereign power seems not merely impossible but misguided. Creating a more just and equitable world begins with recognizing that humans have made the one we live in now and that we can choose to make it differently. As Seyla Benhabib has written about the work of Max Horkheimer, it is only "by disclosing that the world of social facts is not governed by natural laws but *is instead the historical residue of the work* of human beings themselves" that "it will be possible to end the alienation from and enslavement to a social reality that dominates humans."[15] Moreover, I will add, recognition of this fact does not entail any necessary conflict with Islam or any other religious system. The idea that shari'a is a ready-made system of legal administration that requires little in the way of human agency does not belong to traditional Islam—but to twentieth-century thinkers and the modern punitive state.

Yet any attempt to realize democratic sovereignty cannot be backward looking. As in other aspects of political critique, we must not think there was a "good time" circa 1950–60 when labor unions were strong and corporate power was tamed. To start with, this is a story about a handful of countries in the West at a time when we badly need a more global framework. Moreover, today's challenges—from acute climate crisis to capital flight—were not part of the past landscape. Nor should anyone romanticize a past era defined by racial and gender hierarchies at home and Cold War militarism abroad, from Iran to Vietnam. While revisiting the American or French or British past will not provide a path forward, thinking about the struggles of the Global South might prove more fruitful. As Ajay Singh Chaudhary has written about contemporary Western democracies:

They more closely resemble the quasi-sovereign political entities found in the colonized world, tools of a power above, vested with a vastly increased coercive capacity but with weak legitimacy, porous to capture from below. In other words, the beginning of a critical state theory for the twenty-first century suggests a politics and a set of strategies more commonly associated with the Global South— literal decolonization.[16]

This process must begin with the observation—long obvious to many thinkers of the Right—that democracy and capitalism exist in tension if not in out-and-out contradiction. Insomuch as genuine political equality is undermined by vast social and economic inequality, the former has been narrowly redefined to essentially mean formal, legal equality: the right to vote every few years and to be subject to the same laws as everyone else (in theory, if not in practice). Far from the "marriage made in heaven" imagined by liberal thinkers who came of age as the Berlin Wall was coming down, a more nuanced accounting must attend to the fact that capitalism has flourished under all types of governments—from Nazi Germany and Pinochet's Chile to contemporary social democracies and Gulf monarchies. Even short of anything revolutionary, there are a good number of certifiably *liberal* policies—ranging from progressive taxation to enhanced regulatory and anti-trust scrutiny; investments in education, housing, and care; legal reform and decriminalization; and enhanced environmental and labor protections—that would be a welcome change from the rightward drift toward authoritarian capitalism.

Even as I have called to reevaluate—and in some instances suspend—many US military and strategic partnerships abroad, it is crucial not to mistake this stance with isolationism. Given the globalized nature of everything from capital flows to melting icebergs and resurgent nationalism, there is no escaping the need for international cooperation and solidarity. But those differ from US domination and are even undermined by it. Across the globe we will need imaginative thinking at all scales to re-envision the relationship between security and sovereignty along the lines I have suggested here. Doing so entails recognizing that our problems are not the same, but nor are they unrelated. So too our solutions might echo off one another as we try to build a world safe for humans.

However counterintuitive, the work of alternative world-making begins from a place of negation, from refusing to let history end in the way it has been foretold by this age's aspiring prophets. This will require alliances that cross every geographic and cultural boundary, and the building of such coalitions will be difficult enough without imagining an unbridgeable gulf separating "us" from "them." If anything, delving into the history and practice of contemporary jihad reveals striking commonalities between this most vilified phenomenon and political and social formations in the West. But imagining a different, and even better, future for all cannot be done merely by appealing to our better angels—changing hearts and minds without changing anything else. A world safe from authoritarian politics and nihilist violence in all its guises must be built before it can be enjoyed.

Glossary and Notes
on Transliteration

A number of Arabic terms appear in this text, many of which figure prominently in contemporary jihadi writings, even those in English. I have tried to define these terms as they are used throughout each chapter, and a full list with translations is also included below. For transliteration of Arabic words into English, I have relied on a simplified version of the system used by the *International Journal of Middle East Studies*. For the sake of easier reading, I have omitted diacritical marks from familiar terms (e.g. jihad instead of *jihād*) and from most names.

bayʿa (pl. bayʿat): oath of allegiance
farḍ ʿayn: a religious duty that is incumbent upon individuals, such as prayer and fasting
farḍ kifāya: a religious duty that is incumbent upon the community as a whole
fatwa: a legal ruling

hadīth (pl. ahādīth): a report of Muhammad's words and actions, as told by his companions

hākimiyya: (divine) sovereignty

hijra: migration; the original hijra was made by the Prophet and his followers from Mecca to Medina in 622 CE; used recently to indicate moving to Islamic State-controlled territory

ijithād: the practice of independent judicial reasoning (coming from the same Arabic root as jihad, which connotes striving for the sake of something)

jāhiliyya: "ignorance," in classical usage, the time period before Islam

kāfir (pl. kuffār): nonbelievers

khalīfah: Caliph

Khilafah: Caliphate

kufr: disbelief

mujahid (pl. mujahideen): one who engages in jihad

nifāq: hypocrisy; a **munāfiq** is a hypocrite

Salafi: ideological orientation committed to imitating the ways of *al-salaf al-sālih*, the pious forefathers who lived during the first three generations of Islam

shariʻa: "the path" or "the way," shariʻa encompasses Islam's body of laws and varied interpretive traditions

sura: a chapter of the Qur'an

taghut (pl. tawaghit): coming from a root that indicates the transgression of limits, meaning "idol" in classical usage, and used by militants to refer to tyrannical rulers

takfīr: literally, "to make someone an unbeliever," that is, excommunicate

taqlīd: literally, imitation; meaning ruling in the same way as past legal authorities (that is, in accordance with juridical precedent)

umma: the Islamic community, the people

al-wala' wa-l-bara': theological concept meaning "loyalty and disavowal," indicating a commitment to God on the one hand and a withdrawal from all that is contrary to God on the other

Notes

Introduction

1   The quotation is attributed to the Dutch Orientalist Christiaan Snouck-Hurgronje. While this view has been the dominant one for decades, the historian Mustafa Aksakal has recently questioned this narrative by highlighting the Ottoman context of these wartime calculations. See Aksakal, "'Holy War Made in Germany'? Ottoman Origins of the 1914 Jihad," *War in History* 18: 2, 2011, 184–99.

2   The original Arabic text and an English translation are available at the Combating Terrorism Center, "Declaration of Jihad against the Americans Occupying the Land of the Two Holiest Sites," reference number AFGP-2002-003676, ctc.usma.edu.

3   Salo Baron, "Newer Emphases in Jewish History," *Jewish Social Studies*, 25: 4, Oct. 1963, 235–48.

4   As parodied by Bernard Lewis, *The Jews of Islam*, Princeton, NJ: Princeton University Press, 1984, 1.

5   As Mark Cohen argues in an influential book that compares the plight of Jews in medieval Christendom to those in contemporary Islamic societies, the fact that shari'a addressed dealings with the "people of the Book" as a question of law tended to support social and political arrangements that were more secure for Jewish communities than those that lived under the private protection of various European lords. Even though certain restrictions were placed upon protected peoples

(*dhimmis*) so that non-Muslims were in many instances treated like "second-class citizens" (to risk anachronism), living within the law proved substantively superior than living by the whims of the local feudal lord. Cohen, *Under Crescent and Cross: The Jews in the Middle Ages*, Princeton, NJ: Princeton University Press, 1994.

6   Mapping Militant Organizations, "Balochistan Liberation Front," Stanford University, web.stanford.edu.

7   David Cook, *Understanding Jihad*, 2d ed., Oakland: University of California Press, 2015, 4.

8   Cook, *Understanding Jihad*, 178.

9   Faisal Devji, "The Terrorist as Humanitarian," *Social Analysis* 53: 1, 2009, 175.

10   Olivier Roy, *Jihad and Death: The Global Appeal of Islamic State*, Oxford University Press, 2017.

11   Glenn Beck, *It IS about Islam: Exposing the Truth about ISIS, Al Qaeda, Iran, and the Caliphate*, New York: Threshold Edition, 2015, 28.

12   Michel Foucault, "Nietzsche, Genealogy, History," in *Language, Counter-Memory, and Practice: Selected Essays*, ed. D. F. Bouchard, Ithaca, NY: Cornell University Press, 1977, 143.

13   Barack Obama, "Statement by the President on ISIL," September 10, 2014, obamawhitehouse.archives.gov.

14   Cook, *Understanding Jihad*, x–xi.

15   Roxanne Euben, *Enemy in the Mirror: Islamic Fundamentalism and the Limits of Modern Rationalism*, Princeton, NJ: Princeton University Press, 1999.

1   A New Age of Private Violence

1   George W. Bush, "Address to a Joint Session of Congress and the American People," Transcript of Speech, The White House, September 20, 2001.

2   Max Weber, "Politics as a Vocation," in *Max Weber's Complete Writings on Academic and Political Vocations*, ed. John Drejimanis, New York: Algora, 2008.

3   Philip Mirowski, *Never Let a Serious Crisis Go to Waste: How Neoliberalism Survived the Financial Meltdown*, New York: Verso, 2013.

4   David Harvey, *A Brief History of Neoliberalism*, Oxford: Oxford University Press, 2007.

5   Suzanne Schneider, *Mandatory Separation: Religion, Education, and Mass Politics in Palestine*, Stanford, CA: Stanford University Press, 2018, 50.

6   Urban Institute and Brookings Institution Tax Policy Center, "Historical Highest Marginal Income Tax Rates," taxpolicycenter.org; Emmanuel Saez and Gabriel Zucman, *The Triumph of Injustice: How the Rich Dodge Taxes and How to Make Them Pay*, New York: W.W. Norton, 2019.

7   Samuel L. Dickman, Steffie Woodlander, Jacob Bor, Danny McCormick, David H. Bor, and David Himmelstein, "Public Policy and Health in the Trump Era," *Lancet*, February 10, 2021.

8   Ajay Singh Chaudhary, "Toward a Critical 'State Theory' for the Twenty-First Century," in *The Future of the State: Philosophy and Politics*, ed. Artemy Magun, Lanham, MD: Rowman and Littlefield, 2020, 194.

9   We might, for instance, consider the mujahideen who fought in Bosnia alongside the other factions in that war, from the Bosnian Serb Army to UN Peacekeepers, as in Darryl Li's provocative study, *The Universal Enemy*, Stanford, CA: Stanford University Press, 2019.

10   Virginia Held, "Terrorism and War," *Journal of Ethics* 8: 1, 2004, 64.

12   Held, "Terrorism and War," 62.

13   Faisal Devji, *Landscapes of the Jihad: Militancy, Morality, Modernity*, Ithaca, NY: Cornell University Press, 2005, 33. My emphasis.

14   Asma Afsaruddin has noted that "early jurists not aligned with official circles, like Sufyan al-Thawri (d. 161/778) and Hijazi scholars like 'Ata' b. Abi Rabah, Abu Salama b. 'Abd al-Rahman (d. between 94–104/712–722) and 'Abd Allah b. 'Umar, were of the opinion that jihad was primarily defensive and that only the defensive jihad may be considered obligatory on the individual." In contrast, Syrian jurists close to the Umayyad leaders ruled that jihad could be properly understood as an aggressive war, leading her to speculate that "no doubt this last group was influenced by the fact that the Syrian Umayyads during his time were engaged in border warfare with the Byzantines and there

was a perceived need to justify these hostilities on a theological and legal basis. It would not be an exaggeration to state that expressing support for expansionist military campaigns during the Umayyad period was to proclaim one's support for the existing government and its policies." Asma Afsaruddin, *The First Muslims: History and Memory*, Oxford: Oneworld Publications, 2007, 116–17.

15 Khaled Abou El Fadl, "Islam and the Theology of Power," *Middle East Report*, no. 221, 2001, 30.

16 *St. Thomas Aquinas on Politics and Ethics*, ed. P. Sigmund, New York: W.W. Norton, 1988, 64–5.

17 The exceptions, which point to the formative role of foreign occupation in fueling jihad, were the anti-colonial insurgencies that began to emerge in the nineteenth century: Abd al-Qadir, who fought the French invasion of Algeria; Sayyid Ahmad Barelvi, who fought the British and their Sikh allies in India's northwest frontier, now part of Pakistan; and Muhammad Ahmad, the Sudanese Mahdi who fought against Ottoman, British, and Egyptian domination. Within Sunni jurisprudence, jihad does not encompass rebellion against a Muslim ruler; the latter constitutes its own legal category that is dealt with apart from matters of jihad. For an extended discussion, see Khaled Abou El Fadl, *Rebellion and Violence in Islamic Law*, New York: Cambridge University Press, 2001.

18 Suleiman A. Mourad and James E. Lindsay, "Ibn 'Asakir and the Intensification and Reorientation of Sunni Jihad Ideology in Crusader-Era Syria," in *Just Wars, Holy Wars, and Jihads: Christian, Jewish, and Muslim Encounters and Exchanges*, ed. Sohail H. Hashmi, New York: Oxford University Press, 2012, 112.

19 For instance, the Hanafi jurist Ibn 'Abidin wrote, "Jihad becomes *fard 'ayn* if the enemy attacks one of the borders of the Muslims, and it becomes *fard 'ayn* upon those close by. For those who are far away, it is *fard kifaya*, if their assistance is not required." Abdallah Yusuf Azzam included this ruling in his important text, *Join the Caravan*, which encouraged Muslims to join the jihad in Afghanistan. He argued that the impotence of local resistance meant that global help *was* required, effectively transforming jihad into an individual duty regardless of where one was situated geographically.

20 As Abu ʿAbd al-Aziz, a veteran of the Afghan jihad who later fought
    in Bosnia, once retorted, "Will we leave girls to be raped, children to
    be taken away by Crusaders, and youths to be killed and slaughtered
    while standing by and simply invoking [the excuse] of 'secularism'?
    Personally, I believe that a secular Muslim state is much better than a
    Crusader one." As quoted by Li, *The Universal Enemy*, 30.

21 Philip Bobbitt, *Terror and Consent: The Wars of the Twenty-First
    Century*, New York: Anchor Books, 2008, 51.

22 As Charity Butcher has argued, the demonstrable linkage between
    terrorism and civil war demands a greater degree of theorization as to
    how these phenomena are linked in the context of today's New Wars.
    See Butcher, "Civil War and Terrorism: A Call for Further Theory
    Building," *Oxford Research Encyclopedia of Politics*, August 22, 2017,
    oxfordre.com.

23 Mary Kaldor, *New and Old Wars: Organized Violence in a Global Era*,
    3d ed., Cambridge: Polity Press, 2012, 9.

24 United Nations, "Only 4 Per Cent of Iraqis in Syria Plan to Return
    Home: UN Report," *UN News*, April 29, 2008, news.un.org.

25 "Final Report of the African Union Commission of Inquiry on South
    Sudan," Addis Ababa, October 15, 2014, 169, peaceau.org.

26 UNHCR, "South Sudan Refugee Crisis Explained," May 1, 2019,
    unrefugees.org.

27 Pew Research Center, "The Global Religious Landscape," December
    18, 2012, pewforum.org.

28 UN News, "New Levels of 'Brutality' in South Sudan, Says UN Rights
    Report," United Nations, June 30, 2015, news.un.org.

29 Islamic State of Iraq, *Informing the People about the Birth of the Islamic
    State of Iraq*; Uthman bin ʿAbd al-Rahman al-Tamimi is listed as the
    supervisor of the work, rather than its author. Al-Furqan Media,
    December 2006.

30 Steve Niva, "The ISIS Shock Doctrine," *The Immanent Frame: Secu-
    larism, Religion, and the Public Sphere*, February 20, 2005, tif.ssrc.org.

31 Al-Hayat Media Center, "From Hijrah to Khilafah," *Dabiq*, no.1, 2014,
    38.

32 Islamic State of Iraq, *Informing the People about the Birth of the Islamic
    State of Iraq*, 39.

33   Brain Fishman, "Fourth Generation Governance," *Combatting Terrorism Center*, March 23, 2007, ctc.usma.edu.

34   Leo Shane III, "Report: Contractors Outnumber U.S. Troops in Afghanistan 3-to-1," *Military Times*, August 17, 2016; Congressional Research Service, "Department of Defense Contractor and Troop Levels in Afghanistan and Iraq: 2007–2018," everycsrreport.com, May 10, 2019.

35   Congressional Research Service, "Department of Defense Contractor and Troop Levels in Afghanistan and Iraq: 2007–2020," February 22, 2021, 5fas.org.

36   Rita Abrahamsen and Michael Williams, "Security Privatization and Global Security Assemblages," *Brown Journal of World Affairs* 18: 1, 2011, 173–4.

37   David Zucchino, "U.S. Military Stops Counting How Much of Afghanistan Is Controlled by Taliban," *New York Times*, May 1, 2019.

38   The Danish Institute for Human Rights and Geneva Centre for Security Sector Governance, "Private Security Governance and National Action Plans on Business and Human Rights," 2019, 18, www.dcaf.ch/ sites/default/files/publications/documents/NAP_PSP_Supplement. pdf.

39   Ori Swed, "Who Are the Private Contractors in Iraq and Afghanistan?," *Military Times*, March 14, 2019.

40   David Isenberg, "Contractors and Cost Effectiveness," Cato Institute, December 23, 2009, www.cato.org/publications/commentary/ contractors-cost-effectiveness.

41   VisionGain, "Private Military Security Services Market Report 2019–2029," www.marketresearch.com/Visiongain-v1531/Private-Military-Security-Services-12247826/.

42   "Private Security Governance and National Action Plans," 5.

43   Claire Provost, "The Industry of Inequality: Why the World Is Obsessed with Private Security," *Guardian*, May 12, 2017.

44   Organization of American States, "Report on Citizen Security in the Americas," 2012, cidh.oas.org.

45   "Private Security Governance and National Action Plans," 5.

46   Ibid.

47   Ajay Singh Chaudhary, "We're Not in This Together," *Baffler*, no. 51, April 2020.

48 Alexis Madrigal, "Kim Kardashian's Private Firefighters Expose America's Fault Line," *Atlantic*, November 14, 2018.

49 Derek Thompson, "America Is Acting Like a Failed State," *Atlantic*, March 14, 2020.

50 See Muhamad Riad El Ghonemy, *Affluence and Poverty in the Middle East*, London: Routledge, 1998; Jane Harrigan, Chengang Wang, and Hamed El-Said, "The Economic and Political Determinants of IMF and World Bank Lending in the Middle East and North Africa," *World Development* 34: 2, 2006.

51 Stephen J. King, *The New Authoritarianism in the Middle East and North Africa*, Bloomington: Indiana University Press, 2009, 29.

52 "Of course, people feel they have been hurt by the gradual withdrawal of the state from areas they used to be involved in," a Damascus econo-mist stated in a 2011 interview. "The gap between Syria's rich and poor has grown as the economy has liberalized." The article's author noted the growing protest movement, which had at that time killed approx-imately 850 people, was intimately linked to this economic situation. "Many protesters also cite endemic corruption as a primary grievance, pointing out that friends and relatives of the president control huge chunks of the economy." Mark Simpson, "Under Pressure, Syria Ends Economic Liberalization, Worsening Outlook," *Atlantic*, May 25, 2011.

2 The Triumph of the Individual

1 The quote by Abu Bakr al-Baghdadi in the epilogue appears in Paul Kamoinick, "On Self-Declared Caliph Ibrahim's December 2015 Speech: Further Evidence for Critical Vulnerabilities in the Crumbling Caliphate," *Small Wars Journal* 36: 5, 2016, smallwarsjournal.com.

2 NATO Strategic Communications Centre of Excellence, "Daesh Infor-mation Campaign and Its Influence," January 2016, 44, stratcomcoe. org.

3 "There Is No Life without Jihad," al-Hayat Media Center, June 19, 2014, accessible to registered users only /jihadology.net.

4 Open Letter to Abu Bakr al-Baghdadi, September 14, 2014, letterto baghdadi.com.

5 Abdullah bin Khaled Al-Saud, "Saudi Foreign Fighters: Analysis of

Leaked Islamic State Entry Documents," International Center for the Study of Radicalization, February 2, 2019, icsr.info.com.

6   Open Letter to Abu Bakr al-Baghdadi, 4.

7   Indira Falk Gesink, "Madrasa Reform and Legal Change in Egypt," in *Islam and Education: Myths and Truths*, eds. Wadad Kadi and Victor Billeh, Chicago: University of Chicago Press, 2007, 27.

8   Gesink, "Madrasa Reform and Legal Change in Egypt," 34.

9   Ibid., 39.

10 Militant groups have their own scholars, as chronicled in Joas Wagemakers's writings on Abu Muhammad al-Maqdisi and the shariʿa council he formed to adjudicate on matters relating to jihad. Wagemakers argues that there has long been tension between such scholars and fighters in the field, who regard themselves as the true expressions of jihad. Here it is worth noting that the Islamic State ran afoul of many of the most prominent Salafi-jihadist scholars, al-Maqdisi included, who rejected the brutality of its methods and questioned the legitimacy of its self-declared caliphate. See Joas Wagemakers, "What Should an Islamic State Look Like? Jihādī-Salafī Debates on the War in Syria," *The Muslim World* 106: 3, 2016.

11 Gary Bunt, *Hashtag Islam: How Cyber-Islamic Environments Are Transforming Religious Authority*, Chapel Hill, NC: The University of North Carolina Press, 2018.

12 Paul Berman, "The Philosopher of Islamic Terror," *New York Times*, March 23, 2003.

13 Sayyid Qutb, *Milestones (Maʿālim fiʾl-ṭarīq)*, ed. A. B. al-Mehri, Birmingham: Maktabah Booksellers and Publishers, 2006, 24.

14 Though Iraq and Egypt achieved formal independence prior to the war, they largely remained subject to the directives of British "advisers" until a wave of postwar revolutions swept away these vestiges of colonial rule.

15 Roxanne Euben and Muhammad Qasim Zaman, "Introduction," in *Princeton Readings in Islamist Thought: Texts and Contexts from Al-Banna to Bin Laden*, Princeton, NJ: Princeton University Press, 2009, 16.

16 Diego Gambetta and Steffen Hertog, *Engineers of Jihad: The Curious Connection between Violent Extremism and Education*, Princeton, NJ: Princeton University Press, 2016.

17   It is believed that Qutb borrowed this idea of *jahiliyya* from the Pakistani Islamist, Abul A'la Maududi, whom I discuss in more detail in Chapter 4.

18   Roxanne Euben, *Enemy in the Mirror: Islamic Fundamentalism and the Limits of Modern Rationalism*, Princeton, NJ: Princeton University Press, 1999, 57.

19   Qutb, *Milestones*, 27.

20   Wael Hallaq has argued that the demand to govern a modern state in accordance with shari'a is in fact impossible, not because of the "medieval" quality of shari'a but because the political rationality that undergirds the modern state is directly opposed to its ethical concerns. See Wael Hallaq, *The Impossible State: Islam, Politics, and Modernity's Moral Predicament*, New York: Columbia University Press, 2013.

21   Sayyid Qutb, *Social Justice in Islam*, trans. John B. Hadie, North Haledon, NJ: Islamic Publications International, 2000, 121.

22   Roxanne Euben, *Enemy in the Mirror*, 88.

23   Qutb, *Milestones*, 67.

24   Ibid., 70.

25   Abu Qatāda al-Filistini, "Characteristics of the Victorious Party in the Foundation of the State of the Believer," al-Tibyān Publications, 2009.

26   Muhammad Abd al-Salam Faraj, "*Jihād: Al-farīda al-ġā'iba*," 2. The Arabic text is accessible at www.alwahabiyah.com/file/Occation/vijename/T-K55-ar.pdf.

27   Mustafa bin 'Abd al-Qadir Setmariyam Nasar (aka Abu Mus'ab al-Suri), "*da'wa al-muqāwama al-islāmiyya al-'ālamiyya*" (The Call for Global Islamic Resistance), originally published online in December 2004 at archive.org/details/Dawaaah/page/n2/mode/2up.

28   As stated in his December 1998 interview with al-Jazeera, a transcript of which is available in *Messages to the World: The Statements of Osama Bin Laden*, ed. Bruce Lawrence, London and New York: Verso, 2005, 93.

29   Al-Hayat Media Center, "Recit de la terre de la vif: Abu Sohayb al-Fananci," March 2015.

30   Al-Hayat Media Center, "The Fear of Hypocrisy," *Dabiq* no. 3, 2014, 27.

31   Al-Hayat Media Center, "The Concept of Imamah Is from the Millah of Ibrahim," *Dabiq* no. 1, 2014, 24.

32   Shaykh Abul Hassan al-Muhajir, "He Was True to Allah and Allah Was True to Him," lecture, December 2016.

33   Al-Hayat Media Center, foreword, *Dabiq*, no. 2, 2014, 4.

34   Cole Bunzel, "The Kingdom and the Caliphate: Duel of the Islamic States," *Carnegie Endowment for International Peace*, February 18, 2016, carnegieendowment.org.

35   Faisal Devji, "The Terrorist as Humanitarian," *Social Analysis* 53: 1, 2009.

36   Al-Hayat Media Center, "Among the Believers are Men: Abu 'Abdillah Al-Britani," *Rumiya* no. 3, 2016, 14–15.

37   Robert A. Pape, *Dying to Win: The Strategic Logic of Suicide Terrorism*, New York: Random House, 2005, 200.

38   Olivier Roy, *Jihad and Death*, translated by Cynthia Schoch, Oxford: Oxford University Press, 2017, 9.

39   Mary Kaldor, *New and Old Wars: Organized Violence in a Global Era*, 3rd ed., Cambridge: Polity Press, 2012, 78.

40   In this regard, it is noteworthy that one Islamic State fatwa—meant to address the question as to whether it was necessary to secure permission from a leader to engage in jihad—hewed to the traditional Sunni position that permission was required. See Aymen Jawad al-Tamimi, "Unseen Islamic State Fatwas on Jihad and Sabaya," *Jihadology*, September 25, 2015, jihadology.net

3 Making the *Umma* Great Again

1   Eric Hobsbawm and Terence Ranger, eds., *The Invention of Tradition*, Cambridge: Cambridge University Press, 1992.

2   Stuart Hall, "Ethnicity: Identity and Difference" (1989), in *Becoming National: A Reader*, eds. Geoff Eley and Ronald Suny, Oxford: Oxford University Press, 1996, 343.

3   Richard Bulliet, *Conversion to Islam in the Medieval Period*, Harvard: Harvard University Press, 1979.

4   And indeed, the Islamic State would happily dismiss the Ottomans as apostates and reject their political model for a rather different one that arose in the Arabian Peninsula in the eighteenth century out of the marriage of convenience between the House of Saud's

territorial ambitions and Muhammad 'Abd al-Wahhab's puritanical convictions.

5   Benedict Anderson, *Imagined Communities*, New York and London: Verso, 1983.

6   Eugene Weber, *Peasants into Frenchmen: The Modernization of Rural France 1870–1914*, Stanford, CA: Stanford University Press, 1976, 9.

7   Johann Gottfried von Herder, "Materials for the Philosophy of the History of Mankind," in *Modern History Sourcebook*, ed. Jerome S. Arkenber, New York: Fordham University, 2019.

8   Herder, "Materials for the Philosophy of the History of Mankind."

9   Abu Bakr al-Baghdadi, "A Message to the Mujahideen and the Muslim Ummah in the Month of Ramadan," al-Furqan Media, July 1, 2014.

10 Sayyid Qutb, *Social Justice in Islam*, trans. John B. Hadie, North Haledon, NJ: Islamic Publications International, 2000, 70.

11 Qutb, *Social Justice in Islam*, 71.

12 See for instance, Osama Bin Laden, "The Solution," September 7, 2007.

13 Al-Hayat Media Center, "Glad Tidings for the Muslim Ummah," *Dabiq*, no. 1, July 2014, 7.

14 The quotation appears in d'Azeglio's 1867 memoir, *Miei Ricordi*, as cited in Charles L. Killinger, *The History of Italy*, Westport and London: Greenwood Press, 2002, 1.

15 Anke von Kügelgen, "'Abduh, Muhammad," *Encyclopaedia of Islam*, Brill, 2009.

16 As quoted in Seyyed Vali Reza Nasr, *Mawdudi and the Making of Islamic Revivalism*, New York: Oxford University Press, 1996, 64.

17 Muhammad al-Bukhari, *Sahih Bukhari* 8, Book 73, no. 125.

18 Ibn Hajar al-'Asqalani, *Fath ul-Bari*, 12/314.

19 See Abu Amina Elias, "Dangers of Takfir, Declaring Muslims to be Apostates," *Faith in Allah*, November 4, 2014, abuaminaelias.com.

20 For an extended study of both Ibn Taymiyya and Ibn 'Abd al-Wahhab and the intellectual lineage between them, see Samira Haj, *Reconfiguring Islamic Tradition*, Stanford, CA: Stanford University Press, 2008.

21 Nabil Mouline, *The Clerics of Islam: Religious Authority and Political Power in Saudi Arabia*, trans. Ethan S. Rundell, New Haven, CT: Yale University Press, 2014, 59–60.

22   Shiraz Maher, *Salafi-Jihadism: The History of an Idea*, New York: Oxford University Press, 2017, 72, 83.

23   As-Sahab Media, "The Open Meeting with Shaykh Ayman al-Zawahiri, Part 1," www.washingtonpost.com/wp-srv/world/OpenMeeting Zawahiri_Part1.pdf.

24   See Elias, "Dangers of Takfir, Declaring Muslims to be Apostates."

25   Turki al-Bin'ali, as quoted in Aymenn Jawad Al-Tamimi, "Islamic State Training Camp Textbook: 'Course in Monotheism,'" *Muqarrar fi al-tawḥīd*, 30, Aymennjawad.org. The textbook is dated AH 1436 (2015).

26   Delegated Committee of the Islamic State, Fatwa no. 8-13, May 17, 2017, in Bryan Price and Muhammad al-'Ubaydi, "The Islamic State's Internal Rifts and Social Media Ban," Combatting Terrorism Center at West Point, June 21, 2017, ctc.usma.edu.

27   Delegated Committee of the Islamic State, Fatwa no. 8–13.

28   Ibid.

29   As quoted in Faisal Devji, *Landscapes of the Jihad: Militancy, Morality, and Modernity*, New York: Cornell University Press, 2005, 99–100.

30   Abu Mariya al-Shami, "Ān al-Awan yā ahl al-Shām," quoted in Joas Wagemakers, "What Should an Islamic State Look Like? Jihādī-Salafī Debates on the War in Syria," *The Muslim World* 106: 3, 2016, 506.

31   Al-Hayat Media Center, "The Concept of Imamah (Leadership) Is from the Millah (Path) of Ibrahim," *Dabiq*, no. 1, 2014, 21. Note that the translation for *mushrikin* is provided in the original text, as are the those for *imamah* and *millah* in the article title.

32   Hamid ibn 'Atiq, *The Way of Cutting Relations off from the Polytheist and the Apostate*, as quoted in Maher, *Salafi-Jihadism*, 118.

33   Maher, *Salafi-Jihadism*, 121. It is worth noting that for all his radical credentials as a scholar often associated with al-Qaeda, al-Maqdisi has denounced the Islamic State for, among other things, its aggressive use of *takfir*.

34   Qutb, *Social Justice in Islam*, 121.

35   Ibid., 139.

36   Oliver Roy, *Jihad and Death: The Global Appeal of Islamic State*, New York: Oxford University Press, 2017, 63.

37   Al-Hayat Media Center, "Join the Ranks," quoted by Navhat

Nuraniyah, "How ISIS Charmed the New Generation of Indonesian Militants," Middle East Institute, January 9, 2015.

39 Delegated Committee of the Islamic State, Fatwa 8-31, May 17, 2017. This statement originally appeared in an audiotape address given by former Islamic State of Iraq and Syria leader, Abu Umar al-Husayni al-Qurayshi al-Baghdadi, which was released by al-Furqan Media on April 17, 2007.

40 Olivier Roy, *Holy Ignorance: When Religion and Culture Part Ways*, trans. Ros Schwartz, New York: Oxford University Press, 2013.

41 In his study of identity in late Ottoman Palestine, Rashid Khalidi has shown how common it was (at least among the literate upper classes who left records) to simultaneously regard oneself as an Arab, a Palestinian, an Ottoman, a Jerusalemite, and a Muslim (or Christian), among other possible options.

42 In his work on mujahideen who fought in Bosnia, Darryl Li has argued that their solidarity was representative of an aspiring universalism, one that cast itself in contrast to the logic of national sovereignty and identity. In this way it can be viewed as a precursor to today's identarian formations, though the differences between the two instances of jihad are so substantive that one hesitates to place them within the same analytic bucket. See Darryl Li, *The Universal Enemy*, Stanford, CA: Stanford University Press, 2019.

43 Michael Mann, *The Dark Side of Democracy*, New York: Cambridge University Press, 2005.

44 Al-Hayat Media Center, "Remaining and Expanding," *Dabiq*, no. 5, 2014, 22.

45 Joas Wagemakers, "The Concept of Bay'a in the Islamic State's Ideology," *Perspectives on Terrorism* 9: 4, 2015, 99.

46 Elie Podeh, "The Bay'a: Modern Political Uses of Islamic Ritual in the Arab World," *Die Welt des Islams* 50: 1, 2010.

47 Al-Hayat Media Center, "Foreword," *Dabiq*, no. 2, 2014, 3.

48 Ibid.

49 Wagemakers, "The Concept of Bay'a in the Islamic State's Ideology," 101.

50 Al-Hayat Media Center, "Establishing the Islamic State: Between the Prophetic Methodology and the Paths of the Deviants," *Rumiya* no. 8, 2017, 10.

51   This remains true even if we accept Michel Foucault's argument that it is ultimately the populations within such territories that are the central object of sovereignty. Territory remains foundational as the means of demarcating which bodies are to be managed.

52   This argument was adopted by Abu Humam al-Athari as well as al-Shinqiti. For an extended discussion, see Wagemakers, "The Concept of Bay'a in the Islamic State's Ideology."

4 The Democratic Foil

1   Albert Hourani, *Arabic Thought in the Liberal Age: 1798–1939*, Cambridge: Cambridge University Press, 1983, 6. The fear of anarchy is a common theme among classical commentators and found clear expression in the work of the famed medieval theologian and jurist, al-Ghazali, who argued that "that the authority of unjust rulers should be enforced in their land because of the urgent need for authority therein." Al-Ghazali, *Ihyā 'ulūm al-dīn*, Book II, trans. Nabih Amin Faris, *The Foundations of the Articles of Faith*, Lahore: Ashraf Press, 1963, 97.

2   For an extended discussion, see Khaled Abou El Fadl, *Rebellion and Violence in Islamic Law*, New York: Cambridge University Press, 2001.

3   Wael Hallaq, *The Impossible State: Islam, Politics, and Modernity's Moral Predicament*, New York: Columbia University Press, 2013

4   Abu Yusuf, *Kitāb al-kharāj*, trans. Bernard Lewis, *Islam from the Prophet Muhammad to the Capture of Constantinople. Vol. 1: Politics and War*, New York: Walker and Co., 1974, 161.

5   "The Hamidian Despotism" is a chapter that appears in George Antonius's *The Arab Awakening: The Story of the Arab National Movement* (New York: Routledge, 2010), which undoubtedly ranks among the most important artifacts of Arab liberal thought. Though himself a Palestinian Christian, Antonius's view of Arab nationalism afforded Islam (understood in civilizational terms) a place of privilege.

6   'Abd al-Wahab Khayr al-Din, Mustafa 'Ināni, and Hasn Mansur, *kitāb al-dīn al-Islāmī*, Cairo: Dar al-Kuttub, 1930, 100. It is worth noting that this book was co-authored by two affiliates of Dar al-'Ulum, whose alumni also included Hassan al-Banna and Sayyid Qutb.

7   Khaled Abou El Fadl, "Islam and the Theology of Power," *Middle East Report* no. 221, Winter 2001.

8   Nathan Brown, "Post-Revolutionary al-Azhar," Carnegie Endowment for International Peace, September 2011, 6.

9   Al-Hayat Media Center, "The Islamic State is a True Imamah," *Dabiq* no. 1, 2014, 30.

10 Faisal Devji, "ISIS: Haunted by Sovereignty," *Spiked*, December 18, 2015, Spiked-online.com.

11 Seyyed Vali Reza Nasr, *Mawdudi and the Making of Islamic Revivalism*, New York: Oxford University Press, 1996, 20.

12 Nasr, *Mawdudi and the Making of Islamic Revivalism*, 84.

13 Irfan Ahmad, *Islamism and Democracy in India: The Transformation of Jamaat-e-Islami*, Princeton, NJ: Princeton University Press, 2009, 65.

14 As cited in Sayed Khatab, *The Power of Sovereignty*, New York: Routledge, 2006, 32.

15 Sayyid Qutb, *Social Justice in Islam*, trans. John B. Hadie, North Haledon, NJ: Islamic Publications International, 2000, 121.

16 Bin Laden, "The Solution," September 7, 2007.

17 Al-Hayat Media Center, "The Murtadd Vote," jihadology.net.

18 Delegated Committee of the Islamic State, Fatwa no. 8-13, May 17, 2017, available in Bryan Price and Muhammad al-'Ubaydi, "The Islamic State's Internal Rifts and Social Media Ban," June 21, 2017, Combatting Terrorism Center at West Point, ctc.usma.edu.

19 Abu 'Amr al-Kinani, "It's either the Islamic State or the Flood," *Dabiq* no. 2, 2014, 5.

20 Nasr, *Mawdudi and the Making of Islamic Revivalism*, 59.

21 Qutb, *Milestones*, 85.

22 Ibid., 70–71.

23 Qutb's view here bears a striking resemblance to that made by Francisco de Vitoria in the context of the Spanish colonization of the Americas: not that the natives had to accept the Gospels, but that the Christian right to evangelize was a legitimate basis for conquest.

24 Al-Hayat Media Center, "The Murtadd Vote," 4.

25 Ahmad, *Islamism and Democracy in India*, 67.

26 Nasr, *Mawdudi and the Making of Islamic Revivalism*, 86.

27   G.W.F. Hegel, *Introduction to the Philosophy of History*, trans. Leo
     Rauch, New York: Hackett Book Group, 1998, 27.

28   Yoram Hazony, *The Virtue of Nationalism*, New York: Basic Books,
     2019.

29   Wael Hallaq, *Shariʿa: Theory, Practice, and Transformations*, New York:
     Cambridge University Press, 2009, 311-12.

30   Mark Cammack, "Islamic Law and Crime in Contemporary Courts,"
     Berkeley Journal of Middle Eastern and Islamic Law 4: 1, 2012, 3.

31   Hallaq, *Shariʿa*, 313.

32   Ibid.

33   For an extended discussion, see Chaim Saimon, *Halakhah: The Rab-
     binic Idea of Law*, Princeton, NJ: Princeton University Press, 2018,
     Chapter 2, "Non-Applied Law."

34   Hallaq, *The Impossible State*, 56.

35   On the use of shariʿa courts by non-Muslims, see Jessica Marglin, *Across
     Legal Lines: Jews and Muslims in Modern Morocco*, New Haven, CT: Yale
     University Press, 2016; Najwa al-Qattan, *Dhimmis in the Muslim Courts:
     Documenting Justice in Ottoman Damascus: 1775–1860*, Cambridge:
     Harvard University Press, 1996; and Najwa al-Qattan, "Litigants and
     Neighbors: The Communal Topography of Ottoman Damascus,"
     Comparative Studies in Society and History 44: 3, 2002, 511–33.

36   Thus the Caliphate's police forces were known to search cellular
     phones for "infringements in music, videos or communications that
     might threaten ISIS." See Asaad Almohammad, Anne Speckhard, and
     Ahmet S. Yayla, "The ISIS Prison System: Its Structure, Departmental
     Affiliations, Processes, Conditions, and Practices of Psychological and
     Physical Torture," *ICSVE Research Reports*, 2017, 17.

37   Almohammad et al., "The ISIS Prison System."

38   The phrase is Roxanne Euben's, borrowed from the title of her excel-
     lent book about Islamic fundamentalism: *Enemy in the Mirror: Islamic
     Fundamentalism and the Limits of Modern Rationalism*, Princeton, NJ:
     Princeton University Press, 1999.

39   Nasr, *Mawdudi and the Making of Islamic Revivalism*, 85.

40   Hallaq, *The Impossible State*, 58.

41   Al-Furqan Media, "The Structure of the Caliphate," July 2016, acces-
     sible to registered users at jihadology.net.

42 Mara Revkin and William McCants, "Experts Weigh In: Is ISIS Good at Governing?," Brookings Institution, Nov. 20, 2015, brookings.edu.

43 Devji, "ISIS: Haunted by Sovereignty."

44 Milton Friedman, *Capitalism and Freedom*, Chicago: University of Chicago Press, 1982, 21.

45 Philip Bobbitt, *Terror and Consent: The Wars of the Twenty-First Century*, New York: Anchor Books, 2008, 26.

46 F.A. Hayek, *Individualism and Economic Order*, Chicago: The University of Chicago Press, 1948, 7.

5 Means without Ends

1 Khaled Abou El Fadl, "Islam and the Theology of Power," *Middle East Report*, no. 221, 2001.

2 Stuart Carroll, *Blood and Violence in Early Modern France*, New York: Oxford University Press, 2006, 5.

3 Thus far scholars of the Seljuk period (the Seljuks ruled over territory stretching from modern-day Turkey to Iran, encompassing much of the Arabic-speaking Islamic heartlands, from the eleventh to the thirteenth centuries) have only found evidence for a single instance of stoning for adultery, and it was clearly a set-up. The accused was a high-ranking emir who fell victim to a scheme by the vizier to eliminate him. See Christian Lange, *Justice, Punishment, and the Medieval Muslim Imagination*, Cambridge: Cambridge University Press, 2008, 171

4 Al-Hayat Media Center, "Article Title," *Rumiya*, no. 9, May 2017, 47.

5 Philip Bobbitt, *Terror and Consent: The Wars of the Twenty-First Century*, New York: Anchor Books, 2008, 60.

6 Adriana Cavarero, *Horrorism: Naming Contemporary Violence*, New York: Columbia University Press, 2008.

7 Donald J. Trump, "Executive Order on Revocation and Reporting Requirement," The White House, March 6, 2019.

8 Neta Crawford, "Human Cost of the Post 9-11 Wars: Lethality and the Need for Transparency," Watson Institute of International and Public Affairs, Brown University, November 2018.

9 In *Precarious Life: The Powers of Mourning and Violence* (New York:

Verso Books, 2006), Judith Butler has grasped this fact as underscoring that the war on terror divides populations into those who warrant our grief and those who do not, and has argued for a politics of solidarity built around a shared basis of precarity.

10   Lilie Chouliaraki and Angelos Kissas, "The Communication of Horrorism: A Typology of ISIS Online Death Videos," *Critical Studies in Media Communications* 35: 1, 2018, 9.

11   Carroll, *Blood and Violence in Early Modern France*, 5, 7, 6. The defining traits of feuding are here borrowed from William Miller, *Bloodletting and Peacemaking: Feud, Law, and Society in Saga Iceland*, Chicago: University of Chicago Press, 1990.

12   Walter Benjamin, "The Storyteller: Reflections on the Works of Nikolia Leskov," in *Illuminations: Essays and Reflections*, ed. Hannah Arendt, trans. Harry Zohn, New York: Schocken Books, 1968, 84.

13   There have been many calls in recent years to designate domestic terrorism as a federal crime, particularly in the wake of right-wing and white supremacist attacks such as the shooting at Tree of Life synagogue in Pittsburgh or car-ramming into protestors in Charlottesville, Virginia. Still others have voiced caution, like the legal scholar Francesca Laguardia, who points to the politically motivated use of the "terrorist" label. "The primary cause of the disparity in prosecutions between domestic and international terrorists is not a lack of a domestic terrorism statute but rather the lack of a generalized terrorism statute and the failure to designate right-wing organizations as 'terrorists'." See Francesca Laguardia, "Considering a Domestic Terrorism Statute and Its Alternatives," *Northwestern University Law Review* 114: 4, 2020, 212. It is telling that after years of avoiding action on this front, as of this writing in June 2020, the Trump administration is newly enthused about a domestic terrorism law in order to target Antifa and others agitating for racial justice. "To be sure," Sahar Aziz argued, "Trump's primary targets of a domestic terrorism law will be left wing and minority activists." See Sahar Aziz, "A Domestic Terror Law Could Quash Political Dissent in the US," Al-Jazeera, June 13, 2020, aljazeera.com.

14   Khaled A. Beydoun, "Lone Wolf Terrorism: Types, Stripes, and Double Standards," *Northwestern University Law Review* 112: 5, 2018, 1234.

15 Al-Hayat Media Center, "Article Title," *Rumiya* 2: 13, October 2016, 13.

16 Alexander Smith et al., "New Zealand's Mosque Shooting: Attacker's Apparent Manifesto Probed," NBC News, March 15, 2019.

17 For an excellent collection of essays devoted to the issue of ISIS, media, and spectacle, see *Critical Studies in Media Communication* 35: 1, 2018 – Issue 1: "ISIS beyond the Spectacle: Communication Media, Networked Publics, Terrorism." The quotation, from Mehdi Semati and Piotr M. Szpunar, is taken from the volume's introduction.

18 Amanda E. Rogers, "Evil™ – Islamic State, Conflict-Capitalism, and the Geopolitical Uncanny," *Critical Studies on Security* 6: 1, 2018.

19 Walter Benjamin, "The Work of Art in the Age of Mechanical Reproduction," in *Illuminations*, 241.

20 Rebecca Adelman, "One Apostate Run Over, Hundreds Repented: Excess, Unthinkability, and Infographics from the War with I.S.I.S.," *Critical Studies in Media Communication* 35: 1, 2018.

21 Taha Falaha (aka Abu Muhammad al-Adnani), "*Inna Rabaka labil-mirād*," November 11, 2015, archive.org.

22 Patrick Blanchfield, "Guns and the 'Price We Pay for Freedom'," *New York Times*, November 8, 2017.

6 At History's End

1 "In the Hospitality of the Leader of the Faithful" (Video address), April 29, 2019, jihadology.net. A transcript of the speech is available by Haroro J. Ingram, Craig Whiteside, and Charlie Winter, eds., *The ISIS Reader: Milestone Texts of the Islamic State Movement*, New York: Oxford University Press, 2020.

2 Graeme Wood, "What ISIS Really Wants," *Atlantic*, March 2015.

3 Pew Research Center, "The World's Muslims: Unity and Diversity," August 9, 2012, pewforum.org.

4 Notwithstanding this fact, there is a tradition of Orientalism that has tried to argue that Muhammad was a doomsday prophet and that his mission consisted mostly in preparing people for the immanent apocalypse. See Stephen Shoemaker, "Eschatology and Empire in Late Antiquity and Early Islam," *Arabica* 61, 2014, 514–58. Developed largely in conversation with earlier Orientalist scholars rather than

original sources (or the views of Muslims thinkers and theologians), this unconvincing argument remains a minority view.

5	Bernard Lewis, *The Jews of Islam*, Princeton, NJ: Princeton University Press, 1984, 184–85.

6	Ibid.

7	Among the surveys of this literature in English, see Ofer Livne-Kafri, "Some Notes on the Muslim Apocalyptic Tradition," *Quaderni di Studi Arabi* 17, 1999, 71–94; Jean-Pierre Filiu, *Apocalypse in Islam*, trans. M. B. Debevoise, Berkeley: University of California Press, 2011; David Cook, *Studies in Muslim Apocalyptic and Contemporary Muslim Apocalyptic Literature*, New York: Syracuse University Press, 2008.

8	William McCants, *The ISIS Apocalypse*: *The History, Strategy, and Doomsday Vision of the Islamic State*, New York: St. Martin's Press, 2015, Apple Books version, 252.

9	Filiu, *Apocalypse in Islam*, 186.

10	For a more extensive treatment of al-Suri and his ideas, see Brynjar Lia, *Architect of Global Jihad: The Life of Strategist Abu Mus'ab al-Suri*, New York: Oxford University Press, 2009.

11	Mustafa bin 'Abd al-Qadir Setmariyam Nasar (aka Abu Mus'ab al-Suri), *da'wa al-muqāwama al-islāmiyya al-'ālamiyya* (The Call for Global Islamic Resistance), 72. Originally published online in December 2004 at archive.org/details/Dawaaah/page/n2/mode/2up.

12	Suri, *da'wa al-muqāwama al-islāmiyya al-'ālamiyya*, 62.

13	Islamic State Wilayat al-'Iraq, "*al-jihād mādin ila quiyām al-sā'ah*" (Jihad Will Be Performed until the Coming of the Hour), *Jihadology*, September 17, 2018, jihadology.net.

14	"Domination itself which, even as absolute power, is inherently only a means, becomes in untrammeled projection the purpose both of oneself and of others, purpose as such." Theodor Adorno and Max Horkheimer, *Dialectic of Enlightenment*, trans. John Cumming, New York: Verso Books, 1972, 156.

15	"O Media Operative, You Are Also a Mujahid," Al-Himma Library, April 16, 2016, in Ingram et al., eds., *The ISIS Reader*, 438 (epub).

16	Mark Goodwin, *Cabal: An Apocalyptic End-Times Thriller* (The Beginning of Sorrows Book 1), Kindle Edition, 283.

17 Mark Goodwin, *Cabal: An Apocalyptic End-Times Thriller* (The Beginning of Sorrows Book 1), Kindle Edition, 31.

18 Kristi Yeung and Zinan Zhang, "The Neverending Apocalypse," *The Princeton Buffer*, January 23, 2014.

19 Lina Mounzer, "Apocalypse Now: Why Arab Authors Are Really Writing about the End of the World," Middle East Eye, April 1, 2019, middleeasteye.net.

20 Filiu, *Apocalypse in Islam*, xx.

21 Quoted in Filiu, *Apocalypse in Islam*, 84.

22 Adorno and Horkheimer, *Dialectic of Enlightenment*, 141.

23 J. Eric Oliver and Thomas J. Wood, "Conspiracy Theories and the Paranoid Style(s) of Mass Opinion," *American Journal of Political Science* 58: 4, 2014, 953.

24 Ahmed Saadawi, *Frankenstein in Baghdad*, trans. Jonathan Wright, New York: Penguin Books, 2018.

25 Susan Sontag, "The Imagination of Disaster," in *Against Interpretation and Other Essays*, New York: Picador, 1961, 225.

26 *Sawt al-Hind*, "Lockdown Special," June 2020.

27 For a discussion of why this framing is both inaccurate and yet meaningful, see William Cavanaugh, *The Myth of Religious Violence: Secular Ideology and the Roots of Modern Conflict*, New York: Oxford University Press, 2009.

28 Francis Fukuyama, "The End of History?," *National Interest* 16, Summer 1989.

29 There is obvious tension within the argument (based largely on Alexandre Kojeve's assessment of European social democracy) that the conflict between labor and capital had been resolved. If this ever contained a shard of truth, it was only because of the democratic exercise of political power through the state. Yet Fukuyama was not shilling for social democracy but cheering for its destruction at the hands of "conservative parties from Britain and Germany to the United States and Japan, which are unabashedly pro-market and anti-statist."

30 Fukuyama, "The End of History?"

31 Walter Benjamin, "Theses on the Philosophy of History," in *Illuminations*, 256.

32   Fukuyama, "The End of History?"
33   Wendy Brown, *In The Ruins of Neoliberalism: The Rise of Anti-Democratic Politics in the West*, New York: Columbia University Press, 2019.
34   Kamel Daoud, "Paradise, the New Muslim Utopia," *New York Times*, August 2, 2016.
35   Oliver Roy, *Jihad and Death: The Global Appeal of Islamic State*, New York: Oxford University Press, 2017, 69.
36   Ajay Singh Chaudhary, "The Exhausted of the Earth: Political Theory in the Anthropocene" (manuscript in process).

Conclusion

1   Katherine Stewart, "Why Trump Reigns as King Cyrus," *New York Times*, December 31, 2018.
2   As quoted in D. Stammer, "British Colonial Public Finance," *Social and Economic Studies* 16: 2, 1967, 194.
3   According to FBI statistics, the property crime rate declined 42 percent from 1998 to 2017, as did rates of burglary (−50 percent), larceny (−38 percent), and aggravated assault (−31 percent). U.S. Department of Justice, FBI, "Crime in the United States by Volume and Rate per 100,000 Inhabitants, 1998-2017," ucr.fbi.gov.
4   Alex Vitale, "Cut the NYPD Budget Now: We Need to Save Money, and We Just Don't Need This Many Cops," *Daily News*, May 21, 2020.
5   The term as used here is borrowed from John Bailey's *The Politics of Crime in Mexico: Democratic Governance in a Security Trap*, Boulder, CO: FirstForumPress, 2014. John Ikenberry has also used the term but in a slightly different sense more focused on US diplomacy (and implicitly, security for Americans) rather than security for different populations in countries affected by American policies.
6   Bailey, *The Politics of Crime in Mexico*.
7   Kristen Martinez-Gugerli, "The 'Security Trap' in Latin America: Using the State to Fight Violence with Violence," *Panoramas*, February 21, 2019.
8   Franz Neumann, "The Concept of Political Freedom," in *The Democratic and the Authoritarian State*, ed. Herbert Marcuse and trans. Peter Gay, New York: The Free Press, 1964, 168.

9 The quote is borrowed from Ajay Singh Chaudhary, "Toward A Crit-ical 'State Theory' for the Twenty-First Century," in *The Future of the State: Philosophy and Politics*, ed. Artemy Magun, Lanham, MD: Rowman and Littlefield, 2020, 204.

10 Mara Karlin, "Why Military Assistance Programs Disappoint," *Foreign Affairs*, November/December 2017. It is estimated that at least at least 75,000 civilians were killed during the conflict.

11 Andrew Miller and Richard Sokolsky, "What Has $49 Billion in Foreign Military Aid Bought Us? Not Much," *American Conservative*, February 27, 2018.

12 Paul R. Pillar, Andrew Bacevich, Annelle Sheline, and Trita Parsi, "A New U.S. Paradigm for the Middle East: Ending America's Misguided Policy of Domination," Quincy Institute for Responsible Statecraft, July 17, 2020.

13 Robert F. Worth, "Inside the Iraqi Kleptocracy," *New York Times Magazine*, July 29, 2020.

14 David D. Kirkpatrick, "A Cage Fighter with a Soft Touch for Hard-Core Jihadists," *New York Times*, December 29, 2017.

15 Seyla Benhabib, "Below the Asphalt Lies the Beach," *Boston Review*, October 9, 2018, emphasis in original.

16 Ajay Singh Chaudhary, "Toward a Critical 'State Theory' for the Twenty-First Century," in *The Future of the State: Philosophy and Politics*, ed. Artemy Magun, Lanham, MD: Rowman and Littlefield, 2020.

Index